COLLINS POCKET REFERENCE

SCOTLAND

Hilary Macartney

HarperCollins*Publishers*

D0284263

Acknowledgements

The author and publisher would like to thank the following
for their invaluable help in the preparation of this book:
The Scottish Tourist Board, the regional tourist boards, the
tourist offices, the National Trust for Scotland, Historic
Scotland and the many hundreds of attractions which
provided information. The author is also grateful to Craig
Swan and Neil Wilson for additional text.

First published 1996

Reprint 10 9 8 7 6 5 4 3 2 1

© Text and maps, HarperCollins*Publishers* 1996
Photographs by Keith Allardyce (© HarperCollins*Publishers*),
except those on pp. 13 (top), 68-9, 74-5, 76-7, 79, 80-1, 86-7, 141, 158,
159 and 222 (© Dennis Hardley), pp. 48-9 (© James Carney) and
pp. 56-7 (© Douglas Corrance)

Cover photograph: Eilean Donan Castle (© Dennis Hardley)

ISBN 0 00 470870-9
All rights reserved

A catalogue record for this book is available from the British Library

Every effort has been made to provide an up-to-date text but the
publishers cannot accept any liability for errors, omissions or changes
in detail or for any consequences arising from the use of information
contained herein. The publishers welcome corrections and suggestions
from readers. Write to:

Reference Department
HarperCollins*Publishers*
PO Box
Glasgow, G4 0NB

Origination by Arneg Limited, Glasgow
Printed in Italy by Amadeus S.p.A.

Contents

How to Use this Book   6

Introduction   8

EDINBURGH, GLASGOW AND EXCURSIONS

Edinburgh
Attractions 17 • Restaurants 19 • Walk 21

Glasgow
Attractions 29 • Restaurants 31 • Walk 33

Excursion 1	**The Southwest**	41
Excursion 2	**Glencoe, the Great Glen and Perthshire**	55
Excursion 3	**The Trossachs**	71
Excursion 4	**Argyll**	83
Excursion 5	**The Hebrides**	93
Excursion 6	**The Northwest Coast**	109
Excursion 7	**Orkney**	119
Excursion 8	**Caithness, Sutherland and the Black Isle**	125
Excursion 9	**The Northeast Coast**	135
Excursion 10	**Shetland**	143
Excursion 11	**Royal Deeside and Northeast Castles & Distilleries**	149
Excursion 12	**Kincardine and Angus**	157
Excursion 13	**Fife**	165
Excursion 14	**The Borders**	181

CULTURAL GAZETTEER

Aberdeen	190	Ayr	194
Adam, Robert	191	Ben Nevis	194
Antonine Wall	191	Biggar	194
Architecture	192	Broughton	195
Arran	193	Bruce, Sir William	195

CONTENTS

Burns, Robert	195
Bute	196
Carnegie, Andrew	197
Clearances, The	197
Coatbridge	197
Coldstream	198
Coll & Tiree	198
Colonsay & Oronsay	198
Covenanters	198
Cowal Peninsula	199
Cumbrae	200
Doon Valley	200
Drinks	200
Dumbarton	201
Dumfries	201
Dunbar	202
Dundee	203
Dunfermline	204
Duns	205
Edinburgh	206
Elgin	207
Enlightenment, The	208
Eyemouth	208
Festivals	209
Food	212
Forth Bridges	212
Fort William	212
Glasgow	213
Glasgow Boys	215
Glen Affric	215
Glencoe Massacre	215
Great Glen	215
Haddington	216
Hamilton	216
Hebrides	217
Helensburgh	217
Hermitage Castle	218
Inverness	218
Islay & Jura	219
Jacobites	220
Lanark	221
Languages	221
Lismore	222
Loch Lomond	222
Macbeth	223
Macdonald, James Ramsay	223
Mackintosh, Charles Rennie	223
Mary Queen of Scots	223
Moffat	224
Music	224
North Berwick	224
Oban	225
Orkney	226
Paisley	226
Paxton House	227
Perth	227
Picts	228
Prehistory	228
Raeburn, Sir Henry	228
Ramsay, Allan	229
Reformation, The	229
Rennie, John	230
Robert the Bruce	230
Rob Roy	230
St. Andrew	230
St. Andrews	231
St. Columba	234
St. Margaret	234
St. Ninian	234
Sanquhar	234
Scots	234
Scott, Sir Walter	234
Scottish Colourists	235
Shetland	235
Small Isles	235
Staffa	236

Stevenson, Robert Louis	236	Wallace, William	238
Stirling	236	Wanlockhead	239
Telford, Thomas	238	Wick	239
Thomson, Alexander 'Greek'	238	Wolf of Badenoch	239
Thornhill	238		

PRACTICAL GAZETTEER

Accidents & Breakdowns	240	Events	245
Accommodation	240	Ferries	245
Airports	240	Guides	246
Banks	241	Health	246
Best Buys	241	Historic Scotland	246
Bicycle Hire	242	Midges	247
Boat Trips	242	National Trust for Scotland	247
Buses	242	Newspapers	247
Camping & Caravanning	242	Police	247
Car Hire	242	Post Offices	247
Climate	243	Public Holidays	248
Consulates	243	Railways	248
Crime & Theft	243	Sports	248
Currency	243	Tourist Information	249
Customs	244	Transport	249
Disabilities	244	Walking	249
Driving	244	What's On	250
Eating Out	244	Youth Hostels	250

SELECTIVE INDEX OF PLACES AND PEOPLE   252

Pocket Reference *Scotland* will help guide you round the whole of this beautiful country, whether you are following one of the excursions or simply want information on a specific place or attraction. It is divided into three colour-coded sections.

The blue section comprises **14 excursions**, complete with directions and distances, as well as details on the towns, villages and tourist attractions visited. The excursions cover Scotland from the Mull of Galloway to Shetland, and their starting/finishing points are indicated on the map opposite. There is a general route map for each excursion, but it is strongly recommended that you use these maps in conjunction with an up-to-date road atlas. The sections on **Edinburgh** and **Glasgow** at the beginning include listings of major attractions and selected restaurants, plus a guided walk to start your explorations.

The red section is the **Cultural Gazetteer**, packed with information on specific places, personalities and historical events. Listed in alphabetical order, the entries expand on topics referred to in the excursions. Here you can find out about anything from Mary Queen of Scots to the Glasgow Boys or from Architecture to Languages or the Clearances.

The yellow section is the **Practical Gazetteer**, full of invaluable holiday information, and including entries on accommodation, climate, eating out, events, transport and more.

Throughout the book, **cross-references** – *see* Excursion 4, *see* Picts – lead you to extra information on a specific subject. *See* A-Z means that there is an entry in the Cultural Gazetteer on the place or subject just mentioned.

Opening times and indications of **admission prices** (see below) are included for all attractions and sites throughout the book. If opening times are not followed by any details of months, the site or attraction is open all 12 months (though it may only be open on certain days of the week). Similarly, if there is no indication of days of the week after opening times or months, the attraction is open 7 days.

HS denotes that a site is in the care of **Historic Scotland**. Standard HS opening times are given in the entry for Historic Scotland in the Practical Gazetteer, and any exceptions to these are given immediately after the name of the specific attraction. NTS denotes a site in the care of the **National Trust for Scotland**. TIC indicates the location of the nearest **Tourist Information Centre**.

1996 prices			
	Inexpensive	*Moderate*	*Expensive*
Attractions	under £3	£3 – £6	over £6
Restaurants Main course	under £6	£6 – £10	over £10

SHETLAND

Atlantic
Ocean

ORKNEY

THURSO

North
Sea

STORNOWAY

OUTER
HEBRIDES

The Minch

ULLAPOOL

Moray Firth

KYLE OF
LOCHALSH

INVERNESS

S C O T L A N D

ABERDEEN

INNER

HEBRIDES

OBAN

PERTH

Firth of Lorn

Firth of Forth

GLASGOW

EDINBURGH

Firth of Clyde

NORTHERN
IRELAND

GRETNA
GREEN

Solway Firth

E N G L A N D

Introduction

Ceud mille fàilte! – A hundred thousand welcomes! The warmth of the people and their tradition of hospitality is one reason for Scotland's popularity as a tourist destination. In 1994 over 10 million people visited Scotland, spending over £2 billion and accounting for an estimated 8% of all employment.

Piper in Glencoe

Because of tourism's importance to the economy, efforts are constantly being made to improve what is on offer, from training waitresses, taxi drivers and hotel porters how to give good service, to improving food and trying to develop winter as well as summer facilities.

But apart from warm hospitality, Scotland's major attractions are its beautiful scenery and its rich and often romantic history. The much complained-about weather is at least partly responsible for the scenic beauty, from the lush greenery to the mists which shroud the mountains. The frequently changing weather conditions in the west even make it possible to see two rainbows in the sky at once. There are also wide variations in types of scenery, due to the incredible diversity of Scotland's geology. The rolling hills of the Southern Uplands contrast with the relatively flat Central Lowlands. North of the Highland Fault Line, one of the world's major geological faults, landscape is equally varied, from the Cairngorms, rounded by thousands of years of erosion, to the rugged mountains of Torridon, northwest of Inverness. Different again are the curious isolated hills of Sutherland and the strange lunar landscape of parts of the Western Isles.

These differences in landscape also helped to create wide regional variations in traditions and even language. Gaelic culture, scattered rural communities and occupations such as crofting still form a very different way of life in the Highlands and Islands, compared with that of the more industrial Lowlands, where there is a much larger population in cities and towns and the Scots language survives in dialects and accents. Within the same geographic area there are refreshing differences too: Edinburgh and Glasgow are only 50 miles apart yet are totally different in character. Edinburgh people are said to be reserved, a characteristic reflected in the fine Georgian buildings, whereas Glaswegians believe themselves to be much more outgoing, a parallel for which is to be found in the city's flamboyant Victorian architecture.

Glasgow School of Art

Scotland's monuments provide a wonderful insight into the history of the country and its peoples. The numerous stone circles such as at Callanish on the Isle of Lewis suggest a forgotten belief system, while the prehistoric settlement at Skara Brae in Orkney gives a vivid picture of Stone Age life. Pictish sculptured stones dating from around the 6th-9thC AD contain some delightful human and animal figures, even if the exact meaning of the stones and many of their symbols is still not clear. From the 12thC, contact with the Normans is evident in the style of churches and monasteries, though the new buildings were often on earlier sites sacred in Celtic Christianity. Scotland's magnificent castles up to around the 17thC are not only symbols of wealth and power, but as defensive structures they are also reminders of the country's turbulent history. From the 18thC are beautiful stately homes, including Robert Adam's Culzean Castle and Edinburgh's fine New Town. The 19th and 20thC provide a wealth of architectural delights, including the buildings of Charles Rennie Mackintosh. But as well as fine architecture, there is also social and industrial history, with fascinating sites at New Lanark and Summerlee, in Coatbridge.

The stories of less stable times are told by battle sites such as Bannockburn and Culloden, while ruined churches and monasteries speak of the Reformation and there are many memorials to the 'Killing Times' of the 17thC Covenanters. But perhaps individual Scottish figures have captured the world's imagination more than anything else about Scotland. Our image of Mary Queen of Scots, Bonnie Prince Charlie, Rob Roy Macgregor, Robert the Bruce and William Wallace is still over-romanticized due to Sir Walter Scott and recent films. Yet the many

associations which famous figures of the past have with historic sites certainly bring those places alive and may help us appreciate the significance of such sites.

Visitors to Scotland frequently come for the great outdoors. Apart from being the home of golf, Scotland also has trout and salmon rivers which attract anglers from all over the world. Other popular outdoor activities include hillwalking

Iona Abbey, Hebrides

(including 'Munro-bagging'), climbing, birdwatching, skiing, yachting and windsurfing. Perhaps most important, however, is the fact that it is still possible to get away from it all in Scotland and find solitude in the countryside.

Most visitors to Scotland will be touring by car and, apart from a few busy routes, many roads are surprisingly quiet. For those using public transport, there are some good deals by booking in advance and by buying special multijourney tickets for train, bus, ferry and air travel.

Scotland's other major attractions include museums and art galleries. Internationally important art collections are mainly concentrated in the Central Belt and include Edinburgh's national museums and galleries and Glasgow's

IN LOYAL REMEMBRANCE
OF
ROBERT THE BRUCE,
KING OF SCOTS,
WHOSE VICTORY IN THIS
GLEN OVER AN ENGLISH
FORCE IN MARCH, 1307,
OPENED THE CAMPAIGN OF
INDEPENDENCE WHICH HE
BROUGHT TO A DECISIVE
CLOSE AT BANNOCKBURN
ON 24TH JUNE, 1314.

The Bruce Stone, Glen Trool

outstanding municipal collections, among them the prestigious Burrell Collection. There are also interesting local museums throughout the country, for example on the history of fishing and crofting. New attractions like Vikingar in Largs often combine modern multimedia technology with live performances by actors who bring the past to life.

Bannockburn Monument, Stirling

There are a number of important festivals, the best-known being the Edinburgh International Festival held in Aug. each year. Glasgow's Mayfest is a more recent addition. Others include folk and jazz festivals and, of course, Highland Games, held in towns and villages throughout Scotland in summer. Some celebrations like the Viking festival of Up-Helly-Aa in Shetland have fascinating ancient roots.

Scotland has one of the finest larders in the world, producing meats of the

Crathes Castle

highest quality, including venison and grouse, and excellent fresh and smoked fish. In the summer, there are delicious soft fruits, while Scotland's 'tatties' are among the finest. Cooking and presentation were not always up to the standard of the raw materials, however. Fortunately, matters have now improved, partly due to the Taste of Scotland scheme.

Iona Abbey

whisky. Over 85% of it is exported every year and it is one of the top five exports in Britain in terms of the foreign currency it earns. There are over 100 different single malt whiskies, each with a unique flavour. Getting to know them all individually takes a lifetime. To help you, though, many of the distilleries are open for tours and sampling (but don't try

Last but not least, one of Scotland's greatest contributions to the world is sampling and driving!). Slàinte mhath! (pronounced 'slanje va') – Good health!

Mingulay, Outer Hebrides

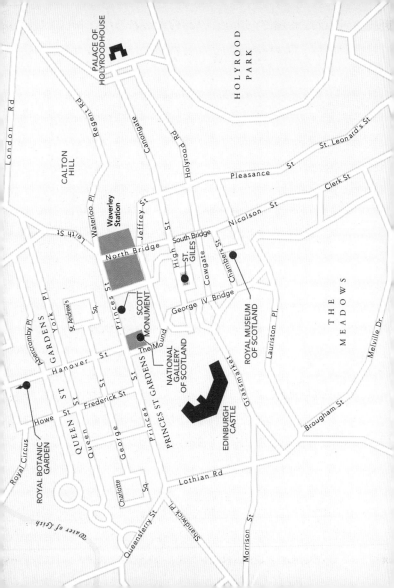

Edinburgh Attractions

EDINBURGH CASTLE
Castlehill, High St.

● HS, 0930-1800 April-Sep., 0930-1700 Oct.-Mar. Last admission 45 min before closing. ● Moderate.
This imposing fortress dominates the city and contains 12thC St. Margaret's Chapel, 15thC Mons Meg cannon, the Great Hall and the Scottish Crown Jewels.

PALACE OF
HOLYROODHOUSE
Canongate.

● 0930-last admission 1715 Mon.-Sat., 1630 Sun., April-Oct.; 0930-last admission 1545, Nov.-Mar. Closed during royal visits. ● Moderate.
Her Majesty's official Scottish residence. The present building dates from the 15th-17thC and has links with Mary Queen of Scots (see A-Z) and Bonnie Prince Charlie (see Jacobites).

NATIONAL GALLERY
OF SCOTLAND
The Mound.

● 1000-1700 Mon.-Sat., 1400-1700 Sun. ● Free.
Though smaller than its London counterpart, this is an excellent collection of Renaissance to Post-Impressionist works.

ROYAL MUSEUM OF
SCOTLAND
Chambers St.

● 1000-1700 Mon.-Sat., 1400-1700 Sun. ● Free.
Decorative arts, archaeology, technology, etc. in an elegant glass-roofed hall.

ST. GILES
High St.

● 0900-1900 Mon.-Fri., 0900-1700 Sat., 1300-1700 Sun. (mid May-mid Sep.); 0900-1700 Mon.-Sat., 1300-1700 Sun. (mid Sep.-mid May). ● Free, but donation for entry to Thistle Chapel.
The Old Town's main kirk, founded 1120, has a distinctive crown tower (1500) and the rich Thistle Chapel (1910). It was a centre of the 16thC Scottish Reformation (see A-Z).

ROYAL BOTANIC
GARDEN
Inverleith Row.

●1000-1800 Mar.-April & Sep.-Oct., 1000-2000 May-Aug., 1000-1600 Nov.-Feb. ● Free.
70 acres of beautifully landscaped gardens and 11 glasshouses.

SCOTT MONUMENT
East Princes St Gardens.

● 0900-1800 Mon.-Sat. (April-Sep.), also 1200-1700 Sun. (June-Sep.); 0900-1500 Mon.-Sat. (Oct.-Mar.). ● Inexpensive.
Romantic Gothic monument to Sir Walter Scott (see A-Z) by George Meikle Kemp. The views are worth the climb!

CALTON HILL
Road access via Regent Rd; pedestrian access via Waterloo Pl. and Royal Terr.

● Open access. ● Admission charges and opening times for Nelson Monument and City Observatory.
This 328 ft hill rises above the east end of Princes St and is topped with several monuments, including the neoclassical National Monument (1819-29).

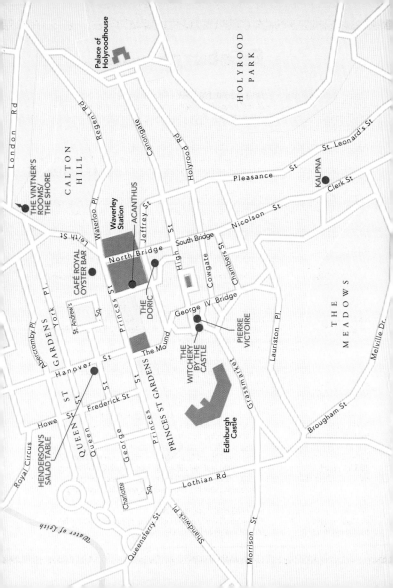

Edinburgh *Restaurants*

THE WITCHERY BY THE CASTLE
352 Castlehill, High St,
tel. 0131 225-5613.

● 1200-1600, 1800-2330. ● Expensive.
One of Edinburgh's best restaurants, serving mainly Scottish dishes. There is also the new Secret Garden downstairs.

CAFÉ ROYAL OYSTER BAR
17a West Register St,
tel. 0131 556-4124.

● 1200-1400, 1900-2215. ● Expensive.
The Oyster Bar has a fine Victorian interior and is believed to be Scotland's oldest seafood restaurant. Other dishes are available.

THE VINTNER'S ROOMS
The Vaults, 87 Giles St,
Leith,
tel. 0131 554-6767.

● 1200-1430, 1900-2230 Mon.-Sat. ● Moderate-Expensive.
Restaurant serving dishes made with fresh local produce in a building once at the centre of the Scottish claret trade.

THE SHORE
3-4 The Shore, Leith,
tel. 0131 553-5080.

● 1200-1430, 1830-2200 Mon.-Sat., 1200-1500, 1830-2200 Sun. ● Moderate.
Excellent fish and other dishes in this restaurant in Edinburgh's now fashionable port.

THE DORIC
5 Market St,
tel. 0131 225-1084.

● 1200-0100 Mon.-Wed., 1200-0200 Thu.-Sat. (all year), 1230-2400 Sun. (summer only). ● Moderate.
Restaurant serving imaginative dishes which combine Scottish cooking with many other influences.

HENDERSON'S SALAD TABLE
94 Hanover St,
tel. 0131 225-2131.

● 0800-2230 Mon.-Sat. ● Inexpensive-Moderate.
Famous self-service vegetarian and wholefood restaurant. An Edinburgh institution.

KALPNA
2-3 St. Patrick's Sq.,
tel. 0131 667-9890.

● 1200-1400 Mon.-Fri., 1730-2300 Mon.-Sat. ● Inexpensive.
A favourite Edinburgh restaurant serving South Indian vegetarian dishes. No smoking.

PIERRE VICTOIRE
10 Victoria St,
tel. 0131 225-1721.

Also at 3-4 Dock Pl., 38-40 Grassmarket & 6-8 Union St (all Edinburgh), & 10a Edinburgh Rd, South Queensferry.
● 1200-1500, 1800-2300 Mon.-Sat. ● Inexpensive.
Unbeatable value French cuisine in relaxed surroundings.

ACANTHUS
17 Waverley Br.,
tel. 0131 556-2358.

● 1000-2200. ● Inexpensive.
This attractive city centre café-bar is right beside Waverley station and serves meals and snacks.

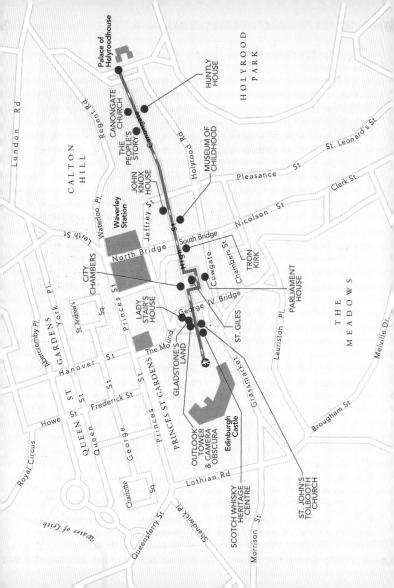

Palace of Holyroodhouse

HOLYROOD PARK

HUNTLY HOUSE

CANONGATE CHURCH

THE PEOPLE'S STORY

MUSEUM OF CHILDHOOD

London Rd

Regent Rd

CALTON HILL

Waterloo Pl

Leith St

Waverley Station

North Bridge

CITY CHAMBERS

LADY STAIR'S HOUSE

GLADSTONE'S LAND

Princes St

The Mound

PRINCES ST GARDENS

OUTLOOK TOWER & CAMERA OBSCURA

Edinburgh Castle

SCOTCH WHISKY HERITAGE CENTRE

JOHN KNOX HOUSE

Jeffrey St

High St

South Bridge

Cowgate

Chambers St

TRON KIRK

Canongate

Holyrood Rd

Pleasance

St. Leonard's St

Clerk St

Nicolson St

PARLIAMENT HOUSE

ST. GILES

George IV Bridge

Lauriston Pl

THE MEADOWS

Melville Dr.

Brougham St

ST. JOHN'S TOLBOOTH CHURCH

Grassmarket

Lothian Rd

Morrison St

Queensferry St

Standrick Pl

Water of Leith

Royal Circus

Abercromby Pl

GARDENS

York Pl

St. Andrew's

Sq.

St. Andrew St

Princes St

Hanover St

George St

Frederick St

Howe St

QUEEN ST

Queen St

Charlotte Sq.

Edinburgh Walk *The Royal Mile*

2 – 5 hr

This historic route began as a track between the Castle and royal hunting grounds. Later it linked the Castle with the royal residence at the Palace of Holyroodhouse and became the main thoroughfare of the cramped Old Town. Today, neither tourists, nor souvenir shops, nor traffic, nor even some new buildings have destroyed its unique atmosphere. There's a lot to see and do, as each 'close' leading to buildings behind has its own story, often told on plaques at the entrances. The time you take will also depend on how many visits you make to the various museums and other buildings open to the public.

Castlehill

Start at the Castle Esplanade looking down the Royal Mile. The first house on the right is Cannonball House (1630), so called because of the cannonball still lodged in the gable wall. One story says it was fired during the Jacobite (*see* A-Z) Rebellion of 1745, though more likely it marked the gravitation level of the city water supply. Opposite is the Witches' Well, where a bronze plaque on the wall of the old reservoir commemorates the site on which 300 women were burned as witches in the 15th-18thC. Further down on the left are Ramsay Lane and Ramsay Gardens, with the remains of 18thC poet Allan Ramsay's 'Goosepie' house, and flats by Old Town improver Sir Patrick Geddes. On the corner of the lane is the **Outlook Tower** and 19thC **Camera Obscura** (0930-1800 Mon.-Fri., 1000-1800 Sat. & Sun., April-Oct.; 1000-1800 all week, Nov.-Mar.; Moderate) and opposite is the **Scotch Whisky Heritage Centre** (1000-1730 all year; Moderate).

Further down on the right is St. John's Tolbooth Church, built in the 19thC for Gaelic speakers. Across from it on the left is the back of the Assembly Hall of the Church of Scotland, whose ministers meet here once a year in May.

Castlehill now becomes Lawnmarket (thought to have been the 'landmarket', where produce of the land was sold). A little way down on the left is **Gladstone's Land** (NTS, 1000-1700 Mon.-Sat., 1400-1700 Sun.; last admission 1630, April-mid Oct.; Moderate), a six-storey 17thC tenement with painted ceilings. It was named after the textile merchant Thomas

Ramsay Gardens

Greyfriar's Bobby Monument

Edinburgh Castle and Princes St Gardens

(see A-Z), Sir Walter Scott (see A-Z) and Robert Louis Stevenson (see A-Z). Across from Gladstone's Land is Riddle's Court, where David Hume, the 18thC philosopher and a major figure of the Edinburgh Enlightenment (see A-Z), once lived. Further down on the right is Brodie's Close, where the notorious Deacon Brodie, said to have been the model for Stevenson's Dr Jekyll and Mr Hyde, lived in the 18thC. By day he was a respectable citizen; by night he robbed the houses of the rich. He is also commemorated by Deacon Brodie's Tavern opposite.

Gledstanes, whose shop or booth was on the ground floor. The 'close' next to it leads to Lady Stair's House, built in 1622 and named after the 18thC Lady Stair. It now houses the **Writers' Museum** (1000-1800 Mon.-Sat., June-Sep.; also 1400-1700 Sun., Aug.; 1000-1700 Mon.-Sat., Oct.-May; Free) with displays relating to Scotland's great writers, Robert Burns

Cross George IV Br., where, on the right are brass strips marking the site of public hangings until 1864. It is at this point that Lawnmarket becomes High St.

On the left is the High Court of

National Monument, Calton Hill

Scott Monument

Justiciary, Scotland's principal criminal court. A short way down, turn right into Parliament Sq. to visit **St. Giles** (*see* Edinburgh in A-Z).

Outside on the cobblestones is the Heart of Midlothian, picked out in stone and, in brass, is the outline of the entrance to the Old Tolbooth which once housed the city's jail, demolished in 1817. To the south of the kirk, under the present parking spaces, was the churchyard where some believe the Protestant reformer John Knox (*see* Reformation) was buried. The equestrian statue in lead is of Charles II. On the south of the square is **Parliament House** (tel: 0131 225-2595, normally open 1000-1300, 1400-1600 Mon.-Fri., all year; Free), a 17thC building with a 19thC exterior, where the Scottish parliament met until the Act of Union in 1707. It houses the

St. Giles

Court of Session, the principal Scottish civil court. Parliament Hall has an impressive hammerbeam roof and a window commemorating the opening of the Court of Session by King James V. At the northeast end of the square is the Mercat Cross, moved from its original position in the middle of the street.

Just down from the Cross on the right

Palace of Holyroodhouse

is the **Edinburgh Festival Fringe Office** (1000-1800 Mon.-Fri., all year). Opposite is the magnificent City Chambers building, originally the Royal Exchange, designed by John and Robert Adam (*see* A-Z). Further down on the left is Anchor Close, where William Smellie printed the first edition of the *Encyclopaedia Britannica* in 1768. On the right, just before the junction with North and South Bridges, is the 17thC Tron Kirk (named after the 'tron' or public weighbeam) with a hammerbeam roof. In it is the **Tron Old Town Information Centre** (1000-1700 Thu.-Sun., mid April-May; 1000-1700 all week, June-Sep.; information service

Free, exhibition Inexpensive), where the remains of an old street, Marlin's Wynd, can also be viewed. On the left, shortly after the junction, is Paisley Close, rebuilt after it collapsed in 1861, killing many inside. Above the entrance is the sculpted head of a boy who had called to rescuers, 'Heave awa' chaps, I'm no dead yet!' Further down on the left, Chalmers Close leads to the **Brass Rubbing Centre** (opening hours as Writers' Museum; Free) in what remains of the beautiful Trinity Church. On the right is the **Museum of Childhood** (opening hours as Writers' Museum; Free) with exhibits mainly for adults and older children, and toys and a play area for kids. Also on the right is Tweeddale Court, in which is the house of the same name, originally a 17thC mansion, then a bank which was the scene of a gruesome armed robbery and murder in 1806. The perpetrator was never caught. Downhill on the left and jutting into the

Remembrance Sunday Parade, Royal Mile

street is **John Knox House** (1000-1630 Mon.-Sat., all year; Inexpensive), 15th-17thC, the oldest surviving house in the Royal Mile, with displays on James Mossman, goldsmith to Mary Queen of Scots (see A-Z), as well as on Knox. Next to it is the Netherbow Arts Centre, named after the lower gate of the city, which stood at the present-day junction with Jeffrey St and St. Mary's St.

Gates to Palace of Holyroodhouse

Outside the gates was the separate town of Canongate, incorporated into the city in 1856. Further down on the left is Canongate Tolbooth (1591), where taxes were collected. Now it contains **The People's Story** (opening hours as Writers' Museum; Free), which describes life in the Old Town. Across from it is Moray House, now a college of education. The entrance has distinctive obelisks and, from the balcony, the Duke of Argyll is said to have watched his arch-enemy the Duke of Montrose being led to execution in 1650.

Just down from here is **Huntly House** (opening hours as Writers' Museum; Free), an attractive house dating from 1517, now a municipal museum with history collections. Across from it is Canongate Church, built in 1688 for parishioners who previously worshipped at Holyrood. Its churchyard contains the graves of the economist Adam Smith, and the young poet Robert Fergusson, whose headstone was erected by Robert Burns. Near the end of the Canongate, on the right, is the picturesque, restored White Horse Close, whose 17thC inn was a departure point

for stagecoaches to London. The Royal Mile finishes on Abbey Strand. Ahead are the fine wrought-iron gates of the Palace of Holyroodhouse (see Edinburgh Attractions), which were erected as a memorial to King Edward VII in 1922.

John Knox House

Edinburgh Castle and Tattoo

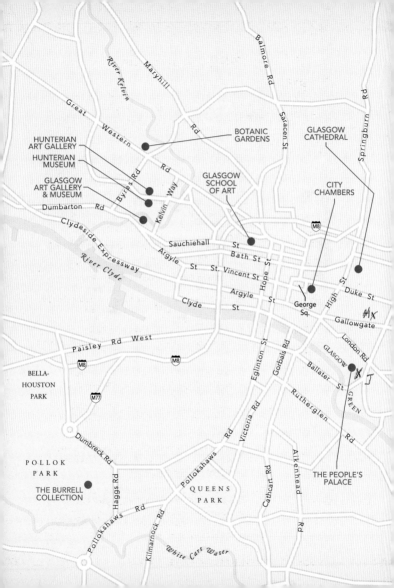

Glasgow Attractions

GLASGOW ART
GALLERY & MUSEUM
Kelvingrove, Argyle St.

● 1000-1700 Mon.-Sat., 1100-1700 Sun. ● Free.
*Built for the 1900 exhibition, this massive building contains the
city's main collections of art, history and natural history.*

THE BURRELL
COLLECTION
Pollokshaws Rd.

● 1000-1700 Mon.-Sat., 1100-1700 Sun. ● Free.
*Sir William Burrell's magnificent collection of ancient, medieval
and Oriental art, plus 15th-19thC fine and decorative art in an
award-winning building. Nearby is 18thC Pollok House, with
important Spanish art and William Blake paintings.*

GLASGOW SCHOOL
OF ART
Renfrew St.

● Guided tours 1100 & 1400 Mon.-Fri., 1030 Sat. Additional
tours may operate in summer, tel. 0141 353-4526.
● Inexpensive.
*Mackintosh's (see A-Z) architectural masterpiece, designed in
1896, still functions as an art school.*

HUNTERIAN MUSEUM
& ART GALLERY
University of Glasgow.

● 0930-1700 Mon.-Sat. Mackintosh House closed
1230-1330. ● Free.
*Scotland's first museum (1807). The art gallery includes a major
collection of Whistlers, plus the Mackintosh House.*

THE PEOPLE'S PALACE
Glasgow Green.

● 1000-1700 Mon.-Sat., 1100-1700 Sun. ● Free.
*Museum on the history of Glasgow from the 12thC to the present
day, plus its social history.*

GLASGOW CATHEDRAL
Castle St.

● 0930-1300, 1400-1800 Mon.-Sat., 1400-1700 Sun. (April-
Sep.); 0930-1300, 1400-1600 Mon.-Sat., 1400-1600 Sun.
(Oct.-Mar.). ● Free.
*This fine Gothic cathedral was built over the tomb of Glasgow's
6thC patron saint, St. Mungo, and survived the Reformation
(see A-Z) intact.*

CITY CHAMBERS
George Sq.

● Guided tours 1030 & 1430 Mon.-Wed. & Fri. ● Free.
*A vast and impressive building, built 1883-8, with a lavish
interior of coloured marble and granite.*

BOTANIC GARDENS
Great Western Rd.

● 0700-dusk; Kibble Palace 1000-1645 (winter till 1615);
Glasshouse 1300-1645 (winter till 1615) Mon.-Sat.,
1200-1645 Sun. (winter till 1615). ● Free.
*19thC gardens with the Kibble Palace, a beautiful Victorian
glasshouse with sculptures, subtropical plants and a fish pond.*

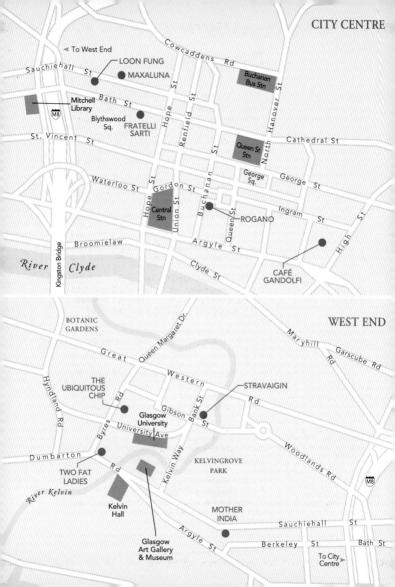

Glasgow Restaurants

ROGANO
11 Exchange Pl.,
tel. 0141 248-4055.

● 1200-1430, 1830-2230 Mon.-Sat. ● Expensive.
Stylish Art Deco restaurant specializing in fish and seafood.
The Oyster Bar and downstairs Café Rogano are less pricey.

THE UBIQUITOUS CHIP
2 Ashton Lane,
tel. 0141 334-5007/7109.

● 1200-1430, 1730-2300 Mon.-Sat., 1230-1430, 1800-2300
Sun. ● Expensive.
The restaurant which revolutionized Glasgow cuisine. Upstairs
at the Chip is much cheaper.

TWO FAT LADIES
88 Dumbarton Rd,
tel. 0141 339-1944.

● 1200-1415, 1730-2230 Tue.-Sat., 1730-2230 Mon.
● Moderate-Expensive.
Stylish modern restaurant specializing in fish and seafood.

CAFÉ GANDOLFI
64 Albion St,
tel. 0141 552-6813.

● 0900-2330 Mon.-Sat., 1100-2300 Sun. ● Moderate.
Restaurant in the Merchant City which serves imaginative dishes
using Scottish produce. Quirky furniture by Tim Stead.

FRATELLI SARTI
121 Bath St,
tel. 0141 204-0440.

● 0800-2300 Mon.-Sat. ● Moderate.
A new and bigger version of this famous Glasgow Italian
restaurant. Round the corner in Wellington St is their
marvellous deli and original tiny restaurant.

LOON FUNG
417 Sauchiehall St,
tel. 0141 332-1240/1477.

● 1200-2330. ● Moderate.
This popular restaurant in a converted cinema serves delicious
Cantonese food.

MAXALUNA
410-414 Sauchiehall St,
tel. 0141 332-1004.

● Café-bar: 1100-2400; Restaurant: 1200-1430, 1730-2230
Mon.-Wed., 1730-2300 Thu.-Sun. ● Moderate.
One of the latest of Glasgow's stylishly designed café-bar/
restaurants serves American, Italian and Chinese dishes.

MOTHER INDIA
28 Westminster Terr.,
Sauchiehall St,
tel. 0141 221-1663.

● 1230-1430, 1730-2300 Mon.-Thu., 1230-1430, 1730-2400
Fri., 1730-2400 Sat., 1730-2300 Sun. ● Moderate.
Delicious and authentic Indian cooking in attractive
surroundings. Bring your own alcohol.

STRAVAIGIN
26 Gibson St,
tel. 0141 334-2665.

● 1200-2300 Mon.-Thu., 1200-2400 Fri. & Sat., 1700-2300
Sun. ● Inexpensive-Moderate.
A restaurant and café-bar with a wide range of influences,
including Lebanese and Thai cooking.

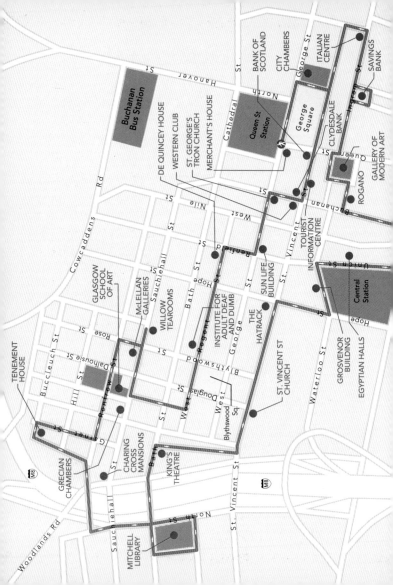

Glasgow Walk The City Centre

3 hr, excluding visits

This walk through the centre of Glasgow focuses on the city's rich architectural heritage of the late 18thC to early 20thC, when the exuberance of the buildings reflected the confidence of the wealthy commercial and industrial city. The route passes through the Merchant City to the southeast of George Sq. and Blythswood to the west (both part of Glasgow's 'new town' development from the 18thC on), as well as Garnethill, northwest of George Sq., originally a prosperous 19thC suburb. Most buildings now date from the 19th and 20thC. Architects include Charles Rennie Mackintosh, Glasgow's best-known architect; Alexander 'Greek' Thomson, the other great Glasgow architect; and Robert Adam, more often associated with Edinburgh.

Start at George Sq., outside Queen St station. Opposite, on the corner of the square, is the Merchant's House (1874-1909), containing Glasgow Chamber of Commerce and Merchant's Hall. It has splendid oriel windows and a gilded merchant ship on the corner dome. On the north side of the square, next to the station, is the former North British Hotel (now the Copthorne Hotel), an early 19thC

George Sq. and City Chambers

neoclassical building. On the east side, and dominating the square, is the magnificent bulk of the **City Chambers** (*see* Glasgow Attractions). The 1882 competition for its design was won by William Young.

In the centre of the square are a number of statues and memorials: west side: equestrian statues of the young Queen Victoria and Prince Albert; north side: Sir Robert Peel, William Gladstone and John Oswald MP; east side: cenotaph; south side: chemist Dr Thomas Graham, poet Thomas Campbell, Lord Clyde, Sir John Moore (by neoclassical artist Flaxman), Robert Burns and James Watt; on top of central column: Sir Walter Scott.

On the corner with St. Vincent Pl. is the Bank of Scotland (1867-70) by J.T. Rochead, with Atlantes figures supporting the coat of arms over the entrance. Continue along St. Vincent Pl. On the right, Nos 12-16 is the former Anchor Line Building (1905-07) by James Miller, with an unusual white ceramic facing. No. 24 (1885-9) was built as Glasgow's *Evening Citizen* newspaper office, on the site intended for the rest of the Italianate Clydesdale Bank (1871-4) next door. Opposite, No. 35 houses the **Tourist Information Centre**.

Glasgow Art Gallery & Museum

Pollok House, Pollok Park

an impressive tower. On the corner is the red sandstone Liberal Club (1907-09), now the Town House Hotel. Next to it on Buchanan St is the tall, narrow **Atheneum Theatre** (1891-3), now occupied by Scottish Youth Theatre. Turn into Nelson Mandela Pl. Next to the hotel is J.J. Burnet's Atheneum (1886) whose austere style is relieved by John Mossman's sculptures. This, the hotel and the theatre all until recently formed the Royal Scottish Academy of Music and Drama (now in Renfrew St). At right angles is the Italianate Royal Faculty of Procurators Building (1854-6) by Charles Wilson.

Continue onto West George St, where, on the right corner with West Nile St is another massive American-influenced building, the former Commercial Bank (1930-7) by James Miller. Carry on along West George St. On the left corner with Renfield St is William Leiper's ornate French-style Sun Life Building (1889-94), now the National and Provincial. Before turning right up Renfield St, look ahead up West George St where, on the right, is James Sellar's House (1877-9), designed by the architect of that name and with unusual oval windows. On Renfield St pass the Odeon cinema. On the far left corner with West Regent St is De Quincey

Before turning right into Buchanan St, look up St. Vincent St to the far side of the next corner on the right for a view of A.D. Hislop's Phoenix Assurance Building (1912-13), considered the first in Glasgow to show the influence of American-style classicism.

On the left in Buchanan St is the former Western Club (1839-42) by David Hamilton and his son James, with bold classical and Italian details. Next to it, John Burnet's Stock Exchange (1875-6) was unusual for its choice of Gothic style for a nonreligious building. St. George's Tron Church (1807) by William Stark, has

The People's Palace, Glasgow Green

taken over as offices and clubs. The east side was altered by James Miller to become the RAC Club. On the north side, at Nos 6-7, lived Madeleine Smith, granddaughter of the architect David Hamilton, accused of poisoning her suitor but found not proven in a famous murder case of 1857. At No. 5 next door, Charles Rennie Mackintosh (*see* A-Z) designed the doorway (1908) for the Glasgow Society of Lady Artists. Leave the square by West George St on the southwest side. On the right is the former St. Jude's Church (1838-9), an extraordinary Greek Revival building by John Stephen, now the stylish **Malmaison Hotel and Restaurant**.

The Burrell Collection, Pollok Park

Turn right into Pitt St. At the Bath St end is Adelaide Place Baptist Church, now with **Adelaide's** café. Cross Bath St and pass a blackened Greek temple, the former Elgin Place Congregational Church (1855-6) by John Burnet, now a disco. Continue to Sauchiehall St. Ahead in Scott St is the hillside façade with long slender windows of Mackintosh's Glasgow School of Art, to be visited shortly. To the left on Sauchiehall St is Alexander 'Greek' Thomson's (*see* A-Z) Grecian Chambers (1865), in fact Egyptian in inspiration with columns at the top. Part of the building is now the CCA (tel. 0141 332-7521), an arts centre.

House (1888-9), named after the Romantic writer who lived on this site in the 1840s. **De Quincey's Bar** retains the remarkable interior of the former insurance offices, with Moorish arches and tiles. Turn left up West Regent St. On the fourth block up on the right is an unusual red sandstone building begun in 1893, the former Institute for Adult Deaf and Dumb and John Ross Memorial Church for the Deaf.

Continue uphill into Blythswood Sq., begun in 1821 by William Hamilton Garden. By the early 20thC, the fashionable houses of the rich had been

Willow Tearooms, Sauchiehall St

Glasgow School of Art

Tenement House, Buccleuch St

Turn right down Sauchiehall St. On the left are the **McLellan Galleries** (1000-1700 Mon.-Sat., 1100-1700 Sun.; Variable), with changing art exhibitions. The 1855-6 building once housed Archibald McLellan's art collection, now at Glasgow Art Gallery and Museum, Kelvingrove. On the right, in the pedestrianized area of Sauchiehall St, are the **Willow Tearooms** (1903), designed by Mackintosh for Miss Kate Cranston. Turn left up Rose St, past **Glasgow Film Theatre** (1938-9). Ahead is St. Aloysius Church with a tall tower.

Turn left up Renfrew St to **Glasgow School of Art** (*see* Glasgow Attractions), Mackintosh's most famous building, restored for its centenary in 1996. Past other art school buildings on the left is the Dental Hospital (1927-31), with Art Deco decoration. Turn right down Garnet St, passing Garnethill Synagogue (1879),

the first to be built in Scotland. Turn left into Buccleuch St, at the end of which is the **Tenement House** (NTS, 1400-1700, last admission 1630, Mar.-mid Oct.; Inexpensive) with original 1911 interior.

Continue round the corner, with the M8 motorway on the right, to Charing Cross and cross by the bridge or pedestrian crossings. Once across, there is a good view of the dramatic Charing Cross Mansions (1889-91) by J.J. Burnet. Pass the leaning fountain, cross Sauchiehall St and go down North St to the **Mitchell Library** (1906-11), with a central dome and grand reading hall. Turn right into Kent Rd and right into Granville St to view the magnificent façade of the **Mitchell Theatre**, originally St. Andrew's Halls (1873-7), by James Sellars, with massive sculpture by John Mossman. Turn right again into Berkeley St and cross the M8 to Bath St. On the

The Hatrack Building, St. Vincent St

Princes Square, Buchanan St

right is the **King's Theatre** (1901-04) by Frank Matcham. On the opposite corner is the **Griffin Bar** with Art Nouveau exterior (1903-04). To the left in Sauchiehall St is Baird Hall, built for Glasgow's 1938 exhibition as the Beresford Hotel and now student accommodation.

Turn right down Elmbank St. On the left is the former Glasgow High School (1846-7). Cross St. Vincent St and turn left past the Abbey National Building with its roof terrace. On the right is 'Greek' Thomson's powerful St. Vincent St Church, completed in 1859 and with Greek and Egyptian features. On the left after West Campbell St is the monumental North British and Mercantile Building (1926-9), now Sun Life, J.J. Burnet's last Glasgow building. Further down on the Wellington St corner is the modern Scottish Amicable Building. Next to it is James Salmon Jnr's

Art Nouveau Hatrack Building (1899-1902), with extraordinary oriel windows.

Turn right down Hope St. On the left at Nos 106-08 is a delightful 1890s building by Salmon and Son. Behind in Renfield Lane is a white-glazed brick building (1901) by Mackintosh for the *Daily Record* newspaper. Continue down Hope St and turn left into Gordon St. On the right is Central Hotel (1880s) by Robert Rowand Anderson and **Central Station**, opened in 1870. On the left is Thomson's massive Grosvenor Building (1859). Turn right down Union St, noting the elegant Ca' d'Oro Building (1872), now Waterstone's, on the left corner. At Nos 84-100 are Thomson's Egyptian Halls (1871) with distinctive top-storey columns. Turning left into Argyle St, look right at the cast-iron viaduct of Central Station, known as the 'Hielan' Man's Umbrella'.

Turn left into Buchanan St. To the right in St. Enoch's Sq. is the diminutive red sandstone Travel Centre. On the left of Buchanan St are grand buildings, now Fraser's department store. Beyond on the right is **Princes Square**, a prestigious new shopping mall with Art Nouveau inspired ironwork. On the left at No. 91 is an attractive little building in red and cream stone, built in 1896 as one of Miss Cranston's tearooms (now the Bradford and Bingley).

Turn right into Exchange Pl. past the 1930s **Rogano** restaurant, and through the columns into Royal Exchange Sq. To the left is the original main entrance to the Royal Bank of Scotland (1827). Dominating the square is the former Royal Exchange, a grand classical temple designed by David Hamilton which until recently housed Stirling's Library, now the new **Gallery of Modern Art** (1000-1700 Mon.-Sat., 1100-1700 Sun.; Free). Cross Queen St into Ingram St. On the right, No. 191 is the High Court of Justiciary (1876-9) or Lanarkshire House, originally by Hamilton, with a rich façade by John Burnet. Next on the right is the baroque Savings Bank by J.J. Burnet.

Turn right down Glassford St. On the right is the Trades Hall, with a neoclassical façade by Robert Adam (*see* A-Z), his only remaining work in Glasgow. Turn right into Wilson St. Ahead is Virginia St, with some of the oldest buildings in the Merchant City. In front are the early 19thC Virginia Buildings, with classical details and old shop signs. Turn right towards the back of Lanarkshire House, then right into Virginia Pl., which leads back to Ingram St. Cross and turn right past Nos 178-82, a new façade with bronze decoration. On the left is the **Italian Centre**, restored buildings with a courtyard, shops, cafés and sculpture. Beyond is **Hutcheson's**

Glasgow University

Kelvingrove Park

Hall (NTS, 0930-1700 Mon.-Fri., 1000-1600 Sat.; Free) of 1802-05 by Hamilton, with 17thC sculptures of the Hutcheson brothers on the façade and a later grand hall. Further along on the right is the Greek Revival style former Sheriff Court. Turn up John St. On the right corner is John St Church (1858-60) by J.T. Rochead, now a pub on the ground floor; the upper floor has a grand ceiling. Ahead are the arches linking the City Chambers to their extension. Turn left to return to George Sq.

City Chambers, George Sq.

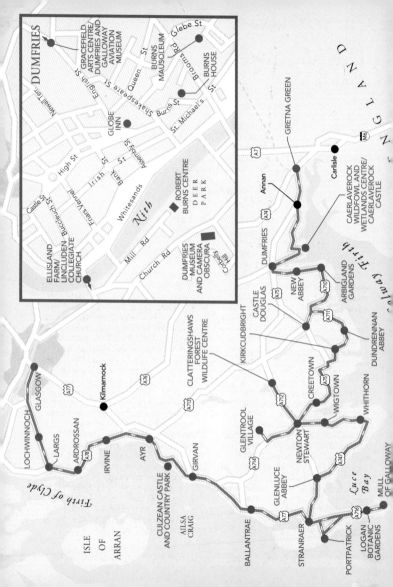

The Southwest

5 days

This excursion explores Dumfries and Galloway, a neglected part of Scotland which even many Scots never visit, yet it has some fine scenery, notably Glen Trool, and pretty towns and villages, including Kirkcudbright and Wigtown. Its attractions include impressive Caerlaverock Castle, beautiful Sweetheart Abbey, the fascinating remains relating to St. Ninian and early Christianity at Whithorn, and the delightful Logan Botanic Gardens. The excursion continues through Ayrshire – 'Burns Country' – and the many resorts of the Clyde coast. Apart from the attractions related to Burns, such as his birthplace at Alloway, there is also Culzean Castle, one of Robert Adam's most spectacular buildings, and the exquisite Skelmorlie Aisle at Largs.

Gretna Green. TIC: Old Blacksmith's Shop, tel. 01461 337834, Easter-Oct.; Gateway to Scotland, M74 service area, tel. 01461 338500. The village is well signposted and easily reached from the main north–south A74(M). In times past young English lovers would elope across the border to be married by the village blacksmith, as up to 1940 Scots Law allowed marriage by declaration before witnesses. Eloping couples over 16 may still marry in Scotland without their parents' consent. **The Old Blacksmith's Shop** (0900-1700 Nov.-Mar., 0900-1800 April, May & Oct., 0900-1900 June & Sep., 0900-2000 July & Aug.; Inexpensive) and the **Gretna Hall Blacksmith Shop** (0900-1700 April-Oct.; Inexpensive) were both used for marriages by declaration. Follow the road south out of the village and turn right at the T-junction on the B721 through Gretna. After 8 miles pass the royal burgh of Annan and beyond it turn left on the B724. In another 6 miles turn left to the village of Ruthwell, whose church (open access) contains the **Ruthwell Cross**, a late 7thC cross, 18 ft high, with runic carvings, one of the

most important of this date in Europe. **The Savings Bank Museum** (1400-1700 May-Sep.; Tue.-Sat., Oct.-April; Free) is housed in the first savings bank, founded in 1810. Turn left to join the B725, heading west through Bankhead. South is **Caerlaverock Wildfowl and Wetlands Centre** (1000-1700; Moderate. Access from Eastpark Farm), with over 13,000 acres of salt marsh, mud and sand flats, and famous for barnacle geese, ducks, swans and waders. Continue to **Caerlaverock Castle** (HS; Inexpensive), an imposing late 13thC castle which has an unusual triangular plan and retains its water-filled moat. Now a well-preserved ruin, it was built for the Maxwell family. Inside are the Renaissance-inspired Nithsdale apartments of 1634. Rejoin the B725 which continues through Glencaple. **30 miles – Dumfries** (*see* A-Z). Leave town by the A710, heading southwest. In 7 miles is the village of New Abbey, built around **Sweetheart Abbey** (HS, except 0930-1300 Thu. and closed Fri., Oct.-Mar.; Inexpensive), founded in 1273 by Devorgilla Balliol, daughter of the last Celtic lord of Galloway, in

Sweetheart Abbey

memory of her husband John Balliol, with whom she also founded Balliol College at Oxford University. The Cistercian monastery was ruined after the Reformation (*see* A-Z) but much remains of the church with its great tower and Gothic arches. Devorgilla was buried with her husband's 'sweet heart' in front of the

New Abbey Corn Mill

high altar and her reconstructed tomb is in the south transept. Nearby is **New Abbey Corn Mill** (same times and ticket as for Abbey), a working Georgian mill. **Shambellie House Museum of Costume** (1100-1700 Mon.-Tue. & Thu.-Sat., 1200-1700 Sun., May-Sep.; Inexpensive) has changing displays from the National Costume Collection. Continue on the A710. 5 miles further south are **Arbigland Gardens** (1400-1800 Tue.-Sun. & hols, May-Sep.; Inexpensive). **The John Paul Jones Birthplace Museum** (1000-1300, 1400-1700 Mon.-Sat., 1400-1700 Sun., Easter-Sep.; Inexpensive) is in the 19thC gardener's cottage, where the founder of the American Navy spent his early years. Continue southwest on the A710, past Sandyhills, which has an extensive but overused beach. 2 miles beyond, turn left down a minor road to Rockcliffe. **Rough Island**, a bird sanctuary where tern and oystercatchers nest on the shingle beaches, lies 200 yd offshore and can be reached by boat, or walked to at low tide if you like mud, but avoid May and June when the birds are nesting. The Jubilee Path leads to the tiny village of Kippford, past the Mark of Motte, a 5th-7thC Celtic hilltop stronghold. Rejoin the A710 and turn left. After 3 miles turn left on the A711.

A detour can be made by turning right on the A745 for 6 miles to the town of **Castle Douglas** (TIC: Markethill, tel. 01556 502611, Easter-Oct.). 3 miles beyond, off the A75, are **Threave Gardens** (NTS, 0900-sunset; Moderate; visitor centre 0930-1730 April-Oct.), set in 60 acres of beautiful grounds, and, on an island in the Dee, the imposing **Threave Castle** (HS, except closed Oct.-Mar.; Inexpensive), built 1360-90 by Archibald the Grim of the Black Douglas family, whose many victims were hung above the doorway. Return to the A711.

After half a mile turn left to visit **Orchardton Tower** (HS, open access; Free. Custodian in nearby cottage), a rare example of a 15thC circular tower house. Continue on the A711. 9 miles southwest is **Dundrennan Abbey** (HS, except 0930-1300 Thu. and closed Fri., April-Sep.; closed Oct.-Mar.; Inexpensive), a Cistercian abbey founded in 1142, and the last place Mary Queen of Scots (*see* A-Z) stayed in Scotland before she fled to England in 1568, never to return. Its architecture is a mixture of Norman and transitional Gothic. It has fine transepts and an interesting doorway to the 13thC chapterhouse. Follow the A711 north past the MOD firing range.

77 miles – **Kirkcudbright**. TIC: Harbour Sq., tel. 01557 330494, Easter-Oct. An attractive town on an estuary dotted with fishing boats. Pronounced 'kirk-coo-bree', the name comes from 'Kirk Cuthbert', a now-disappeared church which housed the bones of St. Cuthbert, a 7thC monk from Northumbria. **MacLellan's Castle** (HS; Inexpensive) on the waterfront was built in 1582 with stones from the old Greyfriars Abbey. The **Stewartry Museum** (1100-1600 Mar., April & Oct., 1100-1700 May, June & Sep., 1100-1930 July & Aug., Mon.-Sat.; Inexpensive) has local history and art collections, including works by 'Glasgow Style' artist Jessie M. King, and exhibits on John Paul Jones, father of the American Navy. On High St is **Broughton House** (NTS, 1300-1730 April-Oct.; Inexpensive), home of the painter E.A. Hornel (1864-1933) (*see* Glasgow Boys), now the Hornel Art Gallery and Library with displays of his work. The **Tolbooth Art Centre** (tel. 01557 331556) recalls the town's artists' colony and has changing exhibitions of contemporary art. Take the A755 northwest and after 5.5 miles turn left on the A75. 3.5 miles beyond is **Cardoness Castle** (HS; Inexpensive), on a crag at the turnoff to Gatehouse of Fleet, a 15thC tower house noted for its original stairway and vaulted basement ceiling. Return to the A75 and after 5.5 miles turn right to **Cairn Holy** (open access; Free), where there are two remarkable chambered cairns dating from 3000 to 2000 BC. Rejoin the A75. 3 miles further on is **Carsluith Castle** (HS, open access; Free), a ruined four-storey L-plan tower house built in the 16thC.

96 miles – **Creetown**. The town itself is off the main road to the right, 1.5 miles

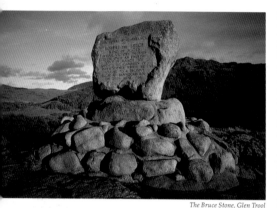

The Bruce Stone, Glen Trool

English. Alternatively, take the A714 north to Bargrennan and turn right for Glentrool Village and beautiful Loch Trool, 10 miles from Newton Stewart, for wide views over the desolate landscape. At the end of the road, on a bluff above the loch stands the Bruce Stone, the site of another skirmish in 1306, when Robert the Bruce and his men rolled boulders onto their English foes. A memorial tomb to six Covenanters (*see* A-Z), killed while at prayer, stands nearby. Above is Merrick, 2766 ft, the highest hill in the Southern Uplands, which can be climbed by a well-marked path. Rejoin the A714 and continue south.

away, and has the **Creetown Gem and Rock Museum** (1000-1800 Easter-Sep.; 1000-1600 Oct.-Dec. & Mar.; 1000-1600 Sat. & Sun., Jan. & Feb.; Inexpensive), an exhibition of minerals from around the world. Rejoin the A75.

101 miles – Newton Stewart. TIC: Dashwood Sq., tel: 01671 402431, Easter-Oct. The late 17thC town takes its name from its founder, William Stewart, a son of the then Earl of Galloway.

A detour can be made 12 miles north-east of Newton Stewart on the A712 to Clatteringshaws Loch, with **Clatteringshaws Forest Wildlife Centre** (1000-1700 April-Oct.; Free) which features natural and local history. Bruce's Stone commemorates the Battle of Rapploch Moss in 1307, one of Robert the Bruce's (*see* A-Z) successful skirmishes against the

106 miles – Wigtown is a small royal burgh whose **Museum** (1400-1600 Mon.-Fri., Easter week and June-Sep.; Free) has local history and the story of the Wigtown Martyrs, two women drowned on stakes in the bay in 1685 for their

Whithorn Dig

Castle Kennedy Gardens

Covenanting beliefs. They are buried in the churchyard, and are also commemorated by Martyrs' Monument on a nearby hill and a pillar on the shore. Continue south on the A714, then turn left on the A746.

117 miles – Whithorn. The first Christian establishment in Scotland was St. Ninian's (*see* A-Z) early 5thC Candida Casa, thought to be on the site of the present graveyard. The ruined early 12thC Whithorn Priory contained his shrine, to which pilgrimages were made. **Whithorn, Cradle of Christianity** (1030-1700 April-Oct.; Inexpensive) gives entry to the priory, museum, the Whithorn Dig, where continuing excavations can be seen, and the Discovery Centre, where finds may be handled. Take the B7004 south for 5 miles to Isle of Whithorn, an attractive village set round a small harbour. St. Ninian's Chapel has associations with early Christianity in Scotland. Take the B7004 back for 0.5 mile, then turn left on the C53. After 2 miles, a detour can be made by turning left for St. Ninian's Cave. The car park is a mile off the main road, and from here it is a walk of 1.5 miles to the cave which was St. Ninian's retreat. Early Christian crosses are carved in the rock. Return to the C53, which becomes the A747 at Glasserton. 5 miles beyond there on the right is Barsalloch Fort, an Iron Age hillfort. The A747 follows the craggy coastline through Port William to the junction with the A75. Turn left then right into Glenluce. Follow a narrow road beneath the old viaduct and signs for the abbey, 2 miles away. **Glenluce Abbey** (HS, except 0930-1630 Sat., 1400-1630 Sun. only, Oct.-Mar.; Inexpensive) was founded in 1192 by Cistercian monks. The elegant 15thC chapterhouse is almost intact. Note the unusual red-clay water pipes. Rejoin the A75 and continue west for 7 miles to the village of Castle Kennedy. To the right are **Castle Kennedy Gardens** (1000-1700 April-Sep.; Inexpensive), set around the Black and White Lochs, with the castle ruins on an isthmus, and including a lily pond, monkey puzzle trees and 35 species of rhododendron. Continue west on the A75.

154 miles – Stranraer. TIC: 1 Bridge St, tel. 01776 702595, Easter -Oct. On the

Logan Botanic Gardens

shores of Loch Ryan, this is the car ferry port for Northern Ireland. **Stranraer Museum** (1000-1700 Mon.-Sat.; Free) in the Old Town Hall has displays on dairy farming and Sir John Ross, the Arctic explorer (1777-1856), whose house, now the Northwest Castle Hotel, can be seen opposite the pier. **Castle of St. John** (1000-1300, 1400-1700 Mon.-Sat., mid April-mid Sep.; Inexpensive), a 16thC tower house, is now a visitor centre with displays on the local area.

A detour can be made to the double-ended peninsula in the southwest corner of Scotland known as the Rhins of Galloway. 7 miles southwest of Stranraer on the A77 stands Portpatrick, a small holiday resort, until 1849 the departure point for sailings to the north of Ireland. With the advent of steam, sailings transferred to Stranraer. The ruins of 15thC Dunskey Castle stand on nearby (dangerous) cliffs. Continue on the B7042 and A716 to **Ardwell House Gardens** (1000-1800 Mar.-Oct.; Inexpensive), with daffodils and rhododendrons, then on the B7065 to

Logan Botanic Gardens (1000-1800 Mar.-Oct.; Inexpensive). This area has the mildest climate in Scotland, and many subtropical plants, such as palms, flourish here. On the north shore of Logan Bay is a fish pond, built into the rock to serve as a larder for Logan House. Now the fish can be fed by hand. The Mull of Galloway, the most southerly point in Scotland, with its lighthouse and 200 ft cliffs, is a further 7 miles south. Return to Stranraer on the A716.

Turn north out of Stranraer on the A77. The road hugs the shore of Loch Ryan for several miles, then turns inland. In 17 miles is Ballantrae, a pretty village with the ruin of Ardstinchar Castle on the hill above it. Continue north on the A77, following the rocky coastline.

181 miles – Girvan. TIC: Bridge St, tel. 01465 714950, April-Oct. This old smuggling town has become a popular resort for its harbour and beaches. Boat trips (tel. 01465 713219) go to **Ailsa Craig**, a 1114 ft-high granite rock 10 miles

Ailsa Craig

offshore, from which curling stones were once made, and now a bird sanctuary which is home to gannets and guillemots. On nearby Dowhill are the remains of a Pictish (*see* Picts) fort. Return to the main road and drive north along the coast, with excellent views of Ailsa Craig. After 4.5 miles turn left on the A719.

186 miles – **Turnberry**, famed for its links golf courses and Edwardian hotel. The much-ruined **Turnberry Castle** (open access; Free) is where Robert the Bruce is believed to have been born in 1274. Beyond Maidens, a detour can be made by turning right to Kirkoswald, 1.5 miles away on the A77. Here, **Souter Johnnie's Cottage** (NTS, 1330-1730 April-Sep.; Sat. & Sun., Oct.; Inexpensive) was the thatched home of

Crossraguel Abbey

souter (cobbler) John Davidson, immortalized in Robert Burns' (*see* A-Z) famous poem *Tam o' Shanter*. On the left 1.5 miles beyond Kirkoswald is **Crossraguel Abbey** (HS, except 0930-1300 Thu. and closed Fri., April-Sep.; closed Oct.-Mar.; Inexpensive), a Cluniac monastery whose 13th-16thC ruins are remarkably complete. Rejoin the A719 and continue north.

192 miles – Culzean Castle and Country Park (NTS, castle 1030-last admission 1700 April-Oct.; park 0900-sunset; Moderate), pronounced 'cul-ane'. Designed 1772-92 by Robert Adam (*see* A-Z) for the Earl of Cassillis, the castle is situated on a clifftop which affords wonderful views of the Firth of Clyde, and is one of Adam's greatest achievements. Inside are the magnificent round drawing room and oval staircase, and many Adam details. There are also displays relating to Gen. Eisenhower, who was given a suite of rooms in recognition of his role as Commander in Chief of Allied Forces in Europe in World War II. There are 565 acres of wooded grounds with an aviary, walled garden and visitor centre. Return to the main road and in 5 miles is the Electric Brae, an optical illusion which makes the road appear to go up when in fact it's going down. Try taking your handbrake off in the layby and see! A short distance beyond is the village of Dunure, reached by turning left

Culzean Castle

off the main road, and overlooked by the ruins of 13thC Dunure Castle, where the Earl of Cassillis is said to have roasted alive the abbot of Crossraguel Abbey to try and force him to give up the abbey lands. Rejoin the A719 and continue north past the cliffs known as the Heads of Ayr. Turn right off the A719.

202 miles – **Alloway** is the village at the heart of 'Burns Country'. **Burns Cottage and Museum** (0900-1800 Mon.-Sat., 1000-1800 Sun., June-Aug.; 1000-1700 Mon.-Sat., 1300-1700 Sun., April- May & Sep.-Oct., 1000-1600 Mon.-Sat., Nov.-Mar.; Inexpensive) is where the poet was born. The Burns Monument and Garden contains the **Land o' Burns Visitor Centre** (1000-1730 July & Aug., 1000-1700 Sep.-June; Free) with material about his

Burns Cottage, Alloway

life, and the new **Tam o' Shanter Experience** (Inexpensive), a multimedia presentation of Burns' famous poem. Opposite is **Alloway Auld Kirk** (open access; Free), the ruined church where

Burns Monument and Garden, Alloway

witches and warlocks danced in the same poem. Nearby is the Auld Brig o' Doon where Tam escaped the witches. **The Maclaurin Gallery and Rozelle House** (1000-1700 Mon.-Sat.; also 1400-1700 Sun., April-Oct.; Free) comprise an 18thC mansion altered in the 19thC and a converted stable block set in extensive parkland. As well as housing local and military history displays, they also have an important contemporary art collection and sculptures by Henry Moore. Continue along Alloway Pl. to Ayr.

204 miles – **Ayr** (*see* A-Z). Leave the town north on the A79.

205 miles – **Prestwick** is a famous golfing resort with three courses. Prestwick Airport was once a famous fog-free airport for flights to North America but has declined since the expansion of Glasgow Airport. Continue north on the A79 and after a mile turn left on the A78. Another mile further on is the turnoff on the A7591 to **Troon** (TIC: Municipal Buildings, South Beach, tel. 01292 317696, Easter-Sep.), a popular Clyde coast resort with six golf courses. Return to the A78 and carry on north.

214 miles – **Irvine**. TIC: New St, tel. 01294 313886. An ancient burgh with a rich maritime history, Irvine became a New Town with Kilwinning in 1966. The old town, created a royal burgh in 1372, contains Glasgow Vennel (or lane), where Robert Burns lived for a short time at No. 4, and worked at the thatched Heckling Shop, where he learned to 'heckle' or comb out flax. Both buildings are now part of the **Glasgow Vennel Museum** (1000-1300, 1400-1700 Mon., Tue. & Thu.-Sat., 1400-1700 Sun., June-Sep.; 1000-1300, 1400-1700 Tue. & Thu.-Sat., Oct.-May; Free). The ruins of the mainly 16thC Seagate Castle overlook Irvine's old harbour. In the Harbourside area is the **Scottish Maritime Museum** (1000-1700 April-Oct.; Inexpensive), a

large-scale, ongoing museum project which has boats including the *Carrick*, the world's oldest clipper, and a Clyde 'puffer' or small cargo boat, as well as part of a shipyard and a reconstructed shipyard worker's tenement flat. Nearby is the massive **Magnum Leisure Centre** (0900-2200; Inexpensive), with an amazing range of sports facilities, plus the Spacebowl water flume, a cinema/theatre and children's play areas. Leave Irvine on the A78 northbound. On the right is **Eglinton Country Park** (dawn-dusk; visitor centre 1000-1630 Easter/April-Sep.; Free), with 400 hectares of parkland and landscaped gardens, plus a ruined castle and Georgian stable block. This was the site of the famous Eglinton Tournament of 1839, a nostalgic re-creation of a medieval event attended by the high society of the day, despite torrential rain. At the Eglinton interchange take the A737 north.

218 miles – **Kilwinning**. **Kilwinning Abbey** (HS, open access; Free) was founded in the 12thC, though its ruins are probably 13thC. Also founded when the abbey was built was Scotland's oldest masonic lodge, known as the Mother Lodge, in Main St. The poet Robert Service lived for a time at 178-180 Main St. On Dalry Rd is Dalgarven Mill (tel. 01294 552448), a working water mill with displays on Ayrshire country life and costume. Leave on the A738, which joins the A78 for the section just before Stevenston. Continue through Stevenston, a former mining town, to visit Saltcoats and Ardrossan. Together these form the Three Towns which were once separate settlements along the bay. **Saltcoats** takes its name from the salt 'cotes' or saltmakers' cottages which once lined the shore. The **North Ayrshire Museum** (1000-1300, 1400-1700 Mon., Tue. & Thu.-Sat; Free) has displays of local history in an 18thC church. The

harbour and promenade recall the town's past as a port and one of the Clyde coast resorts for holidaymakers escaping industrial Glasgow. **Ardrossan** (TIC: Ferry Terminal Building, The Harbour, tel: 01294 601063, April-Oct.), a planned town around a 19thC harbour, is the departure point for ferries to Arran (*see* A-Z). Above the town are the remains of **Ardrossan Castle** (open access; Free), a 12thC castle destroyed by Oliver Cromwell. Rejoin the A78 at the north of the town. On the left after 8 miles is **Hunterston Nuclear Power Station** (visitor centre 0930-1630; Free, tel. 0800 838557 to book guided tours). Beyond the small resort of Fairlie on the right is **Kelburn Castle and Country Centre** (grounds and attractions 1000-1800 April-Oct.; Moderate; grounds only 1100-1700/dusk Nov.-Mar.; Inexpensive; limited summer opening of castle, tel. 01475 568685/554; Inexpensive extra charge), with a wooded glen, gardens with rare trees, and a monument by Robert Adam, as well as riding, a commando assault course and many children's attractions. The castle, still the home of the Earls of Glasgow, is a tower house with later additions and fine 18thC interiors. Continue north on the A78.
236 miles – Largs. TIC: Promenade, tel. 01475 673765. A popular resort for golfing, sailing and watersports, as well as for its ice-cream parlours, Largs is also the terminal for ferries to Millport on Cumbrae (*see* A-Z). The ambitious new **Vikingar Centre** (0900-1800 April-Sep., 1000-1630 Oct.-Mar.; Moderate) celebrates Largs' Viking past in a multimedia presentation on the history of the Vikings which shows their influence in Scotland until the Battle of Largs of 1263, when the Scots defeated the Norwegian King Haakon IV. The battle is also commemorated by the Pencil Tower (1911) on South Shore. The

exquisite **Skelmorlie Aisle** (HS, except 0930-1330 Thu. and closed Fri.; open June-Aug. only; Inexpensive) of 1636 is all that remains of Largs Old Kirk and contains a Renaissance-style tomb and a painted wooden ceiling. **The Christian Heritage Museum** (1000-1230, 1400-1700 Mon.-Sat., 1400-1700 Sun., Easter-Sep.; Free) in the Benedictine monastery has displays on monasticism. The Three Sisters in Waterside St are columns erected by the astronomer Sir Thomas Brisbane. In Douglas Park, the **Haylie Chambered Tomb** (open access; Free) is thought to date from 3000 BC. Leave on the A78 south and turn left on the A760.
244 miles – Kilbirnie. The 15thC **Auld Kirk** (afternoons July & Aug., tel. 01505 682348) is one of the oldest churches still in use in Scotland and includes the beautiful 16thC Crawford Gallery. The **Stables Museum** (1400-1600 Tue. & Thu., 1000-1200 Sat., May-Sep.; Free) has local history collections in the stables of a former coaching inn. **Kilbirnie Place**, or palace (open access; Free), destroyed by fire in the 18thC, is now a ruin. Continue on the A760.
249 miles – Lochwinnoch. The **RSPB Nature Centre** (1000-1700; Inexpensive) has a visitor centre, observation tower, nature trails and hides. Breeding birds include the great crested grebe and the sedge warbler. **Castle Semple Country Park** (0900-dusk; visitor centre 1230-dusk Mon.-Fri., 1000-dusk Sat. & Sun.; Free) is popular for watersports on Castle Semple Loch and also has walks. Continue on the A760 and turn left after 2 miles on the A737. After 7 miles turn left for a mile to Kilbarchan, a well-preserved weaving village. The 18thC **Weaver's Cottage** (NTS, 1300-1730 Easter-Sep.; Sat. & Sun. only, Oct.; Inexpensive) has displays on weaving. Return to the A737. After 6 miles, join the M8 eastbound to Glasgow (278 miles).

Auld Brig o' Doon, Alloway

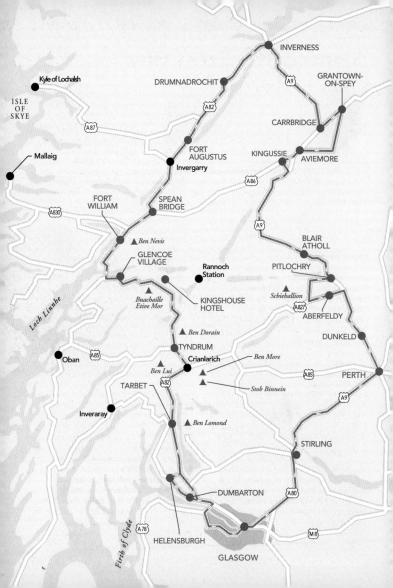

Glencoe, the Great Glen and Perthshire

4 days

This excursion is a variant of one of the most popular routes in Scotland, starting at Loch Lomond and heading up into the Western Highlands through awesome Glencoe, then up the Great Glen to Loch Ness and the Highlands' capital, Inverness. It returns down the centre of Scotland, visiting the Cairngorms and crossing the Grampian Mountains into Perthshire through such picturesque towns as Pitlochry and Dunkeld. The route described is from Glasgow. Visitors travelling from the Edinburgh area can join it via the M8 or may prefer to take the M90 to Perth and do the excursion in reverse.

Leave Glasgow on the A82 for Loch Lomond. Off to the left in 16 miles is **Dumbarton** (*see* A-Z), from where the A814 leads to **Helensburgh** (*see* A-Z). 21 miles from Glasgow is beautiful **Loch Lomond** (*see* A-Z), with views across the loch to Ben Lomond. At Tarbet, follow the A82 round to the right, continuing up the loch. Of several old inns, the Inverarnan is entertainingly eccentric. Up on the hill behind Inverarnan Falls. 2 miles further on is parking for the Falls of Falloch. At the little village of Crianlarich, the A82 continues round to the left. Before reaching Tyndrum the scenery is already changing, with the well-defined outline of Ben Lui, 3708 ft, off to the left, and the twin conical peaks of Ben More, 3852 ft, and Stob Binnein, 3821 ft, back to the right, beyond Crianlarich.
62 miles – **Tyndrum**. TIC: Main St, tel. 01838 400246, April-Oct. This little village is a useful stopping place to eat and is where Excursion 4 may join. Carry on up the A82 which now ascends to Bridge of Orchy, where there is a hotel, and on the right is the dramatic silhouette of Ben Dorain, 3524 ft. Ahead are good views of the Black Mount, a

Glencoe

popular hillwalking area with Loch Tulla in the foreground. The road now winds up past the loch to the desolate expanse of Rannoch Moor, a vast area of peat bog, dotted with lochans, which stretches east for about 12 miles to Rannoch Station on the West Highland railway line. At its summit, over 1500 ft, the road now sweeps left towards the mountains guarding the entrance to dramatic **Glencoe**, notably Buachaille Etive Mor, the 'Great Herdsman of Etive', 3345 ft, an awe-inspiring, pyramid-shaped mountain. Off to the left, a minor road leads to **Glencoe Chairlift** (1000-1700

June-Sep.; Thu.-Mon., Jan.-April, last admission 1600; Moderate), with magnificent views of Glencoe and Rannoch Moor and a popular ski centre in winter. To the right is the Kingshouse Hotel, said to be Scotland's oldest inn and where mountain bikes can be hired. On the left, beyond the bridge, an unclassified road leads 14 miles down beautiful Glen Etive. Continue on the A82 where it reaches its highest point below the Buachaille, popular with rock climbers. Ahead is breathtaking Glencoe, formed by a volcano collapsing on itself during a series of violent eruptions. On the right is the steep mountain wall of Aonach Eagach, while on the left are the brooding crags of The Three Sisters with, high up towards the west end, on the face of Aonach Dubh, a cleft known as Ossian's Cave, said to be the

birthplace of the mythical Gaelic bard. Descend into the upper gorge of the River Coe, past a splendid waterfall on the left, to reach a white farmhouse at the Meeting of the Three Waters.

A few hundred yards further on there is a large layby on the left. From it there is an interesting 2 hr walk to the Lost Valley, a hidden mountain meadow tucked

between the first and second of The Three Sisters. The path descends to the east of the layby towards a footbridge over the river, then climbs steeply by the little stream that falls from the valley, mostly invisible beneath boulders. The path passes between huge rocks amid beautiful birch woods, and finally comes out onto the flat meadow, where cattle-

Loch Rannoch and Schiehallion

raiders once concealed their stolen herds. Return to the layby.

Continue down the glen past Loch Achtriochtan and take the minor road on the right which leads to the Clachaig Inn, a traditional climbers' pub and hotel with live folk music on Sat. night, close to the site of the infamous Glencoe Massacre (*see* A-Z). There are forest walks beyond the hotel. A footbridge across the river leads to the **NTS Visitor Centre** (1000-1700 April-mid May & Sep.-Oct., 0930-1800 mid May-Aug.; Inexpensive), also accessible by car from the main road. The road continues beyond Clachaig to the attractive little Glencoe Village. Turn left to return to the main road.

95 miles – **Ballachulish.** TIC: tel. 01855 811296, April-Oct. The village is surrounded by a number of old slate quarries whose story is told in an exhibition at the TIC. Continue on the A82 at the roundabout, across Ballachulish Bridge. Above the road is a white stone on a rock plinth, commemorating James Stewart, hanged here in 1752 for the alleged murder of Colin Campbell of Glenure, the incident which inspired Robert Louis Stevenson's (*see* A-Z) *Kidnapped*. From the bridge is a good view back up Loch Leven, with the prominent peak of the Pap of Glencoe. From North Ballachulish, the B863 leads round Loch Leven and, at Kinlochleven, is the **Aluminium Story** (1000-1700 Mon.-Fri., 1200-1630 Sat. & Sun., mid April-mid Oct.; 1000-1200, 1300-1700 Tue. & Thu., 1000-1200, 1300-1500 Wed., Fri. & Sat., mid Oct.-mid April; Free), an audiovisual and video presentation on the industry which was brought to this remote area 80 years

ago. Continuing on the A82, at Onich is an ancient standing stone.

109 miles – **Fort William** (*see* A-Z). Take the A82 north. At the edge of the town is a roundabout with a minor road right to Glen Nevis, a beautiful 9 mile drive round the west and south sides of **Ben Nevis** (*see* A-Z). After a mile is a parking area at the foot of a path up the mountain, the highest in the British Isles. The road continues past a caravan/camp site, the Glen Nevis Restaurant and Bar, the youth hostel, and the new **Glen Nevis Visitor Centre, Ionad Nibheis** (0900-1700 Mon.-Fri., 0900-1300, 1400-1700 Sat. & Sun., April-Oct.; 1100-1500 Fri.-Mon., Nov.-Mar.; Free), which gives the history of the glen and Ben Nevis, while a ranger service can provide guided walks for all levels in the summer. The road then crosses the river at a waterfall and passes under Polldubh Crags, popular with rock climbers, before ending at a parking area by a huge waterslide.

Ben Nevis

A 1.5 hr walk starts here. The path is well-marked but stony (stout footwear is recommended) and follows the north bank of the River Nevis as it roars through a rocky wooded gorge for 0.5 mile then emerges unexpectedly into a lovely green meadow ringed by mountains, with the spectacular Steall Waterfall on the hillside opposite. For those with a steady head, there is an Indiana Jones-style wire bridge which crosses the river to a mountain bothy. Beyond, to the south side of the waterfall, there is a

Commando Memorial, Spean Bridge

magnificent view of the back of Ben Nevis. Return to the parking area by the same path.

Back on the A82, 2 miles out of Fort William, a minor road on the left leads to the imposing ruin of the late 13thC Old Inverlochy Castle (exterior only). Nearby is **Ben Nevis Distillery** (0930-last tour 1630, Mon.-Fri.; also Sat., June-Aug.; Free), with tours, exhibition and audiovisual. Turn left at the A830 to cross Neptune's Staircase, Thomas Telford's (*see* A-Z) spectacular entrance to the Caledonian Canal at the beginning of the **Great Glen** (*see* A-Z), where, in a series of eight locks in the space of 500 yd, boats are lifted 65 ft. At Corpach, **Treasures of the Earth** (0930-1900 July-Sep.; Inexpensive) is an award-winning attraction with real gemstones, crystals and minerals set in simulated underground caverns and rocks. Return to the A82 and turn left.

On the right is **Nevis Range** (1000-1700 May-June & Sep.-Nov., 1000-1900 July & Aug., 0900-1700 or dusk, Dec.-April; Moderate), a cable-car system up to Aonach Mor, 4006 ft, beside Ben Nevis. At the top station there's an interpretive display plus a restaurant and marked footpaths. At the base station are forestry walks and mountain bike hire. Continue on the A82.

125 miles – **Spean Bridge**. TIC: tel. 01397 712576, April-Oct. 3 miles along the A86 at Roybridge, a minor road leads left to the strange Parallel Roads, two massive tracks each 30 ft wide, said to have been made by the giant Fingal of Gaelic mythology, but in fact gravel beaches formed on the mountainside as water levels receded in the last Ice Age. Return to Spean Bridge and continue on the A82. In a short distance is the famous Commando Memorial, erected in 1952 in memory of the World War II soldiers who trained in this area.

Caledonian Canal, Fort Augustus

gives the town its name. The abbey has an extensive visitor centre and exhibition on monastic life, the old fort and the area. In the old school-house is located **The Young Clansmen** (0900-2100 May-Oct.; Inexpensive), with an exhibition and a 'blackhouse' (see Architecture) showing Highland life in the past. Cruise Loch Ness (tel. 01320 366221/277) and Loch Ness Ferry Co. (tel. 01320 366233) have cruises on the loch. The road now follows the shores of Loch Ness, famous for its elusive monster (see Great Glen). The greatest number of sightings have been made from **Urquhart Castle** (HS, except 1000-1830 Sun., April-Sep.; 1130-1630 Sun., Oct.-Mar.; Inexpensive), an impressive ruin 18 miles north of Fort Augustus. **169 miles – Drumnadrochit**. The village has two exhibitions dedicated to Loch Ness and its monster. **The Original Loch Ness Visitor Centre** (0800-2130 June-Sep., 0900-1700 Oct.-May; Inexpensive) has an interesting film on the monster which, for some, is more entertaining than the much more authoritative **Official Loch Ness Monster Exhibition** (1030-1730 Easter-May, 0930-1830 June & Sep., 0900-2030 July & Aug., 0930-1800 Oct., 1000-1600 Nov.-Easter, last admission 1 hr before closing; Moderate). There are also cruises with sonar equipment from the Original Loch Ness Centre (tel. 01456 430395) during April-Oct. The latest addition to the Nessie search is the Loch Ness Submarine (tel. 01285 760762;

Continue on the A82 along the banks of Loch Lochy through Laggan Locks. A few miles further on, at a car park opposite a shop, is the Well of the Seven Heads, marked by a monument topped with a sculpture of seven severed heads. This gruesome memorial records a notorious 17thC murder, described on the monument in English, Gaelic, Latin and French. The spring itself is in a low tunnel underneath. Continue north along the side of Loch Oich through Invergarry. To the left, the A87 goes by Lochs Garry and Cluanie and through scenic Glen Shiel to reach the west coast at Kyle of Lochalsh (see Excursion 6). **148 miles – Fort Augustus**. TIC: Car Park, tel. 01320 366367, April-Oct. A pleasant town at the southern end of Loch Ness, Fort Augustus has walks on the towpath of the Caledonian Canal, and in Auchterawe (turn left just beyond the town). Between the town and the loch is **Fort Augustus Abbey** (0900-1800, last admission 1700; Inexpensive), a Benedictine monastery on and around Gen. Wade's (see Jacobites) fort which

Expensive). Continue along the loch shore on the A82. To the left in 6 miles are **Abriachan Gardens** (0900-1900 or dusk; Inexpensive), extensive terraced gardens on the hill above the loch, plus a nursery selling plants. 3 miles further on are **Dochfour Gardens** (1000-1700 Mon.-Fri., 1400-1700 Sat. & Sun., April-Oct.; Inexpensive) at the end of Loch Dochfour, beyond the north end of Loch Ness. Here are specimen trees, yew topiary, rhododendrons and a water garden.

184 miles – **Inverness** (*see* A-Z). Excursion 8 ends here and Excursion 9 begins. Leave Inverness on the A9, heading south. In 2 miles, the B9006 leads left to Culloden (*see* Excursion 9, Jacobites). The main road climbs steadily, crossing Drummossie Muir to **Daviot Wood** (TIC: tel. 01463 772203, April-Oct.). 15 miles from Inverness is Tomatin, where **Tomatin Distillery** (0900-1630 Mon.-Fri., Feb.-Dec.; also 0915-1300 Sat., May-Oct., last tour 1 hr before closing; Free) has a visitor centre and tours. At **Mike Crummy Creative Blacksmiths** (0800-1800 Mon.-Thu., 0800-1300 Fri.; Free) is the working smithy and studio of a well-known artist-blacksmith. Continue south for 5 miles, then left on the A938.

206 miles – **Carrbridge**. TIC: Main St, tel. 01241 552056, May-Sep. The picturesque bridge over Dulnain Water was erected in 1717 after a drowning accident at the ford. The main attraction here is **Landmark Highland Heritage and Adventure Park** (0930-1800 April-June, 0930-2000 July & Aug., 0930-1730 Sep. & Oct., 0930-1700 Nov.-Mar.; Inexpensive), with history and natural history of the Highlands in its multi-vision cinema. Outside are a treetop trail, maze, adventure playground and pine forest nature centre. Continue on the A938 to Dulnain Bridge. To the

Urquhart Castle, Loch Ness

right, off the A95, is the **Speyside Heather Garden and Visitor Centre** (0900-1700 April-Oct., closed Sun. Nov.-Mar.; Inexpensive), detailing the historic uses for heather from thatch to medicine, plus a garden with around 300 different varieties. From Dulnain Bridge continue northeast on the A95.

216 miles – **Grantown-on-Spey**. TIC: High St, tel. 01479 872773, April-Oct. This is a fine 18thC planned town in the Spey valley. Excursion 11 passes nearby at Tomintoul. Leave Grantown on the A939 south and in a mile turn right on the B970. At Nethy Bridge turn left for **Loch Garten (RSPB) Nature Reserve** (1000-2000 mid April-Aug., observation post only; Sep.-mid April, open access; Inexpensive), where ospreys have returned every year to nest since 1959, after they had been extinct in Scotland. Continue on the B970. To the right, in Boat of Garten village, is the small but interesting museum of the Strathspey Steam Railway (see next page). Carry on down the B970, then turn right at Coylumbridge.

Strathspey Steam Railway, Boat of Garten

233 miles – **Aviemore**. TIC: Grampian Rd, tel. 01479 810363. This once small village boomed in the sixties with the development of the ski centre in the Cairngorms. Its range and quality of facilities are currently under review. From Aviemore take the B970 south, then Dalfaber Rd for the **Strathspey Steam Railway** (tel. 01479 810725 for details and timetable) which runs between Aviemore and Boat of Garten. Also off the B970 is the **Rothiemurchus Estate** (visitor centre 0900-1730), with walks, an exhibition, mountain bike and ski hire, trout farm and even clay-pigeon shooting. The ski slopes are 11.5 miles from Aviemore. The **Chairlift** (0900-1630; Moderate) goes almost to the summit of Cairn Gorm and the Ptarmigan Restaurant at 3600 ft. Return to the B970 and turn left to Loch an Eilean, a beautiful loch with a ruined 15thC castle at its centre, surrounded by pine forest. A gentle walk round the

loch takes about 45 min. The **Visitor Centre** (0930-1630; Free) here houses an exhibition on the ecology of the area. Continue south on the B970 to Feshiebridge, a high, single-arch bridge. 200 yd further on is a road on the left leading into secluded Glen Feshie. Continue on the B970 and after a mile turn right towards the B9152. **Loch Insh Watersports Centre** (1000-1800 May-Oct., tel. 01540 651272) is just beyond the intersection. Follow the road over the Spey at the northern shore of Loch Insh into Kincraig. Leave the village and turn left on the B9152, where, a short distance south, is the **Highland Wildlife Park** (1000-1700 June-Aug., 1000-1600 April-May & Sep.-Oct.; Expensive), a drive-through park with Scottish wildlife past and present, including wildcats, deer, lynx, wolves and bears in their natural habitat. Allow at least 2.5 hr; transport can be arranged. Continue on the B9152.

Insh Church, Kincraig

274 miles – **Kingussie** (pronounced 'king-yoosee'). TIC: King St, tel. 01540 661297, May-Sep. A pleasant town whose best-known attraction is the **Highland Folk Museum** (1000-1800 Mon.-Sat., 1400-1800 Sun., April-Oct.; 1000-1700 Mon.-Fri., Nov.-Mar.; Inexpensive). Outside are a number of reconstructed dwellings, including a blackhouse from Lewis and a turf-walled house from the Central Highlands. Inside, see the dairy, stables and exhibits of Highland weapons, furniture and music. Just southeast on the B970 are the extensive

Highland Wildlife Park, Kingussie

ruins of **Ruthven Barracks** (HS, open access), erected in 1719 after the 1715 Jacobite Rebellion (*see* Jacobites) and captured and burned in 1746 by Bonnie Prince Charlie's army. Take the A86 down the Spey valley to Newtonmore, which, like its near neighbour, Kingussie, is famous for its shinty team who play a hockey-like game of Irish origin. Shinty is the subject of a display at the **Highland Folk Park** (1000-1700 Mon.-Sat., April-Sep.; Inexpensive). Others include crofting and crafts.

The Clan Macpherson Museum (1000-1730 Mon.-Sat., 1430-1730 Sun., May-Sep.; Free) has interesting memorabilia. **Waltzing Waters** (shows on the hour 1000-1700, also 2030, Mar.-Dec.; Inexpensive) creates amazing patterns of water synchronized with music. Leave by the B9150 to join the A9 heading south. At Etteridge after 4 miles, an unclassified road leads right to **Dalwhinnie**, whose

Clan Macpherson Museum, Newtonmore

distillery (0930-1700 Mon.-Fri.; Free) is believed to be the highest in Scotland. The A9 is rejoined via the A889. The road now climbs up over Drumochter Pass, a bleak expanse of scree, heather, glaciated valleys and icy lochs. Keep an

eye open for deer. 30 miles south of Newtonmore, turn left on a minor road to Bruar, where a path leads up to the Falls of Bruar, three waterfalls in a narrow cleft. Nearby is the **Clan Donnachaidh (Donnachy) Museum** (1000-1300, 1400-1700 Mon. & Wed.-Sat., 1400-1700 Sun., mid April-mid Oct.; Free) of the clan which includes those with surnames Duncan, MacConnachie, Reid and Robertson. Return to the A9 and continue south.

312 miles – **Blair Atholl** is a pleasant village sitting alongside the River Tilt at the hub of several glens. **Blair Castle** (1000-1800, last admission 1700, April-

Blair Castle, Blair Atholl

Loch Faskally Dam, Pitlochry

Oct.; Moderate) is one of the most popular attractions in Scotland. This white, turreted baronial mansion has a tower dating back to c1269 but there are additions from most centuries. Previous visitors included Mary Queen of Scots (*see* A-Z) and Queen Victoria. Outside are a deer park, pony trekking and nature trails. The castle is home to the Duke of Atholl, who commands the only private army in Britain. **Blair Atholl Mill** (1030-1730 Mon.-Sat., 1200-1730 Sun., April-Oct.; Inexpensive) is a 1613 water mill, producing oatmeal and flour. **The Atholl Country Collection** (1330-1730 Easter, June & Oct., 0930-1730 July-Sep.; Inexpensive) includes a blacksmith's, a crofter's byre and living room, and the Trinafour Post Office. There are beautiful walks in Glen Fender. Leave the village on the minor road and continue on it for 4 miles to the **Pass of Killiecrankie** (NTS visitor centre 1000-1730 April-Dec.; Inexpensive), where in 1689 the first battle of the Jacobites' cause was fought, when 'Bonnie Dundee', John Graham of Claverhouse, led Jacobite rebels to victory over troops of King William. In the gorge where the River Garry thunders between rocks is the Soldier's Leap. Here, a government soldier hurled himself across to escape his pursuers. Just a mile beyond the village of Killiecrankie lies Garry Bridge. Turn left on the B8019.
320 miles – **Pitlochry**. TIC: 22 Atholl Rd, tel. 01796 472215/751. This attractive little town lies at the head of the man-made Loch Faskally. The **Hydro-Electric Visitor Centre** (0940-1730 April-Oct.; Inexpensive) has viewing windows through which salmon can be seen on the fish ladder. Pitlochry Festival Theatre (tel. 01796 472680) has repertory theatre and Sun. concerts May-Oct. in a modern building on the banks of the Tay. Other attractions include **Edradour Distillery** (0930-1700 Mon.-Sat., Mar.-Oct.; Free), said to be the smallest in the world, and **Bell's Blair Athol Distillery** (0930-1700 Mon.-Sat., 1200-1700 Sun., Easter-Oct.; 0930-1700 Mon.-Fri., Nov.-Easter; Moderate), situated to the south of the town. Leave Pitlochry on the B8019

Wade's Bridge, Aberfeldy

back to Killiecrankie, then follow the road west to Loch Tummel. In 7 miles is Queen's View, named after Queen Victoria who visited here in 1866. There are magnificent views down Loch Tummel to Schiehallion, 3554 ft. The road runs along the north side of the loch and past Erochty hydro-electric power station. Turn left at Tummel Bridge on the B846. At Braes of Foss, to the right, is a car park from where the path up Schiehallion (*see* Walking) begins. There are stunning views as the road climbs out of the valley. 2 miles further on, a detour can be made right on the single-track road signposted Schiehallion which crosses the barren moorland lined with snow posts. **Glengoulandie Deer Park** (0900-1 hr before sunset; Inexpensive) has red deer, Highland cattle and a variety of endangered species.

Just over 0.5 mile beyond the deer park, on the right, is a detour leading 3 miles to **Fortingall**, where, in the churchyard, is a yew tree reputed to be 3000 years old. It is also claimed that the nearby Roman fort was the birthplace of Pontius Pilate. Beyond Fortingall, the detour can be continued by turning right up beautiful Glen Lyon. Rejoin the B846.

The road shortly begins to widen out. **Tullochville Farm Heavy Horse Centre** (1000-1700 Easter-Oct.; Inexpensive) has Clydesdale horses and the ploughs they used to pull. Further on is **Castle Menzies** (1030-1700 Mon.-Sat., 1400-1700 Sun., last admission 1630; Inexpensive), standing on the right at the foot of Weem Rock, a particularly large example of a 16thC Z-plan castle whose design allowed for greater accommodation and improved defences. Continue on the B846 to Weem. Weem Hotel is a whitewashed 17thC building where Gen. Wade stayed on his road- and bridge-building expeditions in 1733.

357 miles – Aberfeldy. TIC: The Square, tel. 01887 820276. Beautifully situated on the banks of the Tay, the town has an impressive Wade bridge. Built in 1733, it is the only one still in use in Scotland.

Beside it is the Black Watch Memorial, a cairn topped by a figure of a soldier in a kilt. **Aberfeldy Distillery** (0930-1630 Mon.-Fri.; Free) has tours, while **Aberfeldy Water Mill** (1000-1730 Mon.-Sat., 1200-1730 Sun., Easter-Oct.; Inexpensive) is a working oatmeal mill. Take the A827 from Aberfeldy, east towards the A9, through lovely Perthshire countryside. At Grandtully is 16thC St. Mary's Church with a fine painted wooden ceiling of the 1630s. 9 miles from Aberfeldy is Logierait, with mortsafes to prevent body-snatching, and sculptured stones in the churchyard. Join the A9 heading south and in 6 miles is the **Hermitage** (NTS), a picturesque area of mixed woodland and rivers with two 18thC follies dedicated to the bard Ossian. Continue south on the A9.

375 miles – Dunkeld. TIC: The Cross, tel. 01350 727688, Mar.-Oct. Cross Telford's seven-arch bridge into this pretty little town which became a major site of Celtic Christianity in the 8thC, after Vikings attacked Iona (see Excursion 5), and the relics of St. Columba (see A-Z) were brought here for safety. The town was also the scene of vicious hand-to-hand fighting in the aftermath of Killiecrankie. In Cathedral St and High St are the delightful 'little houses' restored by the National Trust for Scotland (see A-Z), which also has a shop at the Cross. Nearby is the **Scottish Horse Regiment Museum** (1000-1200, 1400-1700 Thu.-Mon, Easter-Sep.; Inexpensive). **Dunkeld Cathedral** (HS; Free) stands on the banks of the Tay. Though mainly 14th-15thC, parts of it date back to the 12thC. The roof was destroyed in the Reformation (see A-Z), but the restored choir is now the parish church. Note the slightly off-centre West Window and the recumbent effigy, perhaps of the Wolf of Badenoch (see

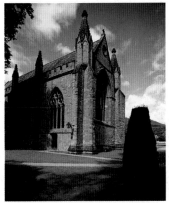
Dunkeld Cathedral

A-Z). Just south of Dunkeld is Birnam Wood, made famous by Shakespeare's *Macbeth* (see A-Z) and reached by the circular Birnam Walk. Rejoin the A9.

390 miles – Perth (see A-Z). Leave on the A9 and after 14 miles take the A823 for 0.5 mile. Gleneagles Hotel, built in 1924, is famed for its championship King's and Queen's Golf Courses. Despite a reputation for exclusivity the hotel does offer some more affordable packages, tel. 01764 662231. At nearby **Auchterarder** is a TIC: High St, tel. 01764 664235. Upstairs is a **Heritage Centre** (0900-1800 Mon.-Sat., June-Aug.; 0930-1730 Mon.-Sat., April-May & Sep.-Oct.; 0930-1330 Mon.-Sat., Nov.-Mar.; Free). **Tullibardine Chapel** (HS, except closed Oct.-Mar.; Free), 15th-16thC, is one of the most complete and unaltered medieval churches in Scotland. Continue on the A9. In 8 miles this excursion meets Excursion 3. Carry on south on the A9 past Dunblane (see Excursion 3), on the A9/M9 to Stirling (see A-Z), and return to Glasgow by the A80/M80 (455 miles).

Glencoe

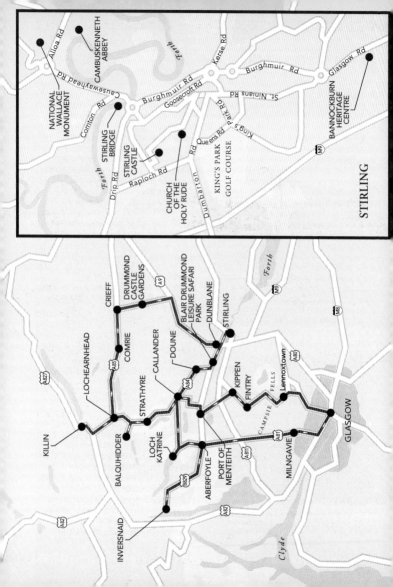

The Trossachs

3 days

One of the most popular areas for day trips and short excursions, the Trossachs (from the Gaelic 'bristly or prickly place'), can be easily reached from the Central Belt in an hour or little more. This excursion starts from and returns to Glasgow. Those travelling from the Edinburgh area could take the M9 to Stirling, then the A811 over to the west and join the excursion by turning right on the A81, 9 miles north of Strathblane. Return by leaving the excursion just after Lennoxtown and turn left on the A803 to Falkirk, then the M9 or see the end of Excursion 12. Because of their rugged beauty, the Trossachs are often known as 'the Highlands in miniature' and, in fact, the Highland Fault Line, the major geological fault which runs between the Highlands and the Lowlands, is crossed and recrossed on the excursion. The area became popular after the publication of Sir Walter Scott's poem *The Lady of the Lake* (1810), set around Loch Katrine. Before that, the Trossachs had been considered a wild and dangerous region, inhabited by outlaws such as Rob Roy. Queen Victoria also fell in love with the area.

Leave Glasgow on the A81 through the suburbs of Bearsden and Milngavie (pronounced 'mill-guy'). Off Milngavie Rd to the left on Roman Rd, Bearsden, is the **Roman Bathhouse** (HS, open access), the best-preserved remains of a Roman building to be seen in Scotland, dating from around AD 140 and built for soldiers in a nearby fort on the Antonine Wall (*see* A-Z). In Milngavie is the **Lillie Art Gallery** (1000-1700 Mon.-Fri., 1400-1700 Sat. & Sun.; Free), with a collection of 20thC Scottish art and temporary exhibitions. Continue on the A81. A mile beyond Milngavie, a road leads left to **Mugdock Country Park** (open access; visitor centre 1000-1700; Free). The park is a large area of woodland, grassland and moor with good views over to Glasgow and containing the fine ruins of 14thC Mugdock Castle by a loch and those of Craigend Castle. The West Highland Way (*see* Walking) starts from here and continues for 95 miles to Fort William. Return to the A81 and continue through the villages of Strathblane and Blanefield, down the steep and twisting Minister's Brae. Up on the right is the kirkyard and 19thC church with, behind, the western slopes of the Campsie Hills.

15 miles – Glengoyne Distillery (1000-1600 Mon.-Sat., 1200-1600 Sun., April-Nov.; Inexpensive) has whitewashed 19thC buildings and, though it lies below the Highland Fault Line, in whisky terms it produces the most southerly of Highland malts. Behind it, the steep hill of Dumgoyne protrudes from the edge of the Campsies and is a popular climb. Continue on the A81 across mainly flat farmland with, on the right, some remaining patches of Flanders Moss, the vast peat bog which once covered this area. After 12 miles turn left on the A821.

28 miles – Aberfoyle. TIC: Main St, tel. 01877 382352, April-Oct. This pleasant village at the foot of the Trossachs hills has become a busy centre with hotels, guesthouses and eating places. **The Scottish Wool Centre** (0930-1800 Mon.-

Fri., 0930-1830 Sat. & Sun., April-Sep.; 1000-1630 Mon.-Fri., 1000-1700 Sat. & Sun., Nov.-Feb.; 1000-1700 Mon.-Fri., 1000-1750 Sat. & Sun., Mar.; Free; theatre shows daily April-Oct., Sat. & Sun., Nov.-Mar.; Inexpensive) has theatre presentations on the history of sheep and the work of the shepherd, and features live specimens. It also has spinning and weaving and, outside, occasional sheepdog demonstrations. South of the River Forth, the kirkyard contains the ruins of the old kirk, the grave of 17thC minister Robert Kirk and cast-iron mortsafes to prevent grave robbing. The signposted Doon Hill or Fairy Knowe walk leads to the place where, in 1692, Rev. Kirk was said to have been carried off by fairies a year after his book, *The Secret Commonwealth of Elves, Fauns and Fairies*, appeared.

A detour can be made from Aberfoyle on the B829 by Loch Ard and Loch Chon to Stronachlachar (11 miles) on Loch Katrine and by Loch Arklet to **Inversnaid** (14 miles) on Loch Lomond. Nearby are Inversnaid Falls. Rob Roy's Cave, 2 miles north, is where the outlaw is said to have hidden when on the run, and can be reached on foot on part of the West Highland Way (*see* Walking).

Leave Aberfoyle on the A821 north on the steep Duke's Pass, named after the Duke of Montrose, the landowner who built it in the early 19thC. It climbs and winds through the Trossachs proper which still 'bristle' with a thick undergrowth of heather and bracken, while native trees such as silver birch and rowan still grow among non-native pines in what is now the massive **Queen Elizabeth Forest Park**, whose visitor centre (1000-1800 Easter-Oct., 1000-1800 Sat. & Sun., Nov. & Dec.; Free) lies off to the right in a mile. It provides information on all aspects of the forest and sells maps of the forest

trails. Walks include the Highland Fault Trail. To the right 1.5 miles further up the Duke's Pass is the start of **Achray Forest Drive** (1000-1800 Easter-Oct.; Inexpensive), a 7 mile route through the forest to Loch Drunkie and Loch Achray, with some spectacular views. The lochs can also be seen from the Duke's Pass as the road descends. Loch Drunkie, on the right, is aptly named, since it is said to have been the site of illicit whisky stills which were emptied into the loch at the approach of government officers. On the far side of Loch Achray is the distinctive conical shape of Ben A'an, 1326 ft, while to the left appears the mass of Ben Venue, 2386 ft. Turn left at the sign for Loch Katrine.

35 miles – Loch Katrine was the setting for Sir Walter Scott's (*see* A-Z) *The Lady of the Lake*, while Rob Roy (*see* A-Z) was born at Glengyle at its northwest end and hid stolen cattle on one of the islands in the loch. Since 1859 it has provided Glasgow with a very pure supply of drinking water via a 26 mile-long aqueduct to Mugdock Reservoir, Milngavie. A second aqueduct was begun in 1885 and, together, these now supply 85 million gallons of water per day. Only authorized vehicles are permitted beyond the car park, leaving the road which runs round most of the loch quiet for walkers and cyclists. The SS *Sir Walter Scott* (sailings 1100, 1345 & 1515 Sun.-Fri.; 1400 & 1530 Sat., April-Sep.; Moderate) has been plying the loch since 1900 and is the last screw steamer in regular passenger service in Scotland. Built by William Denny & Bros of Dumbarton, the parts had to be transported up Loch Lomond in boats to Inversnaid, then by horse-drawn carts to Stronachlachar where the steamer was assembled. **Loch Katrine Visitor Centre** is open 0900-1630 April-

Sep.; Free. Return to the A821 and turn left along Loch Achray. On the left is the former Trossachs Hotel, an extraordinary mid 19thC castle design with 'candlesnuffer' towers. Further along on the right and also dating from the mid 19thC is the tiny, neo-Gothic Trossachs Church with a fish-scale pattern roof. At the end of Loch Achray on the left, at the foot of Glen Finglas, is the hamlet of Brig o' Turk (from Gaelic *tuirc*, 'wild boar'), where a path leads up the glen. The 19thC Pre-Raphaelite Millais painted part of his portrait of the English art critic John Ruskin here. He also fell in love with Ruskin's wife Effie, whom he later married. In the 1880s some of the Glasgow Boys (*see* A-Z) came here to paint. The road now skirts Loch Venachar, dammed at its east end in 1859 as part of the works to supply Glasgow's water. On the nearside is a crannog (*see* Prehistory) or artificial island linked to the shore by a causeway. Beyond the end of the loch on a hill to the left is a large boulder known as Samson's Putting Stone, which, according to Gaelic folklore, was hurled here in a competition between Formorians or giants. Behind it rises Ben Ledi, 2873 ft, while over to the right is the site of a Roman fort at Bochastle.

45 miles – Kilmahog has two mills, one with a working water wheel. The **Trossachs Trundler** (May-Sep., tel. 01877 382352 for times), a 1950s bus which runs between Callander and Aberfoyle, is often parked here when not in service. Turn left on the A84 and in a mile are the Falls of Leny in the narrow Pass of Leny, with Ben Ledi towering above. There is parking space and a path to the falls. Further on on the left is Loch Lubnaig. Near the village of Strathyre are several walks into the eastern edge of the Queen Elizabeth Forest Park. 2 miles beyond Strathyre is

the turnoff on an unclassified road to **Balquhidder** (1.5 miles) with a beautiful setting at the top of Loch Voil. In the churchyard, beside the modern inscription 'Macgregor despite them' (a reference to the fact that the name Macgregor was proscribed in the 16th to 18thC), are three graves believed to be those of Rob Roy, his wife Mary and two of their sons. The ruined old church, dated 1631, replaced an even earlier one. The present 19thC church (open access) by David Bryce contains the 8th/9thC stone of local Celtic St. Angus and the 17thC bell given by the Rev. Robert Kirk, later of Aberfoyle, plus copies of his Gaelic bible and the Psalms he translated into Gaelic.

58 miles – Lochearnhead is a small village spread out round the west end of Loch Earn and has become an important centre for watersports, particularly waterskiing. Leave Lochearnhead on the A85 northbound, which climbs up through Glen Ogle with hills over 2000 ft on either side. After 5 miles turn right on the A827.

65 miles – Killin. TIC: Main St, tel. 01567 820254, April-Sep. A delightful village at the head of Loch Tay, Killin is a popular resort which has the Falls of Dochart running through its centre. St. Fillan's Mill is now shared by the TIC and **Breadalbane Folklore Centre** (1000-1700 Mar.-May & Oct., 1000-1800 June & Sep., 0900-1830 July & Aug., 1000-1600 Sat. & Sun., Nov., Dec. & Feb.; Inexpensive) which has modern installations and displays of historic objects, including the 'healing stones' blessed by Celtic St. Fillan, and material on Clan Gregor and Clan MacNab. Keys are available to visit the MacNab burial place on Inchbuie island. **Killin Church** (0900-2000 Mon.-Sat., Easter-Sep.) of 1744, on the site of an early church, is a whitewashed building of unusual shape

and contains a 9thC font. Outside is
a monument to Rev. James Stewart,
translator of the New Testament into
Gaelic. The A827 continues along
the north side of Loch Tay and
through Kenmore and Aberfeldy
to meet the A9, while a narrow
unclassified road skirts the south
side. Leave Killin and return to
Lochearnhead and follow the A85
round to the left by the north side of
Loch Earn with impressive views
over to Ben Vorlich, 3224 ft. There is
also an unclassified single-track road
round the south side.

78 miles – St. Fillans is a very pretty
little village at the east end of Loch
Earn. Continue east on the A85 to
Comrie. Just outside is **Earthquake
House** (daylight hours; Free), built
in 1874 to record the minor earth
tremors which occur here due to
proximity to the Highland Fault
Line. The seismology displays are
viewed from the doors and windows.

84 miles – Comrie is undoubtedly
one of the prettiest villages in
Scotland for its many picturesque
cottages. On the outskirts is the Glen
Lednock Circular Walk which takes
in the Deil's Cauldron, a rocky
chasm with a waterfall, and the
Melville Monument to Henry
Dundas, 1st Viscount Melville, on
Dunmore Hill. 2 miles south is
Auchingarrich Wildlife Centre
(1000-dusk; Inexpensive) with 17
ponds and more than 100 species of
birds, plus animals and attractions
for children. Continue east on the
A85 from Comrie. To the left after
6 miles is **Glenturret Distillery**
(0930-1630 Mon.-Sat., 1200-1630
Sun., Mar.-Dec.; 1130-1430 Mon.-Fri.,
Jan. & Feb.; Inexpensive), believed
to be Scotland's oldest Highland
malt distillery.

Loch Achray and Ben Venue

91 miles – **Crieff**. TIC: Town Hall, High St, tel. 01764 652578. Up to the end of the 18thC, Crieff was the site of the biggest 'tryst' or cattle market in Scotland, to which drovers brought cattle from all over the Highlands. In Victorian times, when the Hydro and the now-disappeared railway were built, it became an important spa town and it remains a popular and attractive resort town. By the Town Hall are the old 'jougs', a common punishment, and the 1688 cross of the Burgh of Regality of Drummond, the old name of the town. Nearby is a 10thC Celtic cross. On the outskirts is **Crieff Visitor Centre** (0900-1800 Easter-Sep., 0900-1700 Oct.-Mar.; centre Free; tours Inexpensive; guided tours on working days only) which has tours of a pottery and a paperweight factory. **Stuart Crystal Strathearn Glassworks** (0900-1900 June-Sep., 0900-1700 Oct.-May; Free) have tours and demonstrations of the making of crystal. 4 miles southeast of Crieff on the B8062 is **Innerpeffray Library** (1000-1245, 1400-1645 Mon.-Wed. & Fri.-Sat., 1400-1600 Sun., April-Sep.; 1000-1245, 1400-1600 Mon.-Wed. & Fri.-Sat., 1400-1600 Sun., Oct.-Mar.; Inexpensive), Scotland's oldest lending library, founded in 1691 and with books from as early as 1502. Leave Crieff on the A822. 3 miles south is the village of Muthill, where there is a ruined 15thC church with 12thC tower and Drummond family tombs. From Muthill, take the unclassified road right and turn right again in 1.5 miles, following signs for **Drummond Castle Gardens** (1400-1800 May-Oct.; Moderate), a formal garden which featured in the recent film *Rob Roy*, with 1630 sundial by John Mylne, Charles I's master mason, and a spectacular early Victorian parterre laid out in the form of the St. Andrew's Cross. Return to the A822 and carry on

Drummond Castle Gardens

south. On the left, just before entering the village of Braco, are the large and important earthwork remains of **Ardoch Roman Fort** (open access; park in village; signpost at bridge), dating from the 1st and 2nd centuries AD. From

Braco, continue on the A822 and in 2 miles turn right on the busy A9 southbound along the broad valley of Strathallan. To the left is Sheriffmuir, scene of the battle of the same name between Jacobites (*see* A-Z) and Hanoverians early in the first Jacobite Rebellion in 1715. Though indecisive, it was one of the signals of the failure of the rebellion. Behind Sheriffmuir to the left lie the Ochil Hills. After 5 miles take the turnoff left for Dunblane.

113 miles – **Dunblane**. TIC: Stirling Rd, tel. 01786 824428, April-Sep. A pleasant town with attractive old buildings, some dating back to the 17thC, around the 13thC **Dunblane Cathedral** (HS; Free). The cathedral was much admired by the great Victorian art critic John Ruskin, who thought it the most perfect example of Gothic, and the upper window on the west front is still known as the Ruskin Window. The tower is an 11th-12thC survivor of an earlier church. Restoration began in the 19thC and was completed this century. Inside, some 16thC stalls survive, though the choirstalls are early 20thC by Sir Robert Lorimer. In the choir, brass plaques commemorate Margaret Drummond, mistress of James IV, and her two sisters, who are believed to have been poisoned in 1501, shortly before the king was persuaded to marry the English Margaret Tudor. Nearby is **Dunblane Cathedral Museum** (1030-1230, 1430-1630 Mon.-Sat., June-Sep.; Free), housed in the 17thC Dean's house. The **Leighton Library** (1030-1230, 1430-1630 Mon.-Fri., May-Oct.; Free) is thought to be the oldest surviving private library in Scotland, and was formed by Robert Leighton, Bishop of Dunblane in the 17thC. Dunblane also has a Hydro, dating from the town's days as a Victorian spa resort. Leave Dunblane and follow signs for the M9 to Stirling. After the roundabout, the wide valley of the Forth begins to open out ahead. Up on the left is Lecropt Church (1826), and there are some stunning views of the Wallace Monument (*see* Wallace) and Stirling Castle. Leave the motorway at the first turnoff, Junction 10, and follow signs for Stirling town centre.

118 miles – **Stirling** (*see* A-Z). Leave on the A84 which crosses low-lying 'carse' land, or marshland, much of it now drained and its moss removed to create fertile farmland. On the left is Old Drip Bridge (1790) and its tollhouse. After 5 miles is **Blair Drummond Safari Leisure Park** (1000-1730, last admission 1630, April-Sep.; Expensive) with animal reserves, boat trips to see chimpanzees and a wildfowl sanctuary, plus a giant astraglide and other family attractions. It was here in the 18thC that Lord Kames pioneered the removal of the moss from the carse to convert the land to agricultural use.

126 miles – **Doune** is a most attractive village, entered by a bridge, originally of 1535, over the River Teith and paid for by Robert Spittall, James IV's tailor, supposedly after the ferryman refused to take him over. **Doune Castle** (HS, except 0930-1300 Thu. & closed Fri., Oct.-Mar.; Inexpensive) was built at the end of the 14thC and is one of the best-preserved examples of castle architecture of its date in Scotland. It was built for the powerful Duke of Albany, Regent of Scotland during the minority of James I, and contains an impressive gatehouse tower which combined clever defensive features with the height of comfort and fine living in its day. The village became known in the 17thC for the manufacture of pistols. The Mercat Cross and some of the oldest buildings also date from the 17thC, while nearby Deanston is an 18th to 19thC development around the Old Spinning Mill of 1830. Leave Doune on the A84 westbound. On the right in a mile is **Doune Motor Museum** (1000-1700, last admission 1630, April-May & Sep.-Nov.; 1000-1730, last admission 1700, June-Aug.; Inexpensive), a collection of vintage and later cars belonging to the Earl of Moray. Star exhibits include two Hispano-Suizas, the world's second-oldest Rolls Royce and a Sunbeam once buried by the

grieving parents of the car's dead owner. Further on on the right are the splendid Cambuswallace Stables (no access).

134 miles – Callander. TIC: Rob Roy and Trossachs Visitor Centre, Ancaster Sq., tel 01877 330342, Mar.-Dec. Although this is one of the busiest centres of the Trossachs, Callander retains the prettiness which gained it the role of Tannochbrae in

Doune Castle

the first television series of *Dr Finlay's Casebook*. The **Rob Roy and Trossachs Visitor Centre** (0900-2200, audiovisual & exhibition to 1900, July & Aug., 0930-1800 June & Sep., 1000-1700 Mar.-May & Oct.-Dec., 1000-1700 Sat. & Sun., Jan. & Feb.; centre Free; audiovisual and exhibition Inexpensive) is housed in St. Kessog's Church and gives a multimedia presentation on the life and legend of Rob Roy. Some attractive older buildings are round the square and down by the River Teith. Above the village are the Bracklinn Falls where the Keltie Water plunges into a gorge. Leave Callander on the A81, passing tiny Loch Rusky on the left in 4 miles. In a further 3 miles turn left on the B8034.

141 miles – Port of Menteith is a tiny settlement with a 19thC hotel and church by the shores of the Lake of Menteith, Scotland's only natural lake, the others all being called lochs. From here a small boat ferries visitors to **Inchmahome Priory** (HS, except closed Oct.-Mar.; Inexpensive) on the larger island. It was founded as an Augustinian priory in 1238 by Walter

Comyn, Earl of Menteith. In 1547 Mary Queen of Scots (*see* A-Z), then aged four, was brought here for safety after the Scots were defeated by the English at the Battle of Pinkie. Most of this Gothic priory fell into ruin after the Reformation (*see* A-Z), but the vaulted chapterhouse was altered to become a burial chapel of the Earls of Menteith. A number of gravestones and effigies are now displayed here. Return to the A81 and turn right, back towards Callander for a mile, then fork right on the A873. After 1.5 miles is the hamlet of Ruskie. Up to the left is **Dunaverig Farmlife Centre** (1000-1800 April-Oct.; Moderate) which has ponies and farm animals, a collection of old farming implements, and lots of hands-on activities such as milking and making oatcakes. To the right are some undrained areas of Flanders Moss, now protected as a National Nature Reserve. In another 2.5 miles is Thornhill, a pleasant village with a 19thC masonic lodge noted for its unusual tower. Turn right on the B822 which crosses the wide valley of the River Forth before beginning to climb.

150 miles – Kippen is a very attractive village overlooking the Forth valley. Many of the older buildings date from the 18thC, including the two inns and the Smiddy, still a working blacksmith's shop. The present church dates from 1823, while the ruined Old Kirk stands in the churchyard. From Kippen continue on the B822 and climb 2 miles to splendid views with a parking space at a spot known as the 'Top of the World'. The road then descends to the Endrick Water.

156 miles – Fintry has a dramatic situation at the foot of the Campsies, which rise to over 1800 ft. To the east are the lower Fintry Hills. Culcreuch Castle, a fine tower house set in a 1600 acre estate, was once the seat of the Galbraith family and is now a hotel and country park. Continue on the B822, which skirts the Endrick before sweeping up over the Campsies. The B818

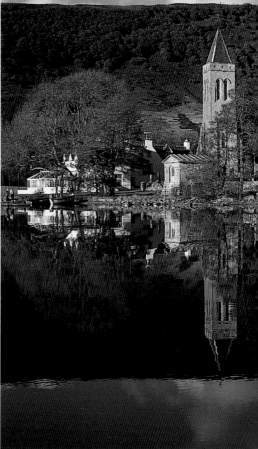

Port of Menteith

off to the left passes the Loup of Fintry, a spectacular 90 ft waterfall. This section of the B822, known as the Crow Road, climbs to over 1000 ft. After 6 miles is a car park with extensive views over the Central Lowlands. Immediately below can be seen the pretty Campsie Glen and village of Clachan of Campsie. In a further 2 miles is Lennoxtown. A mile to the right off the A891 is Clachan of

Campsie, an attractive craft village, with nearby, the tiny modern Schoenstatt Shrine. Return to Lennoxtown and turn right on the B822 through Torrance, then turn left on the A807. Just before the roundabout, the road passes the Forth and Clyde Canal, opened in 1790, and the site of the Antonine Wall. At the roundabout, take the A803 through Bishopbriggs to Glasgow (173 miles).

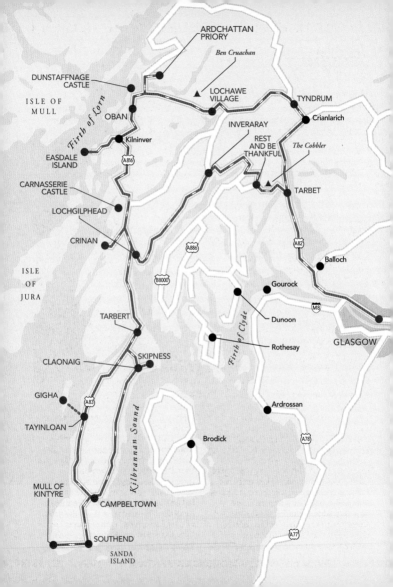

Argyll

2 – 3 days

Argyll is one of the most extensive of the old counties of Scotland, with a distance of over 80 miles separating the towns of Campbeltown on the Kintyre peninsula, opposite Ayr, in the south, and Oban, opposite Mull, in the north. It is an area of beautiful scenery and many sea lochs, and its mild climate has produced some of Scotland's most delightful gardens. There are also historic sites of great importance such as Dunadd Fort, ancient capital of the Scots, while the attractive 18thC planned village of Inveraray makes a fascinating contrast with the nearby former Highland township of Auchindrain.

Loch Fyne

Leave Glasgow on the A82, as for Excursion 2, to Loch Lomond (*see* A-Z) as far as **Tarbet** (TIC: Main St, tel. 01301 702260, April-Oct.). At the hotel, continue straight along the A83 and in 2 miles reach Arrochar, a little resort at the top of Loch Long, from where there are good views, depending on weather conditions, over to the mountains known as the Arrochar Alps, including the distinctively shaped outline of The Cobbler, 2891 ft. Continue on the A83 round the head of Loch Long, and beyond Ardgarten climb steeply up Glen Croe to the highest point on the A83, known as the Rest and Be Thankful, 803 ft, where there are views from the car park. Continue down Glen Kinglas to Cairndow, where **Ardkinglas Woodland Garden** (dawn-dusk; Inexpensive) includes one of Britain's tallest trees, now over 200 ft. Off to the left on the A815 is the Cowal Peninsula (*see* A-Z). The road now skirts the head of Loch Fyne, passing the famous Loch Fyne Oyster Bar and Shop (tel. 01499 600236/276).

61 miles – Inveraray.
TIC: Front St, tel. 01499
302063. The site of this
ancient capital of
Argyll was moved in
the 18thC, when the
Duke of Argyll built
the present fine village
further away from his
castle. **Inveraray
Castle** (1000-1300,
1400-1730 Mon.-Thu. &
Sat., 1300-1730 Sun.,
April-June & Sep.-Oct.;
1000-1730 Mon.-Sat.,
1300-1730 Sun., July &
Aug.; Moderate), seat
of the Campbells and

Inveraray Jail

built for the 3rd Duke of Argyll in the
18thC to replace a 15thC tower, has a
symmetrical plan and turreted corner
towers. The interior is outstanding for its
decorative painting, and has important
collections, including 18thC British

portraits, porcelain,
furniture and
tapestries. In the
grounds is the
**Combined Operations
Museum** (1000-1800
Mon.-Thu. & Sat.,
1300-1800 Sun., April-
Sep.; also open Fri.,
July & Aug., last
admission 1730;
Inexpensive), telling
the story of No. 1
Combined Training
Centre here in World
War II which trained
250,000 troops. In the
village, the 19thC
Inveraray Jail (0930-1800 April-Oct.,
1000-1700 Nov.-Mar., last admission 1 hr
before closing; Inexpensive) is an award-
winning attraction with costumed
figures and an exhibition on crime and
punishment in Scotland. By the pier is

Inveraray Castle

the *Arctic Penguin* (0930-1800 April-Oct., 1000-1700 Nov.-Mar., tel. 01499 302213 for extended hours July & Aug.; Inexpensive), built in 1911 as a lightship in Dublin, and later converted to a three-masted schooner. Now it houses displays on Clyde and West of Scotland maritime history. The Bell Tower of **All Saints' Episcopal Church** (1000-1300, 1400-1700 Mon.-Sat., 1400-1700 Sun., mid May-Sep.; Inexpensive) is said to have the finest bells in Scotland. Continue south on the A83 and after 2 miles is **Argyll Wildlife Park** (0930-1800 or dusk; Inexpensive), which has wildfowl, deer and other Scottish and non-native creatures. In another 3.5 miles is **Auchindrain Township** (1000-1700 Mon.-Fri., April-Sep., also open Sat., May-Sep.; Inexpensive), a fascinating, restored West Highland farming township. 4.5 miles further on is **Crarae Garden** (0900-1800 Easter-Oct., dawn-dusk Nov.-Easter; visitor centre 1000-

1700 Easter-Oct.; Inexpensive), called 'Argyll's great garden'. This gorge with waterfalls has an amazing 400-odd rhododendrons and azaleas, while autumn here is equally spectacular due to the huge variety of deciduous trees. Carry on south. To the left by the shore beyond Tullochgorm is 16thC **Minard Castle** (by arrangement May-Oct., tel. 01546 886272). Continue down Loch Fyne. Just before Lochgilphead are **Kilmory Castle Gardens** (dawn-dusk; Free). Begun in the 1770s, these gardens have fine rhododendrons and are currently being restored.

85 miles – Lochgilphead. TIC: Lochnell St, tel. 01546 602344, April-Oct. This is one of Argyll's major centres. On its western outskirts, on the A816, is **Highbank Porcelain Pottery** (tours 1030 & 1400 Mon.-Fri.; Inexpensive). Continue south on the A83, passing at Ardrishaig the eastern end of the Crinan Canal, planned by John Rennie (*see A-Z*).

99 miles – Tarbert. TIC: Harbour St, tel. 01880 820429, April-Oct. An attractive little fishing port, now a popular resort for yachting. There are a number of craft shops and seafood restaurants. To the south of the village is a steep path up to the remains of 13th-16thC Tarbert Castle, taken by Robert the Bruce (*see* A-Z) after Bannockburn. From Tarbert there is a summer ferry across Loch Fyne to Portavadie on the Cowal Peninsula (*see* A-Z), tel. Caledonian Macbrayne 01475 650100. Carry on down the A83, which now crosses the isthmus between Loch Fyne and West Loch Tarbert. In 5 miles is the Kennacraig Ferry Terminal for ferries to Islay and Jura (*see* A-Z), tel. Caledonian Macbrayne 01880 730253. The road now follows the west coast of the Kintyre Peninsula, with views of the lovely island of **Gigha** (pronounced 'ghee-a'), which can be reached by a 20 min ferry crossing from Tayinloan, tel. Caledonian Macbrayne as above. On the island are **Achamore House Gardens** (1000-dusk; Inexpensive), with camellias and rhododendrons, while trees give beautiful autumn colours. At Kilchattan is a ruined 13thC church. Continue south from Tayinloan and after 7 miles is **Glenbarr Abbey** (1000-1800 Wed.-Mon., Easter-mid Oct.; Inexpensive), an 18th-19thC house and Macalister Clan Centre, where an entertaining tour is given by the laird and lady. Continue south.

132 miles – Campbeltown. TIC: Mackinnon House, The Pier, tel. 01586 552056. A port at the head of Campbeltown Loch, famous in a song, and a market town with a very fine late 14thC carved cross. **Campbeltown Museum** (1000-1300, 1400-1700 Mon.-Sat., also 1800-2000 Mon. & Tue.; Free) in the library building has a good collection of geology, archaeology and other material relating to the peninsula. Along the south shore of the loch is a spit

leading to Davaar Island which can be crossed at low tide (check tides at TIC) to see the cave painting of the Crucifixion by A. MacKinnon (1887). From Campbeltown, the B842 goes south 10 miles to Southend, with sandy beaches on the peninsula's south shore. Dunaverty Rock is the site of a castle

Tarbert

where, in 1647, some 300 Catholic Macdonalds were murdered by Covenanters (*see* A-Z) under Gen. Leslie. The road continues west to Keil, where imprints on a rock by a ruined chapel are said to be Columba's (*see* St. Columba) footsteps. The road ends at the South Point on the Mull of Kintyre, famous in the song by local farmowner Paul McCartney. Leave Campbeltown on the B842 northbound. In 7.5 miles is a car park and stile on the right, with access to the remains of a dun or fort dating from the early centuries AD. In another 1.5 miles are the ruins of 12thC **Saddell Abbey** (open access), thought to have been founded by Somerled, 1st Lord of the Isles. 2.5 miles further on is the **Craft Centre and Kintyre Alpine Nursery** (1000-1700 Mon.-Sat., 1400-1700 Sun., April-Oct.; 1130-1630 Mon.-Sat., Dec.; Free) at a croft overlooking Carradale Bay. The pretty little fishing village and resort of Carradale lies 1.5 miles east of Dippen. Continue north on the B842, overlooking the Kilbrannan Sound. At Claonaig (pronounced 'cloe-naig') is a summer ferry to Lochranza on the island of Arran (*see* A-Z), tel. Caledonian Macbrayne 01475 650100. 2 miles further northeast on the B8001 are the impressive ruins of 13th-16thC **Skipness Castle** (open access), once a Macdonald stronghold, and the 13th-14thC Kilbrannan Chapel. Return to Claonaig and follow the B8001 right to meet the A83 in 5 miles. Turn right and return to Lochgilphead via Tarbert.

185 miles – Lochgilphead. This time, take the A816 northwest. In 2 miles, at Cairnbaan, the B841 leads left along the Crinan Canal, now mainly popular with pleasure boats but built so that fishing boats could avoid the hazardous journey round the Mull of Kintyre. At Crinan is a beautiful bay, plus a hotel and seafood restaurant. Continue on the A816. In 3.5 miles, a road leads left to **Dunadd Fort** (HS, open access), where, on a hill, remains include carvings, a footprint and ogam inscriptions, a form of writing of Irish origin. This fort is thought to have been a capital of the Scots (*see* A-Z) kingdom of Dalriada and where Kings of Scots were proclaimed on the Stone of Destiny, before it moved to Scone and was stolen by Edward I of England (*see* Excursion 12). Return to the A816 and continue north towards Kilmartin, a centre of outstanding importance for its prehistoric cairns from the 2nd millennium BC and later carved stones. About 2 miles after Dunadd is a parking place for visiting South Chambered Cairn, the oldest of the group, in which were remains of both cremation and inhumation. Other cairns, all signposted, are Nether Largie Mid and North Cairns, Ri Cruin Cairn and Glebe Cairn, while at Templewood are two stone circles. In Kilmartin churchyard is a fine group of medieval carved stones, one with a long sword and two with warriors. Continue north from Kilmartin on the A816 and in 2 miles is **Carnasserie Castle** (HS, open access), a 16thC ruined tower house built for John Carswell, superintendent of the Reformed religion in Argyll, who translated some of John Knox's doctrines into Gaelic, the first book to be printed in Gaelic in 1567. Continue on the A816. At Arduaine is the beautiful **Arduaine Garden** (NTS, 0930-sunset; Inexpensive) with rhododendrons, azaleas, a water garden and woodland in a micro-climate created by the Gulf Stream which encourages plants to grow to unusual size. Carry on along Loch Melfort, through Kilmelford. The road then crosses inland to Kilninver, where the B844 goes left to Easdale and the famous **Bridge over the Atlantic**. This graceful stone arch dates from 1791 and spans the narrow stretch of sea separating Seil Island and the mainland. On the far side is a pub, Tigh an Truish or House of the Trousers, said to be where islanders changed from kilt into trousers before visiting the mainland in the period when the kilt was banned after Culloden (*see* Jacobites). At the furthest point, Easdale, with an old slate quarry, a request passenger ferry operates (0900-2100 April-Oct., 0900-1800 Nov.-Mar.) across to Easdale Island where there is a **Folk Museum** (1030-1730 Mon.-Sat., 1030-1630 Sun., April-Sep.; Inexpensive). Continue on the A816. On the right 3 miles beyond Kilninver, **Glenfeochan House Gardens** (1000-1800 April-Oct.;

Loch Creran, north of Oban

Inexpensive) have mature trees planted in the 1850s, plus rhododendrons, azaleas, a walled garden and a large greenhouse.

223 miles – Oban (*see* A-Z). Leave Oban on the A85 and in 3 miles is **Dunstaffnage Castle** (HS, except closed Oct.-Mar.; Inexpensive), a fine 13thC ruined castle on a rock at the entrance to Loch Etive. The nearby chapel is of outstanding quality. Continue to Connel Bridge where the A828 continues up Loch Linnhe to Ballachulish (*see* Excursion 2). On the far side of the bridge, an unclassified road leads right to **Ardchattan Priory** (HS, open access), a ruined Valliscaulian priory founded in 1230 and burned by Cromwell's troops in 1654. Next to it, **Ardchattan Gardens** (0900-dusk, April-Nov.; Inexpensive) has a 2 acre wild garden with shrubs, trees

and roses, plus a herbaceous border and shrub borders, and views of Ben Cruachan. Continue on the A85 to Taynuilt. To the left is **Bonawe Iron Furnace** (HS, except closed Oct.-Mar.; Inexpensive), founded in 1753, an important charcoal-fuelled smelting works, now restored and with displays explaining the process. From Bonawe Pier are daily Loch Etive Cruises (tel. 01866 822430) in the summer. From Taynuilt, an unclassified road leads southwest 3 miles to **Barguillean Garden** (0900-dusk; Inexpensive), a secluded garden with rhododendrons, azaleas, heaths and primulas on a slope leading to a loch and wild garden. Continue on the A85 from Taynuilt. Near Bridge of Awe is **Inverawe Smokery** (0900-1800; Inexpensive), with a shop, an exhibition on fish-smoking, plus a viewing window.

On the left in 3 miles is **Cruachan Power Station** (0930-1630 April-late Oct.; Inexpensive), with fascinating tours into the hydro-electric power station hollowed out of the mountain. Above is Ben Cruachan, 3695 ft. Continue along the narrow Pass of Brander, where Robert the Bruce defeated MacDougall followers of Edward II in 1308. Continue to Lochawe village. The Edwardian steam launch *Lady Rowena* (tel. 01838 200400/449) does summer cruises on beautiful Loch Awe from the pier. Continue round the head of the loch, past the ruins of Kilchurn Castle (no access), with a 15thC keep. Follow the A85 through Dalmally. An unclassified road leads right to Monument Hill, commemorating 18thC Duncan Ban MacIntyre, the 'Burns of the Highlands', and with superb views of Loch Awe. Continue on the A85 through Glen Lochy to Tyndrum. Excursion 4 ends here (260 miles). Excursion 2 can now be joined or, alternatively, take the A82 back to Glasgow.

Loch Awe

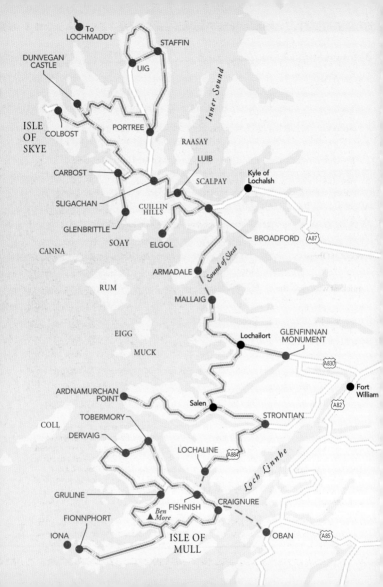

The Hebrides

5 – 10 days

The first part of this excursion covers Mull and Skye, the largest islands of the Inner Hebrides just off Scotland's west coast, plus the small island of Iona off Mull. The second part is the Outer Hebrides and includes North and South Uist, Lewis and Harris. Mull and Skye are beautiful, mountainous islands – Mull with strange basalt formations and Skye with the incomparable Cuillins range of mountains. The Outer Hebrides have a different landscape, in general lower-lying with many little lochs and, on their shores, the 'machairs' or grassy, sandy strips. On these islands further from the mainland, Gaelic language and culture have been preserved. Of monuments, the stone circle at Callanish on Lewis and, on Iona, the abbey and other remains of Celtic Christianity, are among the most important in Scotland. As this route involves extensive use of car ferries, its timing should be planned in advance and ferry times checked. *See* Ferries, Hebrides.

Begin at **Oban** (*see* A–Z), reached via Excursion 4. The quickest way is via the A85 from Tyndrum (*see* Excursion 2) and the drive takes 2.5-3 hr from Glasgow. Take the car ferry to Craignure on Mull. Mull is a scenic island of mountains, cliffs and moors, surrounded by rocky coves, beaches of white shell sand, and columnar, basalt crags.

Duart Castle

The journey across the Firth of Lorn takes 40 min and offers good views of Duart Castle on the final approach to Craignure. From just south of Craignure Pier, the Mull–West Highland Narrow Gauge Railway runs to **Torosay Castle and Gardens** (castle 1030-1700 April-mid Oct.; Inexpensive; gardens 0900-1900 or sunrise-sunset; Inexpensive). The scenic journey takes 20 min (Easter & May-mid Oct.; Inexpensive) and arrives at the Victorian castle, set in 12 acres of

beautiful gardens with outstanding Italian statues. From Craignure, take the A849 towards Fionnphort (pronounced 'finna-fort'). After 2 miles a minor road on the left leads out to **Duart Castle** (1030-1800 May-Sep.; Inexpensive), seat of the Clan Maclean, spectacularly situated on a crag overlooking the sea. The ruined, mainly 14thC, castle was restored in 1911 by Sir Fitzroy Maclean and is now the home of the present chief of the clan. Follow the A849 for 35 miles to Fionnphort, passing through Glen More in the mountainous heart of the island, then along the north shore of the Ross of Mull Peninsula.

A few miles after reaching the shores of Loch Scridain, just beyond the Pennyghael Hotel, a minor road on the left leads across the moors, down through beautiful woods and past waterfalls to Carsaig Bay (where the road forks, take the left, uphill branch). Park at the end of the road to begin a 5 hr walk. Wear stout shoes or walking boots, as the going is sometimes rough. The path follows the shore to the right, passing under huge cliffs. After about 2 hr are the spectacular Carsaig Arches, where the sea has carved the 755 ft-high basalt cliffs into awe-inspiring caves, buttresses and arches. Return by the same route.

The shores of the Ross of Mull contain many secluded rocky coves, many with beaches of white shell sand, which can only be reached on foot. Turn off on any of the minor roads along the Ross and explore. The main road ends at the village of Fionnphort, where a ferry crosses the sound to the famous island of Iona. The crossing takes 5 min and ferries depart at frequent intervals, tel. Caledonian Macbrayne 01681 700559.

38 miles – Iona. This beautiful and historic island, only 3 miles by 1.5, was where St. Columba (*see* A-Z) arrived in AD 563 and established a monastery from which Christianity was spread. The main sights can be seen in 2-3 hr, but the rest of the island is a delight for walkers, birdwatchers, botanists and geologists. Walk up the main street opposite the jetty and turn right through the gate into the lovely grounds of the 13thC Augustinian nunnery, now mostly in ruins. At the far side is the little 14thC St. Ronan's Church, which has been restored to house a collection of medieval sculptured tombstones. Leave by the gate beside the church and, along the road, pass the 15thC Maclean's Cross on the left, then turn right past the St. Columba Hotel to reach **Iona Abbey** (Donation). The mainly 16thC abbey and the surrounding monastic buildings have been restored this century and are now home to the Iona Community, an ecumenical group founded in 1938. To

Iona Abbey

Iona Abbey

the right of the entrance gate is the Reilig Oran, the country's oldest Christian cemetery. The remains of 48 Scottish kings (including Duncan, killed by Macbeth – *see* A-Z), four Irish kings and eight Norwegian kings are said to lie here, though unfortunately their graves are no longer marked. The little chapel of St. Oran (one of Columba's disciples) may date from the 11thC. In front of the main entrance to the abbey itself stand two magnificent 8thC Celtic crosses: St. John's to the left and St. Martin's to the right. Enter the main door of the abbey, where there are self-guided tour leaflets. In the cloisters to the left of the nave are the Community shop (1000-1700) and the coffee house (1000-1700 Mon.-Sat., Mar.-Oct.). Services are held in the abbey at 1400 Mon.-Sat. in summer, with Holy Communion at 1030 Sun.

From Fionnphort, return along the A849, then at the head of Loch Scridain, turn left on the B8035. This leads across the wild, cliff-bound Ardmeanach Peninsula, with Ben More, 3171 ft, to the right. The road then drops down to Loch na Keal, with views westward to the islands of Ulva and Staffa (*see* A-Z), on the latter of which is Fingal's Cave, before squeezing between the sea and the steep basalt cliffs to reach Gruline. Here, a minor road on the right leads to the mausoleum of Lachlan Macquarie, the 'Father of Australia', who was born in

1762 on the nearby island of Ulva, and died here after retiring as governor of New South Wales. Turn left on the B8073, which follows the rugged west coast of northern Mull to windswept Calgary Bay (after which the Canadian city is named), and on to the pretty village of Dervaig. On the right, immediately after the bridge, is a minor road leading to the Druimard Country House and Theatre Restaurant, next to which is Mull Little Theatre (tel. 01688 400245), the smallest professional theatre in the country, with only 38 seats in the auditorium but a full summer programme of entertainment. **The Old Byre** (1030-1730 Easter-Oct.; Inexpensive) has an audiovisual show every hour on the history and natural history of Mull. Continue on the B8073. **109 miles – Tobermory.** TIC: 48 Main St, tel. 01688 302182, April-Oct. This attractive former fishing port was founded in 1788, and is the capital of Mull and a centre for tourism and yachting. Brightly-painted houses line the picturesque harbour, where in 1588 a Spanish galleon, fleeing the aftermath of the Armada, sought shelter and provisions. The ship sank and over the centuries many attempts have been made to recover the treasure she is said to have been carrying. So far only a few cannon and some coins have been found. The story of the galleon, and many other aspects of Mull's culture and history, are given in the **Mull Museum** (1030-1630 Mon.-Fri., 1030-1330 Sat.; Inexpensive) on Main St opposite the pier. A thrice-weekly car ferry service (Mon., Wed. & Sat.) connects Tobermory with Oban, Coll and Tiree (*see* A-Z), and a regular passenger ferry links it with Kilchoan on the Ardnamurchan Peninsula (Mon.-Sat.); for details, tel. 01688 302017. From Tobermory follow the A848 along the Sound of Mull through pretty Salen Bay and turn left.

127 miles – **Fishnish**. From here, take the car ferry to Lochaline on the mainland. The crossing takes 15 min and there are frequent sailings. For details, tel. 01631 566966/562285. At Lochaline is Keil Church, whose churchyard contains a 15thC Celtic cross and commands a splendid view over the Sound of Mull, with 14thC Ardtornish Castle prominent a few miles to the southeast. Take the A884 from Lochaline along lovely, wooded Gleann Geal and over the hills to the head of Loch Sunart. Turn left on the A861 through **Strontian** (TIC: tel. 01967 402131, April-Oct.), in whose 18thC leadmines strontium was discovered, and on to Salen.

From here a detour can be made on the B8007, one of Scotland's most scenic roads, which snakes 23 miles through stunning scenery and rhododendron-clad hillsides to the gale-worn lighthouse on **Ardnamurchan Point**, the most westerly point on the British mainland (it projects a full 23 miles further west than Land's End). There is a hotel and camping at Kilchoan (connected to Tobermory on Mull by a regular

Glenfinnan Monument

passenger ferry), and nearby are the ruins of 13thC **Mingary Castle** (open access). About a mile beyond Kilchoan, on the way out to the lighthouse, a minor road on the right leads to the lovely white-sand beach of Sanna Bay.

The A861 continues north from Salen. A mile or so beyond Acharacle, just after the bridge over the River Shiel, take a minor road on the left (signposted Dorlin) that winds along a rocky ledge beside the river, overhung by trees and ferns, before coming out after 2 miles at a parking place by the shores of Loch Moidart. The ruined 14thC Castle Tioram, ancient seat of the Macdonalds of Clanranald, sits romantically on a small islet near the shore, and is accessible via a sand spit except at high water. The main road follows the north shore of Loch Moidart. Five prominent beech trees are survivors of the original seven planted to commemorate the Seven Men of Moidart who accompanied Bonnie Prince Charlie (*see* Jacobites) on his voyage from France, and continues to Lochailort where it meets the A830.

A detour can be made to the right towards Fort William (*see* Excursion 2, A-Z), to the famous **Glenfinnan Monument** at the north end of Loch Shiel which commemorates the raising of Prince Charlie's standard near here in 1745. The statue on top is not of the prince but represents the brave Highlanders who fought for his cause. The adjacent **Visitor Centre** (NTS, 1000-1300, 1400-1700 April-May & Sep.-Oct., 0930-1800 June-Aug.; Inexpensive) tells the story of the prince's subsequent campaign to regain the Scottish throne, ending in the inglorious defeat at Culloden (*see* Excursion 9).

Continue from Lochailort towards Mallaig. Loch Morar, Britain's deepest at 1017 ft, is reputedly the home of another monster, Morag.

The Cuillins, Skye

200 miles – Mallaig. TIC: Railway Station, tel. 01687 462170, April-Oct. Mallaig lies at the end of the road and the West Highland railway line from Fort William and Glasgow, and is an important fishing port and ferry terminal. Passenger ferries serve the Small Isles (*see* A-Z), and a car ferry makes the 30 min crossing to Armadale on Skye. For details, tel. 01687 462403. **Mallaig Marine World** (0900-2100 June-Sep., 0900-1700 Oct.-Mar.; Moderate) has an aquarium, and a video on local marine life and the fishing fleet.

Cross over the sea to Skye, said to have been called Skuye, meaning 'Island of Clouds', by the invading Norsemen. The aptness of the name will soon become apparent to the visitor. In summer the island is extremely popular with tourists, climbers and walkers. Roadsigns and other notices are in Gaelic and English. Just outside Armadale is the Clan Donald Centre where the **Museum of the Isles** (0930-1730 Easter-Oct.; Inexpensive) in Armadale Castle tells the story of Clan Donald and the Lords of the Isles. Continue on the A851 along the Sleat Peninsula to the A850 (turn right here for the Skye Bridge and the start of Excursion 6) and the village of **Broadford** (TIC: tel. 01471 822461, April-Sep.), spread round Broadford Bay.

A detour can be made left on the A881, which leads for 14 miles through beautiful scenery to the village of **Elgol**, from where there are views to the peaks of the Cuillins and the island of Rum. Weather permitting, there are boat trips from Elgol to Loch Coruisk, whose brooding beauty was admired by the Romantics, including Wordsworth and Scott (*see* A-Z).

North of Broadford, the main road skirts the island's east side and turns sharp left at the mouth of Loch Ainort,

Dunvegan Castle

A detour 6 miles from Sligachan leads left on the B8009 to Carbost and the **Talisker Distillery** (0930-1630 Mon.-Fri., April-Oct.; 1400-1630 Mon.-Fri., Nov.-Mar.; Inexpensive). Before Carbost, a minor road forks left to Glenbrittle, another centre for exploring the Cuillins, where there is a large camp site and a youth hostel. Just before Dunvegan village, the B884 on the left leads 10 miles to the wild cliff scenery of Neist Point, passing on the way **Colbost Folk Museum** (1000-1800 April-Oct.; Inexpensive), and the road to Husabost, on which is the **MacCrimmon Piping Centre** (1200-1730 Tue.-Sun., Easter-May; 1100-1730 June-Aug., 1100-1730 Tue.-Sun., Sep. & Oct.; Inexpensive), a museum devoted to the family of pipers who played for the Clan Macleod chiefs. **263 miles – Dunvegan Castle** (1000-1730 Mon.-Sat., 1300-1700 Sun., mid Mar.-Oct.; Moderate). Skye's most famous attraction has been the seat of the chiefs of Clan Macleod for over 700 years, though the earliest part of the present castle is 14thC. Displays include the Fairy Flag, a silken banner over 1200 years old which is reputed to have the magical power to save the clan from peril three times – it has been used twice already – and documents tracing the history of the clan over 30 generations. From Dunvegan take the A850.

286 miles – Portree. TIC: Meall House, tel. 01478 612137. Portree is the capital of Skye and has a picturesque harbour. **Aros** (0900-2100 June-Sep., 0900-1800 Oct.-May; Inexpensive) is Skye's new heritage centre, with costumed figures, audiovisuals and sound effects. An Tuireann (tel. 01478 613306) is the arts centre with exhibitions, performances and workshops. Take the A855 towards Staffin. Soon the serrated outline of The Storr appears on the left, a mass of crags and pinnacles including the prominent,

with good views to the conical peaks of the Cuillins. At Luib there is a **Folk Museum** (1000-1800 April-Oct.; Inexpensive) in an old, thatched crofter's house. At Sconser, the road passes the ferry to nearby Raasay island. Raasay House, where Dr Johnson and James Boswell stayed in 1773, now has an outdoor centre, tel. 01478 660266. At Sligachan the hotel and camp site are a centre for climbing in the Cuillin mountains, whose jagged, rocky peaks rise impressively to the south. Loch Coruisk can be reached from here by footpath, a 6-7 hr round trip. Take food and all-weather clothing, and wear stout shoes or walking boots. Turn left on the A863, which leads along the west coast of the island, with good views of sea lochs and the flat-topped hills known as Macleod's Tables.

Near The Storr, Skye

165 ft-high finger of the Old Man of Storr, first climbed in 1955. It can be reached by a path along the north side of the forestry plantation at the end of Loch Leathan. Allow 2 hr and wear stout walking shoes or boots. The road now follows the east coast of the Trotternish Peninsula through fertile farmland backed by cliffs of volcanic rock. Spectacular sea cliffs and waterfalls can be seen at the Kilt Rock viewpoint. A few miles beyond Staffin a minor road on the right cuts across the peninsula to Uig, passing on

Flora Macdonald's Grave

the way a parking place from which a footpath leads uphill to the weird pinnacles of The Quiraing, with the 100 ft-tall Needle, an uncannily flat meadow called The Table and good views across the sea to Torridon (*see* Excursion 6). The main road continues around the northern tip of the peninsula. To the right at Kilmuir is the **Skye Museum of Island Life** (0930-1730 Mon.-Sat., April-Oct.; Inexpensive). Further on is the grave of Flora Macdonald (*see* Jacobites). The road then sweeps down to the bay of Uig.

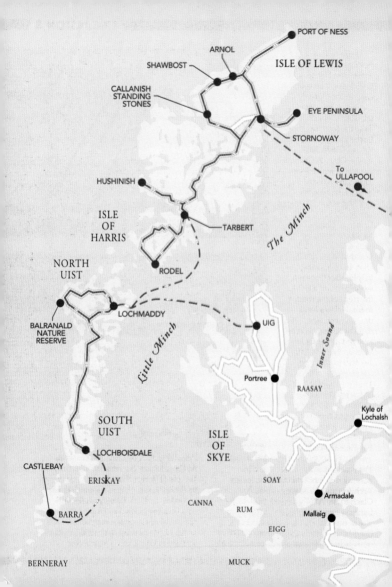

318 miles – **Uig**. A car ferry runs from Uig to Tarbert on Harris, and Lochmaddy on North Uist, in the Outer Hebrides. For details, tel. 01470 542219. Take the ferry to **Lochmaddy** (TIC: Pier Rd, tel. 01876 500321, Easter-Oct.). Follow the A865, which loops round the coast of North Uist before heading south through Benbecula and South Uist (the islands are connected by causeways) to reach Lochboisdale, South Uist, 46 miles away. At Kilphedder there is a stone cross on a rise to the right of the road, a memorial to a local doctor, from where the view northwest can be enjoyed to the serrated Haskeir Islands and beyond to the hazy outlines of St. Kilda, 41 miles away. A few miles further on, turn right at Tigharry for Balranald Nature Reserve, with an RSPB Visitor Centre, **Ionad Fiosrachaidh** (open

Weavers, Harris

Road-side shrine, South Uist

access, April-Sep.) and guided walks. The road skirts the sandy coastline, passing many ruined blackhouses (*see* Architecture) on its way south. At Clachan the A867 goes left, past Barpa Langass (exterior only, inside dangerous), one of the best-preserved of the island's chambered cairns, dating from 4000-5000 BC. Nearby is the standing stone circle of Pobull Fhinn. Continue on the A865. At Carinish are the remains of Trinity Temple (Teampull na Trionaid), founded by Beatrice, daughter of Somerled, Lord of the Isles, c1203. Its monastery and college once formed an important medieval centre of learning. Great care is required in the ruins. Continue south across the tidal flats to Benbecula.

Croft, South Uist

Loop right from the main road on the B892 which passes through Balivanich, Benbecula's main village, home to many of the servicemen who work at the RAF airfield and the missile range on South Uist. The A865 now crosses a causeway to South Uist, and another over freshwater Loch Bee, with views ahead to the hills of Hecla and Ben Mhor, rising to over 1900 ft. On the hillside beyond Loch Bee stands the 33 ft-tall statue of Our Lady of the Isles, erected by the Catholic community in 1957. 1.5 miles south, the road passes through Loch Druidibeg Nature Reserve, an important site for breeding greylag geese and for the rare corncrake. A ruined cottage to the right just before Mingary has a cairn marking the birthplace of Flora Macdonald.

Airport, Barra

374 miles – Lochboisdale. TIC: Pier Rd, tel. 01878 700280, Easter-Oct. The capital of South Uist. From here there are car ferries to Castlebay on Barra, and Oban. From Ludag on the south coast is a passenger ferry to Eoligarry at the north end of Barra, from where it is a short walk to Cille Bharra, with its three 12thC chapels, where the author Compton Mackenzie is buried. Further south on

Church of St. Clement, Rodel

Barra, the A888 leads to Castlebay, the island's capital, where, out in the bay, is 12th-17thC **Kisimul Castle** (1400-1700 Mon., Wed. & Sat., May-Sep.; Inexpensive). From Ludag, South Uist, there are also ferries (tel. 01878 720261) to nearby Eriskay, the setting for Compton Mackenzie's famous book *Whisky Galore*. The Prince's Strand, on the west of Eriskay, is where Bonnie Prince Charlie first set foot on Scottish soil. Return to Lochmaddy and take the ferry to Tarbert on Harris.

Compton Mackenzie's Grave, Barra

431 miles – Tarbert (Tairbeart). TIC: Pier Rd, tel. 01859 502011, Easter-Oct. The capital of Harris has a few shops, a post office, banks, a petrol station and the delightful Rose Villa Tearoom. From Tarbert, a 40 mile detour can be made round South Harris. Start on the A859 and after 4 miles turn left on a minor road (the Golden Road, so named because of the high cost of its construction) which twists and turns for 12 miles down the wild east coast of Harris, through a landscape of hillocky gneiss dotted with lochans and deeply indented by the sea. The bleakness is brightened here and there by splashes of green around crofting communities. At **Rodel** (Roghadal) is the little 15th-16thC church of St. Clement with the magnificent 16thC tomb of Alexander Macleod. Return by the west coast road (much faster than the east) to Tarbert, passing rocky coasts and beautiful sandy beaches at Scarastavore, Borve (Buirgh) and Seilebost.

Take the A859 north from Tarbert to Stornoway through wild hills and across moors. A detour can be made left on the B887 3 miles from Tarbert. This leads along the north shore of West Loch Tarbert, passing an old whaling station built by the Norwegians in 1912 at Bunavoneader. There are views into the mountainous Forest of Harris to the north, before the attractive Amhuinnsuidhe Castle. The road goes through a white iron gate, along the bank of a stream tumbling to the sea, past the door of the castle, now a hunting and fishing lodge, and leaves through an ornamental, turreted arch. It continues to Hushinish (Huisnis), where there is a sandy beach. Return to the A859.

468 miles – **Stornoway (Steornabhagh)**. TIC: 26 Cromwell St, tel. 01851 703088. The main town of the Outer Hebrides is an unexpected oasis of trees, parkland and cosy streets amid the surrounding bleakness of moor and mountain. The **Museum Nan Eilean** (1000-1700 Mon.-Sat., Easter-Oct.; 1000-1300, 1400-1700 Mon.-Fri., Nov.-Easter; Free) has the history of Lewis and its inhabitants. The famous Lewis chessmen may also be on display. **An Lanntair Art Gallery** (1000-1730 Mon.-Sat.; Free) in the Town Hall has exhibitions and events. Stornoway is still a busy fishing port. Its fish market is open from 1900 Tue. & Thu. **St. Peter's Episcopal Church** (0900-1800) contains an ancient font from a hermit's chapel on the remote Flannan Isles, and David Livingstone's bible. About 4 miles east of the town, at Ui (take the A866 to Eye Peninsula, but turn left after the narrow neck of land) are the remains of the early St. Columba's Church and graveyard. Inside are a stone effigy of Roderic Macleod and a beautifully carved stone

slab, possibly from his daughter's grave. From the roundabout north of town, take the A857 to Barvas (Barabhas) across the huge desolate peat moor that covers most of northern Lewis.

A detour can be made from Barvas 12 miles to Port of Ness (Port Nis) and the Butt of Lewis, the most northerly point on the island. At Shader is the Steinacleit, a circular structure dating from the 3rd-2nd millennium BC. Formerly thought to be a cairn, it is now thought to have been a domestic building.

Turn left on the A858 to Shawbost. At **Arnol** is a restored blackhouse (HS,

Callanish Standing Stones, Lewis

except closed Sun., Jan.-Dec., and Fri., Oct.-Mar.; Inexpensive) with original furniture. The **Folk Museum** (1000-1800 Mon.-Sat., April-Nov.; Donation) at Shawbost is housed in an old church and was created by local school children. A minor road on the right leads to Dalmore, where there is a sandy beach, and a few miles further on another leads to Dun Carloway, the best-preserved broch (*see* Prehistory) in the Hebrides. **Callanish Standing Stones** (visitor centre 1000-1700 Mon.-Sat., Easter-Oct.; 1000-1600 Mon.-Fri., Nov.-Easter; Free, video and exhibition Inexpensive) are the best-known prehistoric site in the Hebrides. Dating from the 3rd-2nd millennium BC, this magnificent monument consists of 48 stones, mostly of beautifully banded Lewisian gneiss, arranged in the form of a cross and circle on a hillock above the loch. Two other stone circles are signposted nearby. The excursion ends back in Stornoway (512 miles).

From Stornoway, either return to Tarbert and take the ferry back to Uig, or go by car ferry from Stornoway to Ullapool to join Excursion 6. The latter ferry runs daily Mon.-Sat. (tel. 01851 702361).

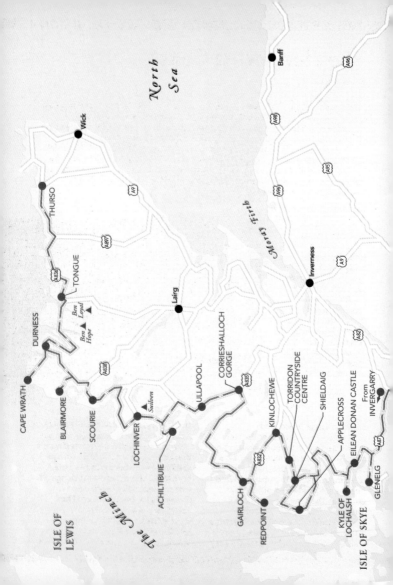

North Sea

The Minch

Moray Firth

ISLE OF LEWIS

ISLE OF SKYE

Banff

Wick

THURSO

Inverness

TONGUE

DURNESS

Ben Loyal
Ben Hope

Lairg

CAPE WRATH

BLAIRMORE

SCOURIE

LOCHINVER

Suilven

ACHILTIBUIE

ULLAPOOL

CORRIESHALLOCH GORGE

KINLOCHEWE

TORRIDON COUNTRYSIDE CENTRE

SHIELDAIG

APPLECROSS

EILEAN DONAN CASTLE

From INVERGARRY

GLENELG

KYLE OF LOCHALSH

GAIRLOCH

REDPOINT

A836
A897
A9
A838
A835
A832
A87
A82
A9
A95
A96
A96
A9

The Northwest Coast

3 – 4 days

This excursion follows Scotland's northwest coast from Kyle of Lochalsh past Cape Wrath and along the north coast to Thurso, the most northerly burgh on the Scottish mainland. It is a journey of surprising contrasts. The rugged beauty of the Northwest Highlands around Loch Carron and Torridon is followed by the attractive scenery of Sutherland, punctuated by the incredible shapes of its isolated hills such as Suilven and Stac Pollaidh (pronounced 'polly'). North again are the vast moorlands of Caithness. Apart from the scenery and quiet, which are the main attractions, there are the beautiful villages of Shieldaig and Plockton and the famous gardens of Inverewe.

This excursion begins at Kyle of Lochalsh, which can be reached from Skye by the Skye Bridge (*see* Excursion 5) or from Invergarry (*see* Excursion 2) via the A87. The latter route descends through lovely Glen Shiel in Kintail and passes the famous **Eilean Donan Castle** (1000-1800, last admission 1730, Easter-Sep.; Inexpensive), whose romantic silhouette is one of the most familiar images of Scotland.

Broch, Glenelg

A detour can be made on the way from Shiel Bridge, 19 miles southeast of Kyle. Turn left on the minor road to Glenelg which climbs steeply to the Pass of Mam Ratagan, 1116 ft above sea level, offering splendid views of the peaks known as The Five Sisters of Kintail, before descending into the lovely wooded valley of Glen More to reach the village of Glenelg after 12 miles. A short distance further on at Bernera a car ferry (July & Aug., tel. 01588 511302) makes the 5 min crossing to Kylerhea (pronounced 'kyle-ray') on Skye. Nearby are **Bernera Barracks** (open access), built after the 1745 Jacobite Rebellion (*see* Jacobites). Fork left at Glenelg and turn left again to visit the interesting brochs (*see* Prehistory) of **Dun Telve** and **Dun Troddan** (HS, open access).

Kyle of Lochalsh. TIC: Car Park, tel. 01599 534276, April-Oct. This is the terminus of the scenic Kyle railway line from Inverness. Nearby is the Skye Bridge. Take the minor road opposite the ferry slip that leads north through unexpectedly green and fertile scenery to the picture-postcard village of **Plockton**, set around an attractive bay. Sailing dinghies can be hired here, or there are boat trips to see seals and other wildlife. Continue towards Achmore. On the way is **Craig Highland Farm** (dawn-dusk, Easter-Oct.; Inexpensive), with rare breeds. Carry on to Achmore and turn left on the A890, which leads round the head of Loch Carron, then turn left on the A896. Beyond Kishorn the main road leads 10 miles to Shieldaig, but a far more interesting detour is the 35 miles of minor road via Applecross. This spectacular road (not suitable for caravans) climbs to 2053 ft over the Bealach na Bà (Pass of the Cattle), before descending more gently to the coast at the attractive village of **Applecross**. Turn right here on the coast road, with views across to Raasay and Skye, passing many ruined crofts. At Fearnmore, the mountains of Torridon come into view as the road swings east, rejoining the main road at the delightful village of Shieldaig.

War memorial, Glen Shiel

Plockton

47 miles – Torridon Countryside Centre and Deer Museum (NTS, 1000-1700 Mon.-Sat., 1400-1700 Sun., May-Sep.; Inexpensive). The centre has an audiovisual presentation on local wildlife, while 600 yd further on is the Deer Museum. The surrounding area contains some of the most impressive mountain scenery in Britain and

Beinn Eighe

provides excellent hillwalking for the experienced walker. The principal peaks are Liathach, 3456 ft, whose great bulk looms above the visitor centre, Beinn Alligin, 3232 ft, to the west, and Beinn Eighe, 3313 ft, at the head of Glen Torridon, part of Britain's first National Nature Reserve. Continue on the A896 to Kinlochewe and turn left on the A832. At Aultroy, just outside the village, is the Beinn Eighe Visitor Centre and, nearby, a circular, self-guided mountain walk, with signs indicating points of natural and geological interest (3 hr). The road follows the shore of lovely Loch Maree, with the distinctive outline of Slioch, 3215 ft, across the water. Near Slattadale, a car park on the left is the start of a forest walk to Victoria Falls, named after Queen

Loch Maree and Slioch

Victoria, who visited the area in 1877. After 6 miles a detour leads 9 miles to the beautiful sandy beach of **Redpoint**, a perfect picnic spot, with views to the hills of northern Skye and the Outer Hebrides (*see* Hebrides).

77 miles – Gairloch. TIC: Auchtercairn, tel. 01445 712130. A popular holiday centre spread along the wide bay. The

Ullapool

Inverewe Gardens

Gairloch Heritage Museum (1000-1700 Mon.-Sat., Easter-Sep.; Inexpensive) illustrates West Highland life from the Stone Age to the present. The road between Gairloch and Poolewe offers splendid views eastwards into the mountains north of Loch Maree; near Loch Tollaidh is the beginning of a pleasant 5 mile footpath along the banks of Loch Maree to Slattadale. Just beyond Poolewe are the famous **Inverewe Gardens** (NTS, 0930-sunset; Moderate), where palm trees and other subtropical plants flourish in the mild climate. Further on, the road touches Gruinard Bay, which is ringed by sandy beaches. Gruinard Island, in the middle of the bay,

has recently been declared safe again, after being contaminated with anthrax during World War II tests of chemical weapons. The road then climbs above Little Loch Broom and drops down to **Corrieshalloch Gorge** (NTS). Turn left on the A835 and stop at the car park to stroll down to the viewing platforms and suspension bridge above the spectacular 200 ft-deep gorge and the 150 ft Falls of Measach.

131 miles – **Ullapool**. TIC: Argyle St, tel. 01854 612135. A pleasant fishing port, tourist and shopping centre, and terminal for the car ferry to Stornoway (*see* Excursion 5). Boat trips to the beautiful Summer Isles leave from the pier and, at nearby Ardmair, canoes, boats and fishing tackle can be hired (tel. 01854 612154). **Ullapool Museum** (1000-1700 Mon.-Fri., April-May & Oct.; 0900-2100 Mon.-Fri., June-Sep.; Inexpensive) tells the town's history since its creation by the British Fisheries Society in 1788 to Thomas Telford's (*see* A-Z) plan. The tiny **Lochbroom Museum** (0900-2200 Mon.-Sat., June-Aug.; 0900-1800 Mon.-Sat., Sep.-May; Free) has geological specimens and memorabilia. 9 miles north of Ullapool, turn left on the minor road to Achiltibuie. This leads through

Lochinver

Inverpolly Nature Reserve and some magnificent mountain scenery. The road passes directly beneath the jagged sandstone crest of Stac Pollaidh, a steep scramble from the parking place by Loch Lurgainn (3 hr round trip; experienced hillwalkers only). A detour continues left to the village of **Achiltibuie**, for boat trips to the Summer Isles or to visit the **Smokehouse** (0930-1700 Mon.-Sat.; Free) where a viewing gallery shows the fish being smoked, or the **Hydroponicum** (guided tours 1000, 1200, 1400 & 1700 Easter-Sep.; Moderate), a unique hi-tech greenhouse where plants are grown using aquaculture – no soil is required. All kinds of fruit are grown, from bananas to lemons. Continue north on the minor road (unsuitable for caravans) that twists through the hills to Lochinver. 161 miles – **Lochinver**. TIC: Main St, tel. 01571 844330, April-Oct. A pleasant lochside village with a fishmarket (2000), Lochinver is famous for its splendid views of the strange-shaped mountains of Assynt, notably Canisp, 2779 ft, and the great sugar loaf of Suilven, 2399 ft. The new **Lochinver Visitor Centre** (1000-1700 Mon.-Sat., April-Oct.; 1000-1800 Mon.-Sat., May; 0930-1800 Mon.-Sat., June & Sep.; 0900-1830 Mon.-Sat., July-

Suilven and Canisp

Aug.; also 1000-1600 Sun., June-Sep.; Donation) tells the story of the land and the people of the area. The steep and winding B869 follows the coast round to Eddrachillis Bay, with sandy beaches at Achmelvich, Clachtoll and Clachnessie. Along the A837 on the shores of Loch Assynt is the ruin of **Ardvreck Castle** (open access), built in the 1590s for the Macleod laird and, nearby, the shell of Calda House, burned in the 18thC. Turn left on the A894, beneath the gullied flanks of Quinag, 2653 ft, a few miles before the modern Kylesku Bridge. From the old ferry pier near the bridge, Statesman Cruises (tel. 01571 844446) do boat trips up Loch Glencoul to see

Lochinver

Handa Island Nature Reserve

wildlife and Eas a'Chual Aluinn, Britain's highest waterfall, 658 ft. Beyond Scourie, a minor road on the left leads to Tarbet, from where a ferry goes to **Handa Island Nature Reserve** (daily from 1000, tel. 01971 502011). The island's cliffs teem with seabirds during the nesting season. A detour can be made on the B801 from Rhiconich to **Kinlochbervie**, an important fishing port where visitors can watch fish being landed. Beyond at Blairmore, a signpost on the right

indicates a farm track leading to **Sandwood Bay**. Park here and follow the track for 2 miles, then its continuation as a footpath for another 2 miles to reach a beautiful sandy beach. Tradition has it that this remote strand, guarded by the sea stack of Am Buachaille ('The Herdsman') at its southern end, is a favourite haunt of mermaids. Just south of Durness is a passenger ferry (daily May-Sep., tel. 01971 511376) across the Kyle of Durness, from where a minibus (tel. 01971 511343) continues 8 miles to the wild most northwesterly point on the Scottish mainland – **Cape Wrath**.

225 miles – Durness. TIC: Sango, tel. 01971 511259, April-Oct. Scotland's most northwesterly village, with a youth hostel and camp site. Its main attraction is **Smoo Cave** (outer cave Free; boat trips 0900-1800 June-Sep. to inner cave; Moderate), a huge limestone cavern cut into the sea cliffs below the road just east of the village. **Durness Visitor Centre** (1000-1700 Mon.-Sat., April & Oct.; 1000-1800 Mon.-Sat., May; 0930-1800 Mon.-Sat., June & Sep.; 0900-1830 Mon.-Sat.,

Dounreay Nuclear Power Station

July-Aug.; also 1200-1800 Sun., June-Sep.; Free) has displays on the local landscape and its people. Nearby are the sand dunes of scenic Balnakeil Bay, with its ruined 17thC church and monument to 18thC Gaelic bard Rob Donn, and Balnakeil Craft Village, where an artists' community has work for sale. From Durness, the road now follows the north coast round Loch Eriboll, with the peak of Ben Hope, 3040 ft, behind. **Choraidh Croft Farm Park** (1100-1830 May-Oct.; Inexpensive) has over 40 breeds of farm animals. A causeway crosses the Kyle of Tongue at the entrance to the delightful village of **Tongue**. To the right is the ruin of 14thC Castle Varrich, guarding the sound and, in the distance, is magnificent Ben Loyal, 2509 ft. Beyond Tongue are some beautiful beaches along this remote coast, notably at Coldbackie, Bettyhill, Strathy and Melvich. At **Bettyhill** (TIC: Clachan, tel. 01641 521342, April-Sep.) is the **Strathnaver Museum** (1000-1700 Mon.-Sat., Easter-Oct.; Free), with displays on Highland life, including the Clearances (see A-Z), plus Clan Mackay

Smoo Cave, Durness

material and the late Pictish Farr Stone. The land becomes flatter crossing into Caithness, and the white dome of **Dounreay Nuclear Power Station** rises on the left. There is a visitor centre (0900-1630 Easter-Sep.; Free) and guided tours of this prototype fast breeder reactor. **306 miles – Thurso** (see Excursion 8). This excursion ends here. Ferries leave from Scrabster for Orkney (see Excursion 7). Alternatively, Excursion 8 continues down the coast to Inverness.

Near Scourie

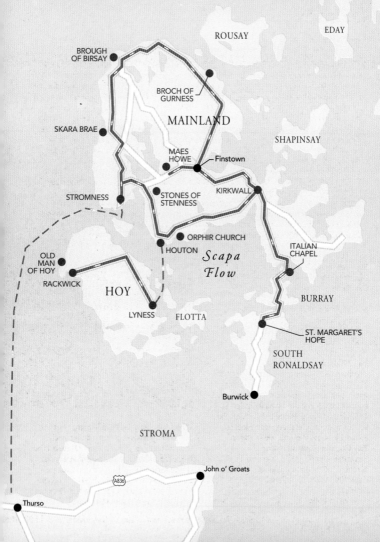

ORKNEY

EDAY

ROUSAY

BROUGH
OF BIRSAY

BROCH OF
GURNESS

MAINLAND

SHAPINSAY

SKARA BRAE

MAES
HOWE

Finstown

STROMNESS

STONES OF
STENNESS

KIRKWALL

ORPHIR CHURCH

HOUTON

*Scapa
Flow*

ITALIAN
CHAPEL

OLD
MAN
OF HOY

RACKWICK

HOY

BURRAY

LYNESS

FLOTTA

ST. MARGARET'S
HOPE

SOUTH
RONALDSAY

Burwick

STROMA

John o' Groats

A836

Thurso

Orkney

1 – 3 days

The Orkney Islands are situated off the northeastern tip of Scotland and separated from the mainland by the 8 mile Pentland Firth. There are over 70 islands, mostly small and uninhabited, a paradise for many species of seabird. The principal island is Mainland, about 20 miles long, which has the two main towns of Kirkwall and Stromness. It is connected to the southern islands of Burray and South Ronaldsay by causeways, and by ferry services to other inhabited islands. There is so much to see that the islands merit a whole holiday devoted to them. Only the major sites are described here. Those on a day trip will have time to see Mainland only, taking in Skara Brae, the Ring of Brodgar, Stones of Stenness, Maes Howe and Kirkwall, as well as Stromness, where the route described starts and ends. *See* Orkney.

P&O Scottish Ferries operate car ferries from Aberdeen to Stromness and on to Lerwick in Shetland up to seven days per week in high season (passage time 8 hr, tel. 01224 572615), and from Scrabster, near Thurso, to Stromness (up to three departures daily, passage time 1 hr 45 min, tel. 01865 850655). A passenger ferry runs between John o' Groats and Burwick, South Ronaldsay, with a bus connection to Kirkwall and Stromness (one-three departures daily May-Sep., passage time 45 min, tel. John o' Groats Ferry 01955 611353/342).

Stromness. TIC: Ferry Terminal Building, Pier Head, tel. 01856 850716. Once a thriving whaling port and outpost of the Hudson Bay Co., this attractive town is clustered along the narrow, winding Main St paved with local flagstone. The **Pier Arts Centre** (1030-1230, 1330-1700 Tue.-Sat.; Free), housed in converted 19thC buildings, has 20thC British art and changing exhibitions. **Stromness Museum** (1000-1700 May-Sep., 1030-1230, 1330-1700 Mon.-Sat., Oct.-April; Inexpensive), south of the ferry pier, was founded in 1837 and has interesting exhibits on the scuttling of the German High Fleet in Scapa Flow in 1919 and the Hudson Bay Co., plus natural history. Leave Stromness by the A965, then turn left on the A967 to Birsay, and left again on the B9056 to Skaill, following signs to Skara Brae.

9 miles – Skara Brae (HS, except 1130-

Skara Brae

1830 Mon.-Sat., 1400-1830 Sun., April-Sep.; Inexpensive, or joint ticket with four other sites). On an eroded site on the Bay of Skaill, this is the best-preserved prehistoric village in northern Europe, dating from about 3100-2500 BC. The site gives a valuable insight into the daily lives of its neolithic inhabitants.

Continue north on the B9056 to Birsay, passing **Marwick Head Nature Reserve** (open access), whose spectacular colonies of seabirds are best seen April-July. In Birsay is the imposing ruin of the **Earl's Palace** (HS, open access), built in 16thC Renaissance style for the Earl of Orkney. Northwest of the village is a car park on the Point of Buckquoy, from where at low tide the Brough of Birsay can be visited via a causeway. The tiny island has the remains of a Norse village and a 12thC church. From Birsay, continue round the north of the island, with views over to Eynhallow and Rousay islands, the latter with a natural arch at Scabra Head. Turn left on a minor road at Aiker Ness to visit the **Broch of Gurness** (HS, except closed Oct.-Mar.; Inexpensive, or joint ticket with four other sites), the best-preserved broch on

Stromness

Orkney, surrounded by the remains of Iron Age and later dwellings. There is also a museum. Continue south on the A966 to Finstown, and turn right on the A965.

36 miles – **Maes Howe** (HS, except closed Wed. & 1400-1630 Tue. & Sun., Oct.-Mar.; Inexpensive, or joint ticket with four other sites). This chambered cairn is the best example of its kind in Europe. The large central chamber with its corbelled roof is approached along a low, narrow passage. Three burial vaults lead off the other walls of the chamber. Runic inscriptions on the walls were made by Vikings who broke in. The great

mound has an atmospheric setting, with fine views, especially at sunset, across the Loch of Harray to the nearby stone circles. Continue west on the A965, then turn right on the B9055 just after Tormiston Mill. On the right the **Stones of Stenness** consist of four impressive standing stones from the original circle of

12. Further on is the even more spectacular **Ring of Brodgar** or Brogar, with 27 stones standing of a possible total of 60. There are also a number of burial mounds and the whole area may have had important ceremonial significance. Return to Finstown and continue to Kirkwall on the A965.

Ring of Brodgar

St. Magnus' Cathedral, Kirkwall

52 miles – Kirkwall. TIC: 6 Broad St, tel. 01856 872856. Orkney's capital is dominated by the impressive pink and yellow masonry of **St. Magnus' Cathedral** (0900-1700 Mon.-Sat., May-Aug.; 0900-1300, 1400-1700 Mon.-Sat., Sep.-April), built in the 12th-15thC and housing the relics of SS Magnus and Rognvald. Next to the cathedral are the imposing ruins of the 12thC Bishop's Palace, with a good view from the top of the 16thC tower, and the splendid Renaissance-style **Earl's Palace** (HS, except closed Oct.-Mar.; Inexpensive, or joint ticket with four other sites), built in the early 17thC. Across the street from the cathedral is the excellent **Tankerness House Museum** (1030-1230, 1330-1700 Mon.-Sat.; also 1400-1700 Sun., May-Sep.; Inexpensive), which covers many aspects of Orkney's history in a 16thC mansion. On the outskirts, off the A965 between the harbour and the Peerie Sea is Grain Earthhouse, a very well-preserved souterrain or underground store dating from the Iron Age. On the road out of town towards St. Margaret's Hope (A961) is the **Highland Park Distillery** (1000-1600 Mon.-Fri., April-Sep.; also tour 1430 Sat., June-Aug. & Mon.-Fri., Nov.-April; Free), with guided tours, sampling and an interesting audiovisual presentation of the islands' history. The A961 continues south, crossing the Churchill Barriers, causeways built by Italian prisoners of war in 1941-3 between Mainland and the islands of Lamb Holm, Glims Holm, Burray and

South Ronaldsay, thus creating a safe anchorage in Scapa Flow for the British fleet. On Lamb Holm is the attractive little chapel created by Italian prisoners of war during 1943-5. Housed in a tiny Nissen hut, it was lovingly fashioned from scrap metal, concrete and any other materials the prisoners could find. The wrecks of old block ships,

Italian Chapel

sunk on purpose to block the way before the construction of the barriers, can be seen rusting in the shallows nearby. At St. Margaret's Hope on South Ronaldsay is the **Orkney Wireless Museum** (1000-1900 April-Sep.; Inexpensive), dedicated to wartime communications. Return to Kirkwall and from there take the A964 which skirts the shore of Scapa Flow, Orkney's great natural harbour, which formed an important naval base during both World Wars. In 1919 the German High Fleet, captured by the British, was scuttled here in an act of defiance. Most of the ships were salvaged, but seven still lie on the seabed, a continuing attraction for scuba divers from all over the world. To the left, off the main road at Orphir, about 9 miles from Kirkwall, is the ruin of the 12thC Orphir Church, with an unusual circular plan perhaps inspired by the builder's pilgrimage to Jerusalem. A short distance beyond is Houton where there is a car ferry to Lyness and Longhope on Hoy. There is also a passenger ferry from Stromness to Moaness on Hoy. 2 miles from Moaness on the road to Rackwick is the Dwarfie Stane. This unique chambered tomb has been hollowed out of a huge block of sandstone. Hoy is the only really hilly

Old Man of Hoy

island in Orkney, and offers excellent walking. A recommended short walk follows a well-worn path from beautiful Rackwick Bay for 2 miles or so to the clifftop opposite the **Old Man of Hoy**, at 450 ft the highest sea stack in the British Isles. Return to Stromness (99 miles).

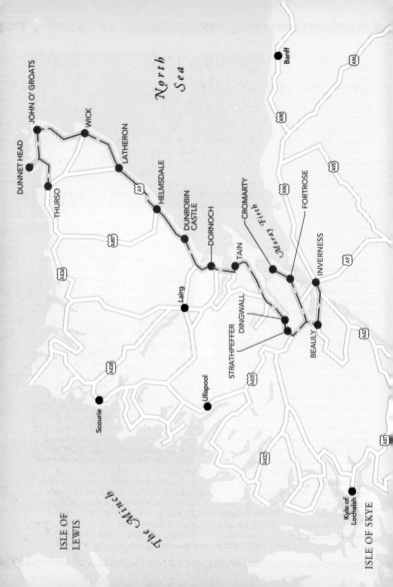

Caithness, Sutherland and the Black Isle

2 – 3 days

This excursion begins in Caithness, the most northerly part of Scotland, and visits John o' Groats, then follows the east coast of Sutherland to the rich and fertile Black Isle – a peninsula, not an island – and on to Inverness. The excursion visits the impressive Dunrobin Castle, the pretty village of Dornoch and its cathedral, the historic town of Tain which has associations with Celtic St. Duthac and James IV, the exquisite little Victorian spa town of Strathpeffer and the picturesque 18thC village of Cromarty. The new bridges across the Dornoch, Cromarty and Beauly Firths mean the journey from Thurso to Inverness can now be driven comfortably in a day, though it is much more rewarding to take longer, exploring the firths.

Thurso. TIC: Riverside, tel. 01847 892371, April-Oct. The principal town of Scotland's north coast, Thurso has many prehistoric remains and had a turbulent Viking history before it became a bishop's seat and integrated with the rest of Scotland in the 12thC. In the Fisher Town are the ruins of the 12th-13thC Old St. Peter's Church, altered in the 17thC. In the 18thC a New Town was built by Sir John Sinclair, while the Town Hall (1870) is a Victorian Gothic building containing **Thurso Heritage Museum** (1000-1300, 1400-1700 Mon.-Sat., June-Sep.; Inexpensive), including the Pictish Ulbster Stone. 2 miles north of the town is Scrabster, the point of departure for the car ferry to Stromness in Orkney (*see* Excursion 7). Follow the A836 east out of Thurso past Castletown. The road flanks the sandy beach of Dunnet Bay. Ahead is the stark, humpbacked outline of **Dunnet Head**, dropping vertically into the sea. At Dunnet is **Mary Ann's Cottage** (tel. 01955 603385), a traditional Caithness crofthouse little changed since the 19thC. To the left the B855 leads to a car park and viewpoint indicator near the lighthouse at the British mainland's

most northerly point. There are grand views to Orkney, dominated by the hills of Hoy, and west along the coast to Ben Loyal and Ben Hope. Return to the A836 and continue east.

20 miles – John o' Groats. TIC: County Rd, tel. 01955 611373, April-Oct. Named after a Dutchman who started a ferry here in the 15thC, this is the northern counterpart to Land's End. In summer the John o' Groats Ferry (tel. 01955 611353/342) takes passengers to Burwick on South Ronaldsay, Orkney (*see* Excursion 7). A minor road on the left leads to the lighthouse at Duncansby Head, with views across the swirling tide races of the Pentland Firth, Britain's most treacherous stretch of water. From the car park at Duncansby Head, a signposted footpath runs south along the clifftops for about 0.75 mile to the spectacular rock needles of the **Stacks of Duncansby**, passing cliffs of seabirds and impressive rock scenery. Take the A9 south, climbing onto a desolate moor, with a magnificent view back over the Pentland Firth and Stroma Island to the low outline of Orkney, then sweeping down to the coast. At Auckengill is **Northlands**

John o' Groats

Stacks of Duncansby

Viking Centre (1000-1600 June-Sep.; Inexpensive), with displays on chambered cairns, brochs (*see* Prehistory), Picts (*see* A-Z) and Vikings. Nearby is the Nyster broch. At Keiss is a fine 19thC harbour, while the ruined castle literally teeters on the edge of a cliff. 3 miles further on are the sandy links of Reiss.

37 miles – Wick (*see* A-Z). Continue south on the A9. After 8 miles, at Whaligoe a minor road leads left to the most unlikely site for a harbour. From the cottages, steep flights of steps lead down the cliff to an inlet offering some protection from the angry North Sea. Extreme caution is required. 3 miles further down the A9, a minor road leads right to the Hill o' Many Stanes at Mid Clyth. These stone rows consist of about 200 stones arranged in a fan pattern. Thought to date from the Bronze Age, their significance is unknown. Another 2 miles down the A9 is the right turn onto a road leading to the Grey Cairns of Camster, two of the best-preserved of all chambered cairns in Britain.

54 miles – Latheron. The **Clan Gunn Heritage Centre** (1100-1700 Mon.-Sat., June-Sep., also 1400-1700 Sun., July & Aug.; Inexpensive), housed in the 18thC parish church, explores the history of Clan Gunn, including its Norse origin and pre-Columbus links with America. 3 miles further on, the **Lhaidhay Croft Museum** (1000-1800 Easter-Oct.; Inexpensive) is a restored thatched croft with household and farm artefacts from the late 19th-early 20thC. There is an

interesting original 'cruck' roof in the neighbouring byre, built entirely from driftwood because of the lack of timber here. Further on, **Dunbeath Heritage Centre** (1000-1700 May-Sep.; Inexpensive), in Dunbeath old school,

has audiovisuals and displays on the social and natural history of the area. At Berriedale is **Kingspark Llama Park** (0900-1800; Inexpensive). Beyond, from Ousdale, are views to the left over the plateau to the rocky Ord of Caithness.

74 miles – **Helmsdale**.
TIC: Couper Park, tel.
01431 821640, April-
Sep. Cross the bridge
on the main road and
turn right into this
small fishing village to
visit **Timespan** (1000-
1700 Mon.-Sat., 1400-
1700 Sun., Easter-Oct.;
Inexpensive), an
award-winning visitor
centre where local
history, including Picts,
Vikings, the Clearances
(see A-Z) and the
Kildonan Gold Rush, is
interpreted through
tableaux and
audiovisual
presentations. The
road runs south from
here to the fishing
village of Brora,
climbing above the
cliff-lined coast and
occasionally sweeping
down to tiny villages.
At Kintradwell are
fascinating guided
tours (tel. 01408 621422
or contact Helmsdale
TIC) of wildlife,
including many
species of birds. Just
before Brora is

Dunrobin Castle

Clynelish Distillery (0930-1630 Mon.-
Fri.; Inexpensive), established in 1819
by the Marquis of Stafford as part of his
improvements to the Sutherland estates.
Nearby are the remains of Carn Liath
Broch.

89 miles – Dunrobin Castle (castle 1030-
1630 Mon.-Sat., 1300-1630 Sun., Easter,
May & Oct.; 1030-1730 Mon.-Sat., 1300-
1730 Sun., June-Sep.; gardens all year;
castle Moderate; gardens Free) is an
extraordinary fairytale castle, largely the
19thC creation of Sir Charles Barry,
architect of the Houses of Parliament in
London, who greatly extended the 14thC
tower. The castle is the seat of the Dukes
of Sutherland and contains fine Mortlake
tapestries, views by Canaletto, and
portraits by Scottish artists Ramsay (see
A-Z) and Michael Wright. In the former
summerhouse is a Victorian museum
with big-game trophies, Pictish stones

and geology. Outside are beautiful formal gardens. Continue to **Golspie**, where the village is still dominated by the huge monument to the 1st Duke of Sutherland and Marquis of Stafford, who, in the name of liberal reform, forced thousands of tenants from their homes during the 19thC Clearances.

Dunrobin Castle gardens

18thC **St. Andrew's Church** (0900-2000 June-mid Sep.) contains a fine laird's loft or gallery for the Sutherlands. 19thC **Golspie Mill** (1300-1700 Mon.-Fri., June-mid Sep.; Inexpensive) has self-guided tours. Follow the A9 south through Golspie and across the head of Loch Fleet via a causeway built by Thomas Telford (*see* A-Z) in 1815. The loch is a shallow inlet frequented by many species of wading birds. Turn left on the B9168.

100 miles – Dornoch. TIC: The Square, tel. 01862 810400. A delightful little town built of attractive yellow stone, Dornoch also has sandy beaches and the famous Royal Dornoch Golf Course. Dominating The Square is **Dornoch Cathedral**, now the parish church, founded in 1224 but much restored, particularly in the 19thC. Across the street, the 16thC Bishop's Palace is now incorporated in the Dornoch Castle Hotel. The old post office houses the TIC and a little **Visitor Centre** (0900-1700 Mon.-Sat., April & Oct.; 0900-1800 Mon.-Sat., May, June & Sep.; 0900-1830 Mon.-Sat., July & Aug.; 0900-1700 Mon.-Fri., Oct.-Mar.; also 1000-1600 Sun., June-Sep.; Free). **Dornoch Craft Centre** (0930-1700 Mon.-Sat., Easter-Sep.; also 1200-1700 Sun., July & Aug.; 1000-1600 Mon.-Fri., Oct.-Easter; Free), in the 19thC

Dornoch Cathedral

town jail, includes a museum on the jail. Leave Dornoch on the A949 then turn left on the A9 to cross the new Dornoch Bridge. Once across, continue left on the A9.

108 miles – Tain is thought to have been a royal burgh as early as 1066, though the earliest surviving royal charter is of 1587-8. The present Tolbooth dates from 1706. Nearby in the old schoolhouse is a visitor centre containing **The Pilgrimage** (0930-

1730 April-Oct., 1200-1600 Nov.-Mar.;
Inexpensive), a multimedia presentation on
Tain's importance as a place of pilgrimage to
the shrine of the 11thC Celtic St. Duthac,
notably by James IV. The 14th-15thC St.
Duthac Memorial Church was the focus of
the cult of the saint, while the ruined **St.
Duthac's Chapel** (open access) by the shore
was believed to be the site of the saint's
birthplace. **Tain Museum** (1000-1700 April-
Oct., 1230-1600 Nov.-Mar.; Inexpensive) has
local history and displays on Clan Ross.
Glenmorangie Distillery (tours 1030 & 1430
Mon.-Sat., April-Sep.; 1430 Mon.-Fri., Oct.-
Mar.; Inexpensive) dates from 1843, though
distilling on the site is said to go back 250
years or more. From Tain, backtrack west
on the A9 as far as the bridge, then take the
A836 which continues along the southern
shore of the firth, through Bonar Bridge and
all the way to Tongue on the north coast (*see*
Excursion 6). 11 miles from Tain, turn left on
the B9176 which cuts south through the
peninsula over high moorland. In 2.5 miles
at Struie is a parking place and viewpoint
looking back into the hills of Sutherland.
Rejoin the A9 by turning right along the
north shore of the Cromarty Firth, through
Evanton. To the right a minor road, then a
forestry track on the left, lead to the
spectacular **Black Rock Ravine**, which is
200 ft deep and 11 ft wide. Great care is
required. Also to the right of Evanton is a
rounded hill topped by the Fyrish
Monument, a replica of an Indian temple
gateway erected in 1782 by Sir Hector
Munro, in an effort to ease unemployment in
the area. Continue on the A9, then, instead
of crossing the bridge, take the A862 to the
head of the firth.

143 miles – Dingwall. A royal burgh since
1226, Dingwall was the county town of
Ross-shire. Its name, meaning 'field of the
parliament', comes from Norse. The **Town
Hall** on High St houses a small museum of
local history (0900-1700 Mon.-Sat., May-
Sep.; Free). Take the A834 east.

Dunrobin Castle

150 miles – **Strathpeffer**. TIC: The Square, tel. 01997 421415, April-Nov. An extremely picturesque Victorian spa town. In the pavilion opposite the TIC are four brass hand-pumps where the very sulphurous spring waters can be sampled. The restored Victorian railway station now houses the **Highland Museum of Childhood** (1000-1600 Mon.-Sat., 1300-1600 Sun., Mar.-May; 0900-1700 Mon.-Fri., 1000-1700 Sat., 1300-1600 Sun., June-Sep.; 1300-1600 Tue.-Sun., Oct.-Dec.; Inexpensive). In a nearby field is the Pictish Eagle Stone. Continue on the A834 and turn right on the A832 at Contin to reach the **Falls of Rogie** after a further 2 miles. From a car park on the right there are a number of forest walks centred on the scenic waterfall where salmon can be seen leaping in July and Aug. Return on the A832 through Contin, which turns right to Muir of Ord. At Marybank, a minor road leads right 22 miles up secluded Strathconan. On the outskirts of Muir of Ord is **Glen Ord Distillery** (0930-1200 Mon.-Fri.; Inexpensive), a large distillery offering guided tours. Continue on the A832 through Tore. At Avoch old post office is a **Heritage Exhibition** (1000-1700 Mon.-Sat., July-Sep.; Inexpensive), mainly on education. 2 miles beyond is the pleasant little town of **Fortrose** with views over the Moray Firth to Fort George (*see* Excursion 9). The ruined **Fortrose Cathedral** (HS, open access) dates from the 14th-15thC and contains the burial aisle of Euphemia, Countess of Ross, widow of the Wolf of Badenoch (*see* A-Z). Adjacent is the 13thC chapterhouse. Almost adjoining Fortrose is the attractive village of **Rosemarkie**. **Groam House Museum** (1100-1700 Mon.-Sat., 1430-1630 Sun., May-Oct.; Inexpensive) contains important Pictish stones, including one with remarkably fine carving, plus other material on the

Picts and the Brahan Seer, a Gaelic prophet who is said to have foreseen, among other things, the Clearances (*see* A-Z) of the Highlands. Continue on the A832, which now crosses northeast through the Black Isle.
187 miles – **Cromarty** became a royal burgh in 1264 and is now a very attractive and well-preserved 18thC village. The fine **Cromarty Courthouse** (1000-1800 April-Oct., 1200-1600 Nov.-Mar.; Inexpensive) has an award-winning museum with computer-controlled, costumed figures in a reconstruction of a trial. **Hugh Miller's Cottage** (NTS, 1000-1300, 1400-1700 Mon.-Sat., 1400-1730 Sun., May-Sep.; Inexpensive) is the late 17thC thatched cottage where the stonemason and important geologist was born in 1802. The house has furnishings plus an exhibition and video on Miller, who committed suicide in 1856. Leave Cromarty on the B9163, which follows the southern coast of the Cromarty Firth. At Shoretown, after 15 miles, veer left on the B9169. Continue on this road through Duncanston and cross the A9, the A835 and A832 to Windhill. Turn left on the A862.
216 miles – **Beauly**. At the end of the wide Main St on the right is the impressive ruin of **Beauly Priory** (HS, open access), founded around 1230. Little remains of the monastic buildings but the roofless church still stands. Nearby is the monument to the Lovat Scouts, originally raised for the Boer War. Continue on the A862. In 5 miles, at Moniack Castle, are **Highland Wineries** (1000-1700 Mon.-Sat.; Free), with tours and tastings of their wines made from flowers, berries and tree sap. Carry on along the shores of Beauly Firth, with views across the water to the distant outline of Ben Wyvis, 3433 ft, to reach Inverness (229 miles).

Falls of Rogie

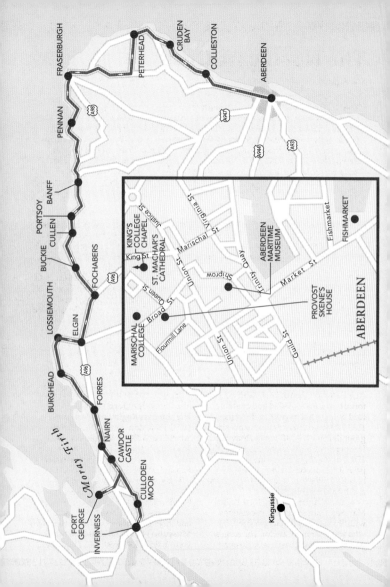

The Northeast Coast

5 – 6 days

The Northeast of Scotland, though north of the Highland Fault Line, consists of a fertile coastal plain which broadens out to the extensive farmlands of Aberdeenshire. Linguistically it is also distinct in its rich Northeast Scots dialect (*see* Languages). The fishing industry flourished here in the 19thC, hence the many attractive fishing villages, while the large modern port of Peterhead is important for North Sea oil as well as fish. Monuments range from prehistoric Clava Cairns and Pictish Sueno's Stone to the magnificent ruins of Elgin Cathedral and the castles of Cawdor and Brodie. From the 18thC, the Northeast offers such contrasts as the site of the Battle of Culloden and Duff House, William Adam's masterpiece.

Leave Inverness by the B9006 and after 5 miles reach **Culloden Moor** where, at the Battle of Culloden in 1746, the last battle on British soil, the Jacobite army of Bonnie Prince Charlie (*see* Jacobites) was finally crushed by Hanoverian troops led by the Duke of Cumberland. The **Visitor Centre** (NTS, 0900-1800 April-Oct., 1000-1600 Nov., Dec., Feb. & Mar.; Inexpensive) has an audiovisual presentation and facilities for visual, hearing and wheelchair disabilities. Continue on the B9006 and turn right at signposts for **Clava Cairns** (HS, open access), two chambered cairns and a ring cairn from the neolithic or early Bronze Age. Return to the B9006. Take the right fork at Croy on the B9091 and continue for 2 miles to **Kilravock Castle** (castle 1100-1700 Wed., May-Sep.; Inexpensive; grounds 0900-1700 Mon.-Sat., May-Sep.; Inexpensive), a 15thC tower house with 17thC additions and, outside, an early privy-cum-doocot (dovecote) and beautiful old trees. Return to Clephanton and turn left on the B9090.

15 miles – Cawdor Castle (1000-1730 May-Sep.; Moderate) has associations with Shakespeare's Macbeth (*see* A-Z), who was Thane of Cawdor. The earliest part of the present castle is the tower house, thought to date from 1372, built for the Calder family, Thanes of Calder or Cawdor. The 17thC range has Flemish tapestries made for it in 1682. Well-preserved Cawdor village has 19thC buildings and a 17thC kirk. Return on the B9090 to Clephanton and continue north on the B9006, crossing the A96 and passing Ardersier, where oilrigs are built and refurbished.

22 miles – Fort George (HS, except last admission 45 min before closing; Inexpensive) is a massive fort and barracks planned immediately after Culloden to discourage further rebellions. Built 1748-69, partly by John Adam, brother of Robert (*see* Adam), it also houses the **Queen's Own Highlanders Regimental Museum** (1000-1800 Mon.-Fri., 1400-1800 Sun., April-Sep.; 1000-1600 Mon.-Fri., Oct.-Mar.; Free). The fort is still in use by the British Army. Return to Ardersier and turn left on the B9092, which joins the A96 just before Nairn.

29 miles – Nairn. TIC: 62 King St, tel. 01667 452753, April-Oct. A very pleasant seaside resort with beach, watersports and three golf courses. **Nairn Fishertown Museum** (1430-1630, 1830-2030 Mon., Wed. & Fri., 1430-1630 Tue., Thu. & Sat.,

Standing stone at Clava Cairns

June-Sep.; Inexpensive) tells the story of fishing in the area, while **Nairn Museum** (1430-1630 Mon.-Sat., June-Sep.; Inexpensive) has local history and fossils. Leave Nairn on the A96 eastbound, passing, at Auldearn, Boath Doocot, where in 1645 the Marquis of Montrose raised the standard of Charles I after defeating the Covenanters (*see* A-Z). After 6 miles turn left for **Brodie Castle** (NTS, 1100-1730 Mon.-Sat., 1330-1730 Sun., Easter-Sep.; 1100-1730 Sat., 1330-1730 Sun., Oct.; Moderate), a 16thC Z-plan tower house with additions including extraordinary plasterwork and containing important collections of paintings, porcelain and furniture. Outside is the Pictish Rodney Stone. On either side of Brodie Castle, unclassified roads lead to walks into Culbin Forest, planted on the shifting sands which, in 1694, destroyed the Barony of Culbin in a great sandstorm. The area is now a haven for rare birds, plants and animals,

including capercaillie, ospreys, wildcats and pine martens. A short distance on, to the right off the A96, **Darnaway Farm Visitor Centre** (1000-1700 May-Sep.; Inexpensive; estate tours and castle 1300 & 1500 Wed., Thu. & Sun., July & Aug.; Inexpensive) has displays on the farms and forests of this large estate, plus walks. Darnaway Castle, now mainly 19thC, retains the banqueting hall in use around 1500, when James IV visited his mistress Janet Kennedy here. It has a splendid hammerbeam roof. Continue on the A96 and follow Forres signposts. **39 miles – Forres**. TIC: Falconer Museum, Tolbooth St, tel: 01309 672938, April-Oct. An ancient royal burgh now with mainly 18th and 19thC buildings and a fine High St. The **Falconer Museum** (1000-1700 Mon.-Sat., April-Sep.; 1000-1700 Mon.-Fri., Oct.-Mar.; Free) has local collections, including fossils. Good views of the countryside and firth can be had from the top of

Cawdor Castle

Nelson Tower (1400-1600 Tue.-Sun., May-Sep.; Free). On this hill, witches were put in barrels, rolled down, then burned, and Shakespeare's Macbeth (*see* A-Z) met his witches near here too. To the east of the town is **Sueno's Stone**, a magnificent Pictish stone with battle scenes, perhaps recording a 9thC campaign against Norse invaders. A detour may be made 2 miles south off the A940 to **Dallas Dhu** (HS, except 0930-1300 Thu. and closed Fri., Oct.-Mar.; Inexpensive), a perfectly-preserved distillery no longer producing but still with supplies to sample. Rejoin the A96 and turn left on the B9011, turning left at RAF Kinloss.

43 miles – Findhorn, at the estuary of the river of the same name, has a beach, famous yacht club and the internationally-known **Findhorn Foundation** (visitor centre 0900-1200, 1400-1700 May-Sep.; 1400-1700 Mon.-Fri., 0900-1200, 1400-1700 Sat. & Sun.,

Oct.-April; Free), a community founded in 1962 and dedicated to spiritual growth and cooperation with nature. Return to Kinloss and turn left on the B9089.

50 miles – Burghead (known locally as 'the Broch') is a small fishing town built in the early 19thC on the site of an important Pictish fort. Burghead Well, often described as a Roman well or early Christian baptistry, is now thought to be Pictish instead. Leave Burghead and turn left on the B9012 through the attractive fishing village of Hopeman.

54 miles – Duffus. Turn left to visit St. Peter's Church, a ruined, late medieval church altered in the 18thC, with St. Peter's Mercat Cross and fine tombs in the kirkyard. Further southeast are the imposing remains of Duffus Castle, originally a 12thC Norman motte and bailey timber castle. The late-13thC stone keep was too heavy for its gravel mound and collapsed. Return north on the B9012 and turn right on the B9040, passing RAF Lossiemouth.

59 miles – Lossiemouth, a fine fishing town and seaport, was the birthplace of James Ramsay Macdonald (*see* A-Z). **Lossiemouth Fisheries and Community Museum** (1100-1700 Mon.-Sat., April-Sep.; Inexpensive) has material on him, as well as on the fishing industry. Leave Lossiemouth by the A941.

65 miles – Elgin (*see* A-Z). Leave by the A96 eastbound. Pass Lhanbryde and Mosstodloch, at the end of which, on the banks of the Spey, is **Baxters** (0930-1800 Mon.-Fri., 1000-1800 Sat. & Sun., June-Sep.; 0930-1700 Mon.-Fri., 1000-1700 Sat. & Sun., Oct.-May; Free; tel. 01343 820666 for factory tours and cookery demonstrations), the fine foods manufacturers, with a visitor centre and reconstruction of the original 1868 Baxters grocery shop. Cross the Spey by the modern bridge alongside the old one.

72 miles – Fochabers is a handsome planned village laid out by the Duke of Gordon in 1776. On the left just before the present village are the gates of Gordon Castle (closed to the public). The earlier village stood within its grounds. **Fochabers Folk Museum** (0930-1300, 1400-1800 April-Oct., 0930-1300, 1400-1700 Nov.-Mar.; Inexpensive) has local history and horse-drawn carts in a converted church. Leave Fochabers uphill through Speymouth Forest on the A98, signposted Fraserburgh.

75 miles – Tynet. Turn left at the sign for **St. Ninian's Chapel** (dawn-dusk), the oldest post-Reformation Roman Catholic church still in use in Scotland. Built just after Culloden, when persecution of Catholics was common, it is no accident that this simple building looks like a row of cottages. Continue for 4 miles on the A98 and turn left.

80 miles – Buckie. TIC: Clunie Sq., tel. 01542 834853, May-Sep. This 19thC fishing port still has a busy harbour and

fishmarket (tours: July-Sep., booking essential, tel. 01542 834646). **The Buckie Drifter** (1000-1800 Mon.-Sat., 1100-1700 Sun., April-Oct.; Inexpensive) tells the story of the herring industry using hi-tech, while Buckie Library has the **Anson Gallery** (1000-2000 Mon.-Fri., 1000-1200 Sat.; Free), with works by Peter Anson, painter of Northeast fishing villages. Leave Buckie by the A942 past the harbour to the delightful fishing villages of **Findochty** (locally 'Finechty') and **Portknockie**. The latter has remains of an early fort at Green Castle and, further east, the Bow Fiddle, a huge rock with an impressive natural arch. Rejoin the A942 and turn left at the A98.

87 miles – Cullen. TIC: 20 Seafield St, tel. 01542 840757, May-Sep. Dominated by now-disused railway viaducts, Cullen has a good Seatown (fishermen's quarter), a fine main square, a beautiful beach and a golf course. Cullen Old Kirk or **St. Mary's Collegiate Church** (1400-1600 April-Sep.) is a medieval church enlarged in the 16thC. Inside are the tomb and effigy of Alexander Ogilvie and a laird's loft or private gallery of 1602. The 2nd Earl of Fife stole tombs from here for his mausoleum at Banff, and had the dates altered to pretend he was of ancient family. These have now been returned. Continue on the A98 and in 3.5 miles on the left is **Sandend** (locally 'Sanyne'), a tiny fishing village with a long beach. A mile up to the right is **Fordyce**, a beautiful and well-preserved village with a 16thC tower house, a ruined church and interesting tombs. Fordyce Academy was founded in 1790 for boys named Smith! **Fordyce Joiner's Workshop** (1000-1700 Easter-Oct.; Inexpensive) has a visitor centre and Victorian garden. A short distance along the A98 on the left is a ruined windmill.

92 miles – Portsoy has a fine old harbour of 1692 and good vernacular architecture.

Pennan

Serpentine, called Portsoy Marble, was once quarried here and used for fireplaces at Versailles and Hopetoun House (*see* Excursion 13). Only small pieces are available now at the workshop by the harbour. Rejoin the A98.

100 miles – Banff. TIC: Collie Lodge, tel. 01261 812419, April-Oct. An ancient royal burgh, Banff has some excellent 17th-19thC buildings and a kirkyard with the ruins of old St. Mary's Church and fine tombs. Banff Castle was replaced by John Adam's 18thC building. **Banff Museum** (1400-1720 Fri.-Wed., June-Sep.; Free) has local hallmarked silver, natural history and displays on James Ferguson, 18thC pioneer of modern astronomy. Banff's major attraction is the wonderfully extravagant **Duff House** (1000-1700 Mon.-Sat., 1400-1700 Sun., April-Sep.; 1400-1700 Oct.-Mar.; Moderate) by William Adam, father of John and Robert (*see* Adam). The house has paintings and furniture from the collections of the National Galleries of Scotland. Further into the park is the icehouse and the mausoleum,

still with an effigy stolen by the 2nd Earl of Fife. Nearby is Duff House Royal Golf Club. Leaving Banff, cross the 18thC bridge over the Deveron and turn left.

101 miles – Macduff, with a hilltop church, is still a fishing port with a fishmarket (0800 Mon.-Fri.). Follow the A98 through, then turn left on the B9031. After 2 miles, the Law of Melrose cairn can be seen to the left. In another 4 miles turn left to visit **Gardenstown** (or Gamrie), a fishing village at the foot of a steep hill. Beyond it is tiny Crovie. Return to the B9031 and in 3 miles a track leads to a car park. Along a narrow path is Castle Point, a clifftop promontory with evidence of settlements from the Bronze Age on and many seabirds. Return to the road and shortly turn left for **Pennan**, the picturesque village used in the film *Local Hero*. Continue on the B9031. Just before New Aberdour, a road leads to Aberdour Beach with caves and the ruins of St. Drostan's Church. 2 miles south of New Aberdour is **Northfield Farm Museum** (1100-1730 May-Sep.; Inexpensive).

119 miles – Rosehearty was a port dating back to 1684 and has the remains of a 16thC dower house. Turn right on an unclassified road to visit the ruins of old Pitsligo Church with a laird's loft, and 15thC Pitsligo Castle a mile south of Rosehearty. Rejoin the B9031 and continue to Fraserburgh via Sandhaven.

123 miles – Fraserburgh (also locally called 'the Broch'). TIC: Saltoun Sq., tel. 01346 518315, April-Oct. A seaside resort and still a major fishing port with a fishmarket (0730 Mon.-Sat.), Fraserburgh has a 19thC town house and 18thC Mercat Cross. Scotland's **Lighthouse Museum** (HS, 0930-1830 Mon.-Sat., 1400-1830 Sun., June-Sep.; 0930-1630 Mon.-Sat., 1400-1630 Sun., Nov.-May; Inexpensive) includes Kinnaird Head Lighthouse, the first in Scotland, adapted from a 16thC tower house and lit with whale-oil lamps, and the curious 16thC Wine Tower which has heraldic bosses. **Fraserburgh Library** (0930-1900 Mon.-Wed. & Fri., 0930-1700 Thu., 1000-1300, 1400-1700 Sat.; Free) contains the Glover Room, with material on Thomas Glover, founder of the Japanese Navy, who spent his childhood here. Leave Fraserburgh on the A92 south to Mintlaw, and turn right on the A950.

135 miles – Aden Country Park (heritage centre 1100-1700 May-Sep., 1200-1700 Sat. & Sun., April & Oct.; Inexpensive; park 0700-2200; Free; TIC: tel. 01771 623037, April-Oct.), pronounced 'aa-den', has been created from the great Aberdeenshire estate of the Russell family. The fine stable block contains the award-winning NE Scotland Agricultural Heritage Centre and there are also nature trails and a wildlife centre. Nearby at Old Deer is **St. Drostan's Episcopal Church** (0900-1700 Mon.-Sat.), built for the Russell family in 1851 with stained glass of 1870. Further west is **Deer Abbey** (HS, open access), the remains of a Cistercian monastery founded in 1219. Return to Mintlaw and continue on the A950. After 2 miles is Longside village. **Longside Parish Church** (1000-1700 Mon.-Sat., June-Aug.) is a plain building of 1835-6 with, in the kirkyard, the roofless old kirk and some interesting 18thC graves, including that of Jamie Fleeman, the Laird of Udny's 'feel' or jester, and John Skinner, Episcopalian minister and poet praised by Robert Burns (see A-Z). **St. John's Episcopal Church** (0800-1630 Mon.-Sat., April-Oct.) of 1854 has fine stained glass, including a window dedicated to John Skinner, and a memorial made from the propellor of a destroyed airship. Continue on the A950.

139 miles – Peterhead. TIC: 54 Broad St, tel. 01779 471904, April-Oct. Called 'the Blue Toon' because of the blue hats worn by the whalers during Peterhead's preeminence as a whaling port, the town is in fact built of local pink granite. It is now Europe's busiest white fish port with a huge harbour begun in 1773. The fishmarket is best visited 0730-0900 Mon.-Sat. Recently Peterhead has also flourished as a supply port for the North Sea oil and gas industries. North Sea gas comes ashore 5 miles north at St Fergus. **Arbuthnot Museum** (1030-1300, 1430-1700 Mon., Tue. & Thu.-Sat., 1030-1300 Wed.; Free) has displays on fishing, granite and whaling, with important Inuit collections. **Ugie Salmon Fish House** (0900-1200, 1400-1700 Mon.-Fri., 0900-1200 Sat.; Free), dating from 1585, is the oldest working fish house in Scotland. Leave Peterhead on the A952 south, past the remains of Boddam Castle and **Buchan Ness** lighthouse, Scotland's most easterly point. After 5 miles, turn left on the A975 and in 2 miles turn left to park and follow a narrow path to the **Bullers o' Buchan**, magnificent 200 ft cliffs, and the Bow of Pitwartlachie, a

Slains Castle

great rocky arch, with important colonies of seabirds. Continue south.

148 miles – Cruden Bay has a beach, golf course and harbour, and has become the oil terminal for the North Sea Forties Field. Out on the headland to the north are the dramatic ruins of **Slains Castle** (open access), begun in 1597, once home of the Earls of Errol and an inspiration for *Dracula* by Bram Stoker, who spent much time in this area. Carry on south for 8 miles and turn left at the sign for Collieston. After a mile turn right to **Forvie Nature Reserve** (visitor centre 1000-1700 May-Aug., 1000-1700 Sat. & Sun., Sep.-April; Free) by the extensive Sands of Forvie north of the River Ythan estuary, important for eider duck and greylag and pink-footed geese. Forvie village disappeared in a great sandstorm. Further down the same road is Collieston, visited by T.E. Lawrence, 'Lawrence of Arabia', a former fishing village whose nearby caves also made it a haunt of smugglers. Return to the A975 and carry on south, crossing the Ythan, and through Newburgh. After 6 miles turn left on the A92.

169 miles – Balmedie has a beach and country park (visitor centre 0900-1700 April-Sep., 0900-1700 Mon.-Thu., 0900-1600 Fri., Oct.-Mar.; Free) with sand dunes and two shipwrecks occasionally visible. Enter Aberdeen (177 miles) by King St, passing on the right Brig o' Balgownie, built in 1329.

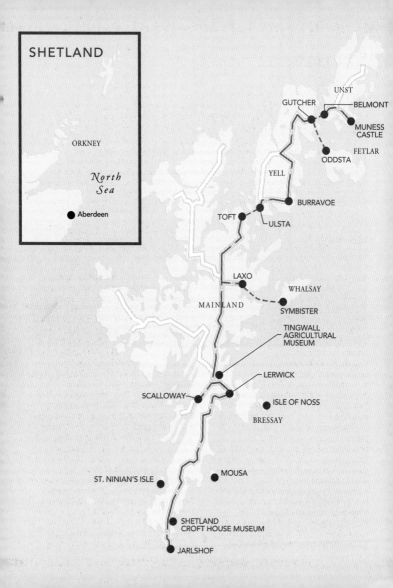

Shetland

2 – 3 days

The Shetland Isles form the most northerly group of islands in Britain, lying 60 miles north of Orkney and around 200 miles from Aberdeen, about the same distance as from Bergen in Norway. There are over 100 islands, only 12 of which are now inhabited. By far the largest is Mainland. These windswept islands are also home to many thousands of seabirds which nest in and around the 900 mile coastline. Despite (or because of) their remoteness and the often harsh climate, the islands have a unique appeal. The excursion and distances described here are for the Mainland as far north as Toft, but details of ferries for other major islands and what there is to see on them are also given. *See* Shetland.

P&O Scottish Ferries operate an Aberdeen–Lerwick service which runs up to six days a week and takes 14 hr. It also operates a Stromness (Orkney)–Lerwick service up to twice a week – an 8 hr crossing. There are a number of special round trip deals which include Orkney and offer good value. For details, tel. 01224 572615. Flights to Sumburgh on Shetland depart from Glasgow, Edinburgh and Aberdeen airports. Services are operated by British Airways.

Lerwick. TIC: The Market Cross, tel. 01595 693434. Shetland's capital was founded as a fishing port in the 17thC and has attractive old buildings and narrow streets. The **Shetland Museum** (1000-1900 Mon., Wed. & Fri., 1000-1700 Tue., Thu. & Sat.; Free) chronicles the history of human settlement on the islands. **Fort Charlotte** (HS, open access), on the waterfront, was first built in 1665 to guard the Sound of Bressay. On the southern outskirts of town is **Clickhimin Broch** (HS, open access). This fortified Iron Age site contains a 17 ft-high broch (*see* Prehistory) constructed inside it. To the east of Lerwick is the island of Bressay, reached by a frequent car ferry (tel. 01595 692024). Off its east shore is the **Isle of Noss**, now a nature reserve with 600 ft cliffs and huge colonies of auks, gulls and gannets, reached by inflatable boat (1000-1700 Tue.-Wed. & Fri.-Sun., May-Aug.; Inexpensive, tel. 01595 693345). At Sandwick, 14.5 miles south of Lerwick on the A970, is a boat (contact TIC for details) for the little island of **Mousa** whose 40 ft broch (HS, open access) is the best example of a broch tower anywhere in Scotland. 7 miles further south and just off the A970 is the **Shetland Croft House Museum** (1000-1300, 1400-1700 May-Sep.; Inexpensive), a typical 19thC thatched house which shows the traditional lifestyle on a Shetland croft (smallholding). Continue south to the very tip of the island. **25 miles – Sumburgh** is the site of the modern airport. Nearby is **Jarlshof** (HS, except closed Oct.-Mar.; Inexpensive), first excavated in 1933 and containing the remains of settlements from the Bronze Age to c1600. Particularly important and extensive are the 9thC Viking remains. From Grutness, there are regular sailings in summer on the *Good Shepherd IV* (tel. 01595 760222) to **Fair Isle**, 27 miles southwest (also accessible by air from Tingwall, tel. 01595 840246, or Kirkwall, Orkney, tel. 01856 872421). Knitting is still exported from the island. Fair Isle Bird Observatory is open May-Oct., tel. 01595 760251. A little further down the coast at Sumburgh Head, puffins can be spotted. Backtrack towards Lerwick on the A970 and at Boddam a minor road leads left. Turn left again at the signpost for **St. Ninian's Isle**. The island is reached on foot by a causeway and has a ruined 12th-13thC church where Celtic silver now in the Royal Museum of Scotland, Edinburgh, was discovered in the 1950s. Return towards Lerwick and 2 miles beyond Quarff turn left on the B9073, then left again for Scalloway. **50 miles – Scalloway**, on the west coast, has the extensive ruin of Scalloway Castle (1600), built for Earl Patrick Stewart of Orkney. **Scalloway Museum** (1400-1700 Tue.-Thu., 1000-1300, 1400-1700 Sat., May-Sep.; Donation) tells the story of the 'Shetland bus', the small boats from here which maintained

Jarlshof

Shetland Croft House Museum

links with Norway's resistance during German occupation in World War II. Leave on the B9074 north which skirts the Loch of Tingwall and passes a standing stone on the right. At the north end is a promontory, Law Ting Holm, thought to have been the meeting place of the Norse parliament, the *thingvollr* or 'parliament field'. At Veensgarth is the **Tingwall Agricultural Museum** (1400-

1700 June-Aug.; Inexpensive), with displays on Shetland crofting, and 18thC granary, stables and smithy. Leave Veensgarth on the A970 to explore north Mainland and the northern islands. The interior is mainly peat bog, while round the shores are beautiful beaches and cliffs teeming with seabirds. In 7 miles turn right on the B9075 round South Nesting Bay and up to Dury Voe. From **Laxo** a car ferry (tel. 01806 566259) crosses to Symbister on the island of Whalsay, where a restored Hanseatic Booth (keyholder next door; all reasonable times) commemorates trade between Shetland and the Hansa ports. Rejoin the A970 by the B9071 and continue north, veering right in a mile on the A968.

81 miles – Toft has a car ferry (tel. 01957 722259) to Ulsta on Yell, one of the larger islands, where the A968 continues north. The B9081 leads east to Burravoe, where the **Old Haa** (1000-1600 Tue.-Thu. & Sat., 1400-1700 Sun., April-Sep.; Free), the oldest building on Yell, houses a local museum. The B9081 continues north and joins the A968 beyond Mid Yell. From Gutcher are car ferries (tel. 01957 722259) to Oddsta on Fetlar and Belmont on Unst. To

Shetland ponies

Lighthouse, Sumburgh Head

the east of Unst, on a minor road off the A968, is **Muness Castle** (HS, details of keyholder at site; all reasonable times), Britain's most northerly castle, now an extensive ruin. It was begun in 1598 for Laurence Bruce, half-brother of the Earl of Orkney, and notoriously corrupt local sheriff.

Back on Mainland, 2 miles south of Toft the B9076 passes Sullum Voe oil terminal to join the A970 which continues north as far as Isbister on Mainland. Return to Lerwick by the main road (105 miles). On the northern outskirts is the 18thC **Böd of Gremista** (1000-1300, 1400-1700 Wed.-Sun., June-mid Sep.; Inexpensive), where Arthur Anderson, co-founder of the P&O shipping line, which still serves Shetland, was born.

Lerwick

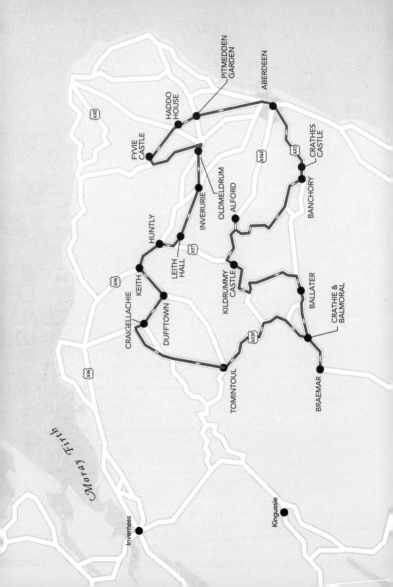

Royal Deeside and Northeast Castles & Distilleries

2 – 3 days

This excursion includes Royal Deeside, where Queen Victoria, enchanted by the Highlands, built her beloved Balmoral which is still visited each year by the present Queen. Deeside, and the valleys of Strathdon and Ythanside, have some of the finest examples of castle architecture in Scotland. A number, including Huntly Castle, are in ruins, yet remain incredibly evocative. Others, like Fyvie Castle, have a history which spans the centuries, while 16th-17thC Castle Fraser is a superb example of the sophistication achieved in these buildings. The other focus of this excursion is the Northeast's distilleries which produce the famous Speyside malts. These seven distilleries together form a recognized tourist route known as the Whisky Trail.

Leave Aberdeen on the A93 North Deeside road, passing some of Aberdeen's wealthier suburbs. The South Deeside road, the B9077, runs parallel and at Maryculter (pronounced 'mary- cooter') is **Storybook Glen** (1000-1800 Mar.-Oct., 1100-1600 Sat. & Sun., Nov.-Feb.; Inexpensive), 20 acres of gardens containing lifesize models of fairytale characters. The B979 goes from Maryculter to Milltimber, connecting the North and South Deeside roads. Continue on the A93. Just beyond Peterculter (same pronunciation as in Maryculter) on the right, by the bridge over the Leuchar Burn, is a brightly-coloured statue of Rob Roy (see A-Z), who is believed to have crossed this burn (stream). 3 miles after Peterculter on the right is **Drum Castle** (NTS, 1330-1730 Easter-June & Sep., 1100-1730 July & Aug., 1330-1730 Sat. & Sun., Oct., last admission 1645; Moderate; garden 1000-1800 Easter-Oct.; grounds 0930-sunset; Inexpensive), whose great tower is one of the three oldest in Scotland, dating from the 13thC and built by Richard Cementarius, royal master mason and

first provost (mayor) of Aberdeen. The contents include fine Georgian furniture, while the grounds contain a natural oakwood. Continue west through the village of Crathes. A short distance beyond on the right is **Crathes Castle** (NTS, 1100-1730, last admission 1645, April-Oct.; Moderate; grounds 0930-sunset; Inexpensive), built in the 16thC, although the lands were given to the Burnett family by Robert the Bruce (see A-Z). Inside are fine painted ceilings, unusual vernacular furniture and the fascinating Horn of Leys, a jewelled ivory horn said to have been given by Bruce. Outside is yew topiary and a delightful walled garden. Continue on the A93.

18 miles – Banchory. TIC: Bridge St, tel. 01330 822000. A busy local centre, Banchory is also now a commuter town for Aberdeen. Just south on the B976 is Bridge of Feugh, where the River Feugh joins the River Dee. Here there is parking and a special bridge from which to watch salmon leap. **Banchory Museum** (1100-1300, 1400-1700 Sat.-Sun. & hols, Easter-May & Oct.; 1030-1300, 1400-1730 June-

Sep.; Free) has local history, including material on Scott Skinner, a famous 19thC fiddler known as the 'Strathspey King'. Leave Banchory on the A980 north and in 3 miles turn right on the B977. After 4 miles the road veers left. 3 miles northeast, to the right off the B9125, is the **Cullerlie Stone Circle** (open access), probably dating from the late 2nd millennium BC. Return to the B977 and continue north through the agricultural villages of Echt and Dunecht. Just after the latter, turn left on an unclassified road through Achath. On the right 4 miles from Dunecht is **Castle Fraser** (NTS, 1330-1730 Easter-June & Sep., 1100-1730 July & Aug., 1330-1730 Sat. & Sun., Oct., last admission 1645; Moderate; garden 0930-1800; grounds 0930-sunset; Inexpensive), one of the most spectacular and sophisticated of the so-called 'Castles of Mar', referring to this ancient Aberdeenshire province. It dates mainly from the 16th-17thC and has typical 'pepperpot' towers. Outside is a walled garden. Return to the unclassified road which sweeps north through Craigearn. In 2 miles turn left on the B993, which in 3 miles reaches Monymusk. The 12thC Norman parish church or St. Mary's (tel. 01467 651470) is on the site of an earlier priory. **Monymusk Walled Garden** (1000-1700 Mon.-Sat., 1400-1700 Sun., Mar.-Oct.; Free) dates back to the 18thC. **Monymusk Arts Centre** (1000-1600 May-Sep.; Free), housed in an 18thC lapidary mill, tells the story of agricultural reform in that century. Continue on the B933 and at Tillyfourie turn right on the A944.

57 miles – Alford. TIC: Railway Museum, Station Yard, tel. 01975 562052, April-Oct. This former market town is still an important centre of the mainly agricultural area. **Grampian Transport Museum** (1000-1700 April-Oct.;

Inexpensive) has vintage vehicles, from penny-farthings and horse-drawn trams to a strange steam car built by a local postman. Its Railway Museum has a Victorian booking office. **Alford Valley Railway** (1100-1700 June-Aug.; Sat. & Sun., April, May & Sep.; Inexpensive) is Scotland's only 2 ft narrow gauge passenger railway and operates between Alford Station and Haughton Country Park, which has fine birch woods. **Alford and Donside Heritage Centre** (1000-1700 Mon.-Sat., 1300-1700 Sun., April-Oct.; Inexpensive) is a museum of farming life, housed in the former cattle mart. A mile to the north is the water-powered **Montgarrie Oatmeal Mill** (tours 1400 & 1530 Tue. & Thu., April-Oct.; booking essential, tel. 01975 562209). From Alford, follow the A980 south for 6 miles, then turn right on an unclassified road to visit **Craigievar Castle** (NTS, 1330-1730, last admission 1645, May-Sep.; Moderate; grounds 0930-sunset; Inexpensive), perhaps the most delightful of 17thC castles, with many little turrets sprouting from the top. Inside are important plaster ceilings and 17th-18thC furniture. Backtrack on the A980 to Muir of Fowlis, then turn left on a minor road. A mile after Ley, turn right, then right again. At Milltown, take the left fork and buchat Glenbuchat Castle on the A97. A short distance on the right is **Kildrummy Castle** (HS, except 0930-1630 Sat., 1400-1630 Sun., Oct.-Mar.; Inexpensive), a ruined 13thC castle around a courtyard, following the design of the French Château de Coucy at Lyons. Its destruction was ordered after the 1715 Jacobite Rebellion (*see* Jacobites). A garden has been created in the nearby 'Back Den' of Kildrummy, an old quarry. Continue on the A97, passing on the right at Bridge of Buchat Glenbuchat Castle (no access), a 16thC tower house built for the Gordon family. 2 miles beyond the

Balmoral Castle

road veers left. **Old Semeil Herb Garden** (1000-1700 May-Aug., 1000-1700 Sat. & Sun., April; 1000-1700 Fri.-Wed., Sep.; Free) has herb displays. Carry on down the A97. To the right is the distinctive hill of Morven, 2861 ft, and in the kirkyard at Logie Coldstone is the 9thC Migvie Stone, while to the left 5 miles along the B9119 is **Culsh Earth House** (HS; access via Culsh Farmhouse; Free), an important example of a souterrain or underground store dating from the early 1st millennium AD. Continue on the A97 and turn right on the A93.

99 miles – Ballater. TIC: Station Sq., tel. 01339 755306, Easter-Oct. A pleasant old spa resort, Ballater has also benefited from its proximity to Balmoral. At **Dee Valley Confectioners** (0900-1230, 1400-1700 Mon.-Thu.; Free) visitors can watch hand production of sweets. Beyond Ballater on the A93, at the junction with the A939 is the **McEwan Gallery** (1000-1800; Free), a mainly Scottish art collection in the house built by Swiss artist Rudolphe Christen. Continue on the A93.

107 miles – Crathie. TIC: Car Park, Balmoral Castle, tel. 01339 742414, Easter-Oct. On the hill on the right is **Crathie Church** (0930-1300, 1400-1730 Mon.-Sat., 1400-1730 Sun., April-Oct.), built in 1895, where the Royal Family worship when in residence at Balmoral. To the left a short way up the B976 is **Balmoral Castle** (1000-1700 Mon.-Sat., May-July; Inexpensive), the turreted Scots baronial (*see* Architecture) castle (1855) designed by William Smith of Aberdeen with Prince Albert. The estate was a personal purchase by Queen Victoria and her extraordinary new castle replaced a 16thC tower. The queen's love of the area more or less created tourism on Royal Deeside, while the castle itself influenced a Scots baronial revival. Only the exhibition of works of art in the Ballroom can be visited inside the castle. Outside in the grounds are many royal memorials. Continue up the B976 to the **Royal Lochnagar Distillery** (1000-1700 Mon.-Sat., 1100-1600 Sun., Easter-Oct.; 1000-1700 Mon.-Fri., Nov.-Easter; Inexpensive), founded in Victoria's reign and given its royal appointment by her. Return to the A93 and turn left. A mile before Braemar itself is **Braemar Castle** (1000-1800 Sat.-Thu., May-mid Oct.; Inexpensive), built by the Earl of Mar in 1620. In the 18thC it became a garrison post for Hanoverian troops after the Jacobite Rebellions and later became a residence of the Farquharsons.

Linn o' Dee

117 miles – Braemar. TIC: The Mews, Mar Rd, tel. 01339 741600. This attractive village is best known for the Braemar Royal Highland Gathering (*see* Events, Festivals), the most famous of Highland Games, held at the beginning of Sep. each year and usually attended by the Royal Family. The first Braemar Gathering is said to have been held by King Malcolm Canmore in the 11thC in order to choose the finest clansmen for his warriors. Like other Highland traditions, the Gathering was banned for a time after the Jacobite Rebellions. Its continuing popularity is still in part due to the enthusiastic support which Queen Victoria gave it in the 19thC. There are only scant 14thC remains of Kindrochit Castle, whose predecessor is believed to have been occupied by Malcolm Canmore. **Braemar Highland Heritage Centre** (0900-1800 April-June & Sep.; 0900-2000 July & Aug.; 1000-1700 Oct.-Mar.; Inexpensive) tells Braemar's story through displays and film. A plaque marks the cottage where in 1881 Robert Louis Stevenson (*see* A-Z) worked on *Treasure Island*. The A93 continues south through Glenshee, popular with skiers in winter, and the eastern Grampian mountains to Blairgowrie (*see* Excursion 12), while an unclassified road goes west 8 miles to the Linn o' Dee, a popular beauty spot and waterfall. Return by the A93 to Crathie and turn left on the B976. In 5 miles turn left on the A939, a mountain road which in 8 miles passes **Corgarff Castle** (HS, except 0930-1630 Sat., 1400-1630 Sun., Oct.-Mar.; Inexpensive), a 16thC tower house which became a barracks for Hanoverian troops after Culloden (*see* Jacobites). In the 19thC unpopular 'redcoats' were stationed here to try to control smuggling of illicit whisky. The castle retains its star-shaped ramparts. Continue to Cock Bridge, where snow gates are a reminder that the stretch of road between here and Tomintoul is among the most commonly blocked by snow in winter. 4 miles after the snow gates are the **Lecht Ski Centre** (tel. 01975 651440).

149 miles – **Tomintoul**. TIC: The Square, tel. 01807 580285, April-Nov. A tiny village in the bleak moorland between Deeside and Speyside. **Tomintoul Museum** (1000-1730 Mon.-Sat., 1400-1730 Sun., April, May & Oct.; 0930-1800 Mon.-Sat., 1400-1800 Sun., June & Sep.; 0930-1900 Mon.-Sat., 1400-1800 Sun., July & Aug.; Free) has reconstructions of a farm kitchen and a blacksmith's shop. Leave Tomintoul on the B9008. At Tomnavoulin is the **Tamnavulin Distillery** (0930-1630 Mon.-Sat., April-Sep.; 0930-1630 Mon.-Fri., Mar. & Oct.; last tour 1545; Free), one of several distilleries in the famous Glenlivet, where some of the finest malt whiskies are made. Continue on the same road and in 2 miles is **The Glenlivet Distillery** (1000-1600 Mon.-Sat., Easter-Oct.; Free). It has displays of old tools and other whisky artefacts. Further on is Bridge of Avon. A short distance to the left is **Ballindalloch Castle** (1000-1700 April-Sep.; Moderate), a 16thC tower house still owned by the Macpherson-Grant family. Outside is a 17thC doocot and a famous herd of Aberdeen Angus cattle. Take the A95 north. On the right after Marypark is **Glenfarclas Distillery** (1000-1600 Mon.-Sat., June-Sep.; Mon.-Fri., Oct.-May; Inexpensive). Return to Marypark and turn right on the B9012 and, after 4 miles, is **Cardhu Distillery** (0930-1630 Mon.-Sat., May-Sep.; Mon.-Fri., Mar., April, Oct. & Nov.; Inexpensive). Continue on the B9012 to **Craigellachie**, where there is a fine iron bridge (1812-15) built by Thomas Telford (*see* A-Z) and thought to be the oldest of its type in Scotland. 2 miles southwest is (Charlestown of) Aberlour, where the fascinating **Village Store** (1000-1800 Mon.-Sat., 1400-1730 Sun.; Free) is now a museum. After the owner retired, much of the old stock remained, from corsets and woollie knickers to hardware and

haberdashery, as well as the shop accounts. North of Craigellachie on the A941 is the **Glen Grant Distillery** (1000-1600 Mon.-Fri., Easter-June & Sep.; Mon.-Sat., July & Aug.; Free), dating from 1840 and one of the most famous of all malts. Leave Craigellachie on the A941 south. Just outside is the **Speyside Cooperage** (0930-1630 Mon.-Fri., Oct.-Easter; Mon.-Sat., Easter-Sep.; Inexpensive) where oak casks are made for the whisky industry. Continue south on the A941.

178 miles – **Dufftown**. TIC: Clock Tower, The Square, tel. 01340 820501, April-Nov. An attractive little town, Dufftown is situated at the heart of the whisky industry. **Mortlach Church** (daylight hours, Easter-Oct.) has an ancient history dating back to its founding around AD 566 by St. Moluag. Part of the present building dates from the 11th or 12thC and the church is one of the oldest in Scotland in continual use for public worship. **Balvenie Castle** (HS, except closed Oct.-Mar.; Inexpensive) is a ruined 13thC castle with moat, courtyard and curtain wall. **Dufftown Museum** (1000-1730 Mon.-Fri., April, May & Oct.; 0930-1800 Mon.-Fri., 1000-1700 Sat., June & Sep.; 0930-1800 Mon.-Fri., 1000-1800 Sat. & Sun., July; 0930-1900 Mon.-Fri., 1000-1900 Sat., 1230-1900 Sun.; Free), housed in the Clock Tower, has a reconstruction of a laundry, plus whisky displays. 2 miles south off the A941 are the remains of Auchindoun Castle (exterior only), surrounded by prehistoric earthworks. Leave Dufftown on the B9014. In 3 miles is **Drummuir Castle** (tours 1400, 1445 & 1530 Sun., May-Sep.; Inexpensive), the 19thC castle home of the Duff family, with a spectacular lantern tower. Continue along the B9014. After 3.5 miles is **Mill of Towie** (1030-1730 Wed.-Mon.; booking, tel. 01542 810307; Inexpensive), a restored, working 19thC water-powered mill.

188 miles – Keith. TIC: Church Rd, tel. 01542 882634, May-Sep. On the site of an early Christian settlement by the River Isla was the medieval town of Old Keith whose Auld Brig dates from 1609. The present town was mainly planned in the 18th and 19thC. The beautiful 18thC **Strathisla Distillery** (0930-1630 Mon.-Fri., mid Feb.-mid Nov.; also 0930-1600 Sat., July & Aug.; Moderate) has a water wheel and incorporates stones from the nearby ruined Milton Castle (open access). Leave Keith on the main A96 road southbound. After 6 miles, to the left is the **Northeast Falconry Visitor Centre** (1000-1800 Mar.-Sep., 1000-dusk Oct.-Nov.; Moderate). Further up the unclassified road is **Borve Brew House** (1230-2000; Free), a small family-run brewery. Continue on the A96.

199 miles – Huntly. TIC: 7a The Square, tel. 01466 792255. A pleasant 18thC planned town between the rivers Deveron and Bogie, laid out by the Duke of Gordon near the family's former principal seat. **Huntly Castle** (HS, except 0930-1300 Thu., and closed Fri., Oct.-Mar.; Inexpensive), in a beautiful woodland site, was first a Norman motte and bailey, then an early 15thC tower house and finally a sophisticated 16thC Renaissance palace whose substantial ruins we see today. The palace entrance has a spectacular carved stone heraldic panel with the shield of the 4th Earl of Gordon and his wife, while from the early 17thC are fine oriel windows and a carved heraldic mantelpiece. The **Brander Museum** (1000-1200, 1400-1600 Tue.-Sat.; Free) has material on the town's development. Leave Huntly on the A97 south and in 6 miles turn left on the B9002 to visit **Leith Hall** (NTS, 1330-1730, last admission 1645, Easter-Sep.; Inexpensive; garden 0930-sunset; Inexpensive), a fine mid 17thC mansion containing the military history of the

Leith-Hay family, including a rare Jacobite pardon. Continue on the B9002 and a mile beyond Oyne turn right on the A96. Almost immediately, an unclassified road leads right to Chapel of Garioch and signposts indicate the 9thC **Maiden Stone**, one of the finest Pictish stones in the Northeast. To the southwest is Bennachie, 1733 ft, the highest hill hereabouts and with the remains of the Mither Tap Iron Age fort on top. Continue on the A96.

224 miles – Inverurie. TIC: Town Hall, Market Pl., tel. 01467 620600, April-Oct. A busy market town which now holds all the Northeast's major livestock markets at the **Agricultural Centre** (auction 1000-1600 Sun.; centre 0900-1700 Mon.-Fri.; Free). Inverurie is also the centre of an area rich in Pictish and earlier remains. **Carnegie Museum** (1400-1700 Mon.-Tue. & Thu.-Fri.; Free) contains interesting archaeological material. Just southeast of the town on the B993 is the Bass of Inverurie (open access), the 12thC motte of a Norman castle with, beside it, three Pictish stones. A mile further south are the ruins of 16thC Kinkell Church (open access), with a fine sacrament house (a decorated niche in which the items used in the sacrament were kept). 5 miles north off the B9001 is **Loanhead of Daviot Stone Circle** (open access), an important recumbent stone circle from at least the 2nd millennium BC. Leave Inverurie on the B9170 to **Oldmeldrum**, a pleasant old town. Turn left here on the A947 north to **Fyvie**, famed in the ballad of *The Bonnie Lass o' Fyvie*. Fyvie Church (tel. 01651 891230/413) is an attractive 19thC building with Tiffany stained glass on the site of earlier churches and with Celtic stones incorporated in its gable. **Fyvie Castle** (NTS, 1330-1730 April-June & Sep.; 1100-1730 July & Aug.; 1330-1730 Sat. & Sun., Oct.; last admission 1645; Moderate; grounds 0930-sunset;

Inexpensive), a short distance beyond the village on the B9005, began as a 13thC square tower with a great curtain wall and projecting corner towers. To this have been added four other towers and additions up to the 19thC. It thus illustrates much of the development of Scottish castle architecture. Inside is a very fine collection of paintings, including a number of Raeburns (*see* A-Z), plus the fabulous Pompeo Batoni portrait of Gen. William Gordon (1776) in full Highland dress standing among the ruins of classical Rome. Continue on the B9005, then at Methlick turn right on the B999 through Tarves, where, in the kirkyard, is Tarves Medieval Tomb, the remarkable carved altar tomb of William

Fyvie Castle

Forbes. Just beyond the village, turn left to visit **Haddo House** (NTS, 1330-1730 Easter-June & Sep.; 1100-1730 July & Aug.; 1330-1730 Sat. & Sun., Oct.; Moderate; garden and country park 0930-sunset; Inexpensive), a fine William Adam house of 1731. Later developments include a 19thC cedar-panelled library in a former hayloft and a chapel with stained glass by 19thC Pre-Raphaelite Burne-Jones. The country park is rich in wildlife. On the right 2 miles south on the B999 is the ruin of **Tolquhon Castle** (HS, except 0930-1630

Sat., 1400-1640 Sun., Oct.-Mar.; Inexpensive), an early 15thC tower house enlarged in the 16thC by William Forbes and with fine carving on the gatehouse. A short distance beyond is **Pitmedden Garden** (NTS, 1000-1730, last admission 1700, May-Sep.; Moderate), with the reconstructed parterres of this great formal garden laid out in 1675 by Sir Alexander Seton, perhaps due to contact with Lenôtre in France. There is also an interesting Museum of Farming. Continue south on the B999 which joins the A92 outside Aberdeen (265 miles).

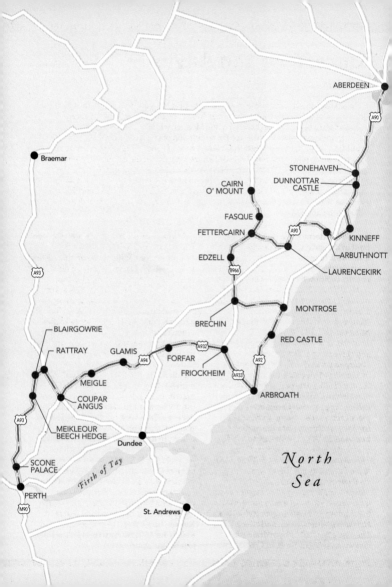

ABERDEEN

A90

Braemar

STONEHAVEN
CAIRN
O' MOUNT
DUNNOTTAR
CASTLE

FASQUE
FETTERCAIRN
A90
KINNEFF

EDZELL
ARBUTHNOTT
B966
LAURENCEKIRK

A93

MONTROSE
BRECHIN

RED CASTLE
BLAIRGOWRIE
RATTRAY
GLAMIS
A932
FORFAR
A94
FRIOCKHEIM
MEIGLE
A933
COUPAR
ANGUS
A92
ARBROATH

A93
MEIKLEOUR
BEECH HEDGE
Dundee

SCONE
PALACE
Firth of Tay

North

PERTH
Sea

M90

St. Andrews

Kincardine and Angus

3 – 5 days

This excursion explores one of the least well-known areas of Scotland, though it has a wealth of history and monuments. Much of Kincardine is rich farmland on the red earth of the Howe (hollow) o' the Mearns, while wide and fertile Strathmore (big valley), famed for the cultivation of soft fruit, runs across the middle of Angus. North of Strathmore and west of Kincardine are the Grampian Mountains, while the Sidlaw Hills lie to the south. Down the east coast are cliffs and beaches and the coastal towns of Stonehaven, Montrose and Arbroath. The whole area is extremely important for Pictish remains, with museums of sculptured stones at Meigle and St. Vigeans. Other major monuments include Arbroath Abbey, site of the famous Declaration of Arbroath, and the castles of Dunnottar and Glamis.

Leave Aberdeen by the Bridge of Dee, built in the early 16thC and widened in the 19thC. Take the A90 south, then turn off left at the Stonehaven road.

15 miles – Stonehaven. TIC: 66 Allardyce St, tel. 01569 762806, Easter-Oct. A very pleasant little town with a 19thC centre and an older town around the picturesque harbour. **The Tolbooth Museum** (1000-1200, 1400-1700 Mon. & Thu.-Sat., 1400-1700 Wed. & Sun., June-Sep.; Free) was a 16thC store which became a prison for Episcopal ministers in 1748-9, yet they still managed to baptize children through the windows. Now it has displays on local history and fishing. The Fireball Ceremony takes place each year on Hogmanay, when fireballs are thrown into the harbour. Leave on the A92 and shortly turn left, following signs for Dunnottar Castle.

16 miles – Dunnottar Castle (0900-1730 Mon.-Sat., 1400-1630 Sun., April-Oct.; 0900-sunset, Mon.-Fri., Nov.-Mar.; Inexpensive) is a magnificent ruin on an incredible clifftop site and is now probably best known as the setting for Zeffirelli's *Hamlet* with Mel Gibson and Glenn Close. The castle has had its own dramatic history. In 1651 the Scottish Crown Jewels

(*see* Edinburgh in A-Z) were brought here from Edinburgh while Cromwell's troops were in Scotland. When this castle too came under siege by Cromwell's men, the jewels were smuggled out, either in a local minister's wife's apron and basket according to one story, or lowered down the cliff in another. In 1685 a number of Covenanters (*see* A-Z) died when 167 of them were imprisoned here. Return to the A92 and in 2 miles turn left for **Fowlsheugh Nature Reserve** (open access). Along a clifftop path are views of mainland Britain's biggest seabird colony, with 80,000 pairs and six species breeding April-July. Continue south on the unclassified road to Catterline, a tiny fishing village where artist Joan Eardley painted. Carry on south to Kinneff, where, in **Kinneff Old Kirk** (0900-dusk, Easter-Oct.), the Scottish Crown Jewels were hidden under the floor during the siege of Dunnottar in 1651-2. The church was largely rebuilt in the 18th-19thC and has memorials to John Grainger, the minister who hid the jewels, and George Ogilvie, keeper of Dunnottar. Out of Kinneff, turn left on the unclassified road. Rejoin the A92 and turn right on the B967 just before Inverbervie.

Dunnottar Castle

28 miles – Arbuthnott village has several attractions. **Arbuthnott Church** (open access) or St. Ternan's is one of the few pre-Reformation churches still in use in Scotland. Its chancel dates from 1242 and the Lady Chapel or Arbuthnott Aisle from 1500. The 1896 restoration included stained glass by Daniel Cottier.

Arbuthnott House (open certain days each year, tel. 01561 361226; Inexpensive) is 15thC with 17th and 18thC additions, including fine plasterwork. The gardens (0900-1700; Inexpensive) have a 17thC parterre. The **Grassic Gibbon Centre** (1000-1630 April-Oct.; Inexpensive) is dedicated to the 20thC writer Lewis Grassic Gibbon (James Leslie Mitchell), author of the trilogy *A Scots Quair*, who is buried in the churchyard. Continue on the B967, turn left on the A90 and in 4 miles take the turning right for **Laurencekirk**, an 18thC weaving village. Turn right on the B9120.

39 miles – Fettercairn has an arch erected for the visit of Queen Victoria in 1861 and an old Mercat Cross brought from the now-disappeared village of Kincardine. **Fettercairn Distillery** (1000-1630 Mon.-Sat., May-Sep.; Free) is one of the oldest licensed distilleries in Scotland. Just north of Fettercairn on the B974 is **Fasque** (1100-1730 May & Sep.; 1100-2000 June-Aug.; Moderate), bought by the Gladstone family in 1829 and the home of prime minister William Gladstone. Further up the B974 are spectacular views over the Mearns and Angus from the car park at Cairn o' Mount, 1488ft. Return to Fettercairn and take the B966.

45 miles – Edzell also has an arch commemorating Queen Victoria's visit. **Edzell Castle** (HS, except 0930-1300 Thu. and closed Fri., Oct.-Mar.; Inexpensive) is a ruined early 16thC tower house extended by Sir David Lindsay, Lord Edzell c1580. He was also responsible for the important walled garden of 1604 with a parterre and relief sculpture panels with figures copied from prints by German Renaissance artist Dürer.

Continue on the B966, crossing the A90.
51 miles – Brechin. TIC: St. Ninian's Pl.,
tel. 01356 623050, April-Sep. The
attractive old town centre around High
St grew up next to the **Cathedral** (0830-
1600 Mon.-Sat.), now mainly 13thC and
restored this century. Inside are fine
examples of carved stones from the 8th-
17thC. The unusual **Round Tower**
(exterior only) is of a Celtic type and
probably dates from the 11thC. **Brechin
Museum** (0930-2000 Mon. & Wed., 0930-
1800 Tue. & Thu., 0930-1700 Fri. & Sat.;
Free) in the library has local collections.
The **Caledonian Railway** (timetable:
01356 622992, enquiries: 01674 810318;
Inexpensive) runs a steam train on Sun.
in summer from Brechin station to Bridge
of Dun. Leave Brechin on the A935 and in
6 miles is **House of Dun** (NTS, 1330-1750
Easter-June & Sep., 1100-1730 July &
Aug., 1330-1750 Sat. & Sun., Oct.;
Moderate; gardens 0930-sunset;
Inexpensive), a fine William Adam house
with stunning plasterwork and a
Victorian walled garden. Continue on the
A935, passing the tidal Montrose Basin.
60 miles – Montrose. TIC: The Library,
High St, tel. 01674 672000, April-Sep. An
ancient royal burgh with an old market
square and fine High St containing the
18thC Old Town Hall and Old Church
whose much-admired steeple was added
by Gillespie Graham in 1834. **Montrose
Museum and Art Gallery** (0930-2000
Mon. & Wed., 0930-1800 Tue. & Thu.,
0930-1700 Fri. & Sat.; Free) has geology,
natural history and Pictish stones, plus
Montrose silver. The **William Lamb
Memorial Studio** (1400-1700 Sat., July &
Aug., or tel. 01674 673232; Free) is the
studio of this early 20thC sculptor and
etcher and contains his heads of royalty
and the furniture he designed for
himself. Montrose Bay has golf courses
and miles of beach. **Montrose Basin
Nature Reserve** (1000-last admission

Brechin Cathedral

1800 April-Sep.; 1000-last admission 1500
Sat.-Mon., Oct.-Mar.; Inexpensive) has a
new visitor centre from where there are
walks with stunning views of the basin
and its seals, migratory waders, ducks,
pink-footed geese and ospreys. Leave
Montrose on the A92 south and in 5 miles
turn left for the tiny village of Lunan,
once a busy fishing station whose old
icehouse has survived. Turn right on the
unclassified road south. After a mile is
Red Castle (open access), a 15thC ruin
originally built in the 12thC for King
William the Lion, overlooking the
singing sands of Lunan Bay. A short
distance on, turn right for Inverkeilor
and rejoin the A92. On the outskirts of
Arbroath, turn right to St. Vigeans where,
in a cottage below the church, is **St.
Vigeans Museum** (HS, 0930-1800 Mon.-
Sat., April-Sep., or key from nearby
cottage, tel. 01241 872433; Free), with an
outstanding collection of 32 Pictish
stones discovered when the church was
rebuilt.

75 miles – **Arbroath**. TIC: Market Pl., tel. 01241 872609. This royal burgh, with a pleasant old town around the harbour, is famed for its Arbroath smokies, a type of smoked haddock. **Arbroath Abbey** (HS; Inexpensive), now an imposing red sandstone ruin, was founded by King William the Lion in 1178. Here in 1320 the famous Declaration of Arbroath was signed by Scottish nobles. This remarkable document asserted Scotland's right to remain independent of England. The Abbot's House is the most complete of its type in Scotland and today houses a museum. **Arbroath Signal Tower Museum** (1000-1700 Mon.-Sat.; Free) is housed in the former signal tower for the Bell Rock Lighthouse designed by Robert Stevenson, grandfather of Robert Louis Stevenson (*see* A-Z), on a rock in the North Sea southeast of Arbroath. The museum has displays on local life, including fishing. **Arbroath Art Gallery** (0930-2000 Mon. & Wed., 0930-1800 Tue. & Thu., 0930-1700 Fri. & Sat.; Free) has two paintings by Flemish artist Pieter Breughel the Younger, plus local artists' works. There is also a beach, a golf course and **Kerr's Miniature Railway** (July & Aug.; Inexpensive). Leave Arbroath by the A933 and at the village of Friockheim turn left on the A932. In a short distance are **Pitmuies Gardens** (1000-1700 April-Oct.; Inexpensive), delightful old walled gardens with roses and delphiniums and a riverside walk. Continue on the A932 past lochs, including **Balgavies Loch**, a nature reserve (open access) with heron, roe deer and otters.

91 miles – **Forfar**. TIC: The Library, West High St, tel. 01307 467876, April-Sep. Here King Malcolm Canmore held his first parliament in 1057, and his queen, St. Margaret (*see* A-Z), founded a religious house. Today Forfar has a pleasant old centre and is the home of the

Glamis Castle

Forfar bridie, a savoury meat pasty. The **Meffan Institute** (1000-1700 Mon.-Sat.; Free) has a local history museum and a Scottish art collection. Just outside the town are the ruins of **Restenneth Priory** (HS, open access), whose foundation dates back to the early 8thC by Nechtan, King of the Picts. The present building is a very early example of Romanesque style in Scotland and has a tall tower. Forfar Loch has a sensory garden, bird garden and watersports. Further north, at **Aberlemno**, is a group of four Pictish stones. Leave Forfar on the A94 and cross the A90. Turn right after 6 miles.

97 miles – **Glamis** is a picturesque village

which contains the **Angus Folk Museum** (NTS, 1100-1700 Easter-Sep., 1100-1700 Sat. & Sun., Oct.; Moderate). This important collection relating to domestic life and agriculture is housed in a row of cottages and a farm steading. **Glamis Church** (open access) was founded by early 8thC Celtic St. Fergus. Most of the present church dates from 1790 and the Strathmore Aisle from 1459. In the manse garden is a Pictish stone. **Glamis Castle** (1030-1730 April-Oct.; Moderate), seat of the Earls of Strathmore and Kinghorne, was the childhood home of the Queen Mother and birthplace of Princess Margaret. Macbeth (*see* A-Z) became

Thane of Glamis in Shakespeare's play. The L-plan tower house was added to in the 17thC and, from the same century, are paintings in the chapel by Jacob de Wet and an important series of English tapestries. Return to the A94 and continue west through wide Strathmore. Turn right off the main road to visit **Eassie Sculptured Stone**, a fine Pictish stone in the ruined Eassie Church (HS, open access). Return to the main road and continue to Meigle, whose museum (HS, except closed Oct.-Mar.; Inexpensive) contains the **Meigle Sculptured Stones**, 25 outstanding examples of 8th-10thC Pictish art.

Continue on the A94 to **Coupar Angus**, with some older streets and a Jail Tower or Tolbooth. Turn right on the A923.
114 miles – Blairgowrie and **Rattray**. TIC: 26 Wellmeadow, tel. 01250 872960/873701. A busy route centre, Blairgowrie is also the heart of the soft fruit industry. Leave by the A93. On the right after 4 miles is the famous **Meikleour Beech Hedge**, an impressive stretch of copper beech hedging planted in 1746, 100 ft high and over 1500 ft long.

128 miles – Scone Palace (0930-1700 May-Oct.; Moderate), home of the Earls of Mansfield, is now a 19thC neo-Gothic building by William Atkinson and contains important collections of ivories, porcelain, French furniture, rare papier-mâché by the French Martin family and embroideries by Mary Queen of Scots.

Scone Palace

Scone was the Pictish capital where, in the 9thC, the kingdoms of the Scots and the Picts were united under Kenneth MacAlpine. On the Moot Hill where the chapel currently stands, kings of Scots were proclaimed, seated on the Stone of Scone or Stone of Destiny which was stolen by King Edward I of England and is still used in the coronation of British monarchs at Westminster Abbey. Little remains of Scone Abbey and Bishop's Palace, ransacked in 1559 after a sermon at Perth by Protestant reformer John Knox (*see* Reformation). The Mercat Cross of old Scone village remained after the village was moved several miles to New Scone. The 19thC pinetum includes a Douglas fir, named after local gardener David Douglas. Return to the A93 and continue to Perth (103 miles).

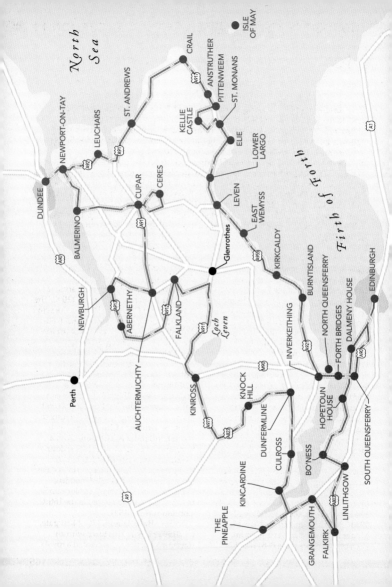

Fife

4 days

The 'Kingdom' of Fife is bounded by the Firths of Forth and Tay, the North Sea, and, to the west, by the Ochil Hills. Nowadays, it is easily accessible from Edinburgh by the Forth Road Bridge. From Glasgow, take the M8, then the M9, following signs for the Forth Road Bridge, and return from the Kincardine Bridge on the M876 and the M80/A80. Fife has a long history of seafaring, trade and fishing. It is also one of the most outstanding architectural areas in Scotland, and its many pretty villages have fine vernacular examples. Other important buildings include the beautiful Falkland Palace, a stark contrast to Loch Leven Castle, where Mary Queen of Scots was imprisoned. Fife's towns include St. Andrews, home of golf and of Scotland's oldest university, and historic Dunfermline, with associations with St. Margaret and Andrew Carnegie. It is feasible to do a day trip to Fife but there is so much to see that an excursion of several days is more rewarding.

Leave Edinburgh on the A90 and cross the Firth of Forth by the Forth Road Bridge, with views of the Forth Rail Bridge (*see* Forth Bridges) and of some of the islands in the Forth. Take the first turnoff on the B981 for North Queensferry. The Forth Road Bridge TIC, Queensferry Lodge Hotel, tel. 01383 417759, is also signposted.

11 miles – North Queensferry was at the northern end of the ferry crossing over the Forth which St. Margaret (*see* A-Z) is said to have introduced in the 11thC. It continued until 1964 when the Forth Road Bridge was opened. In summer the *Maid of the Forth* (tel. 0131 331-1451/4857) sails regularly to **Inchcolm** island, where the ruined 12th-14thC Abbey (HS, except closed Oct.-Mar.; Inexpensive) is unusually well-preserved. The church has a rare fragment of wall painting. In North Queensferry is **Deep Sea World** (0930-1800 April-June & Sep.-Oct., 0930-1900 July & Aug., 0930-1600 Mon.-Fri., 0930-1800 Sat., Sun. & hols, Nov.-Mar.; Moderate), a spectacular aquarium. Retrace the route on the B981 but this time continue under the A90 to Inverkeithing.

13 miles – Inverkeithing is an ancient royal burgh dating back to the 12thC. The 14thC Mercat Cross is one of the finest in the UK. **Inverkeithing Museum** (1100-1700 Wed.-Sun.; Free), in a 14thC friary, has material on Sir Samuel Greig, admiral and reformer of the Russian Navy for Catherine the Great. St. Peter's Church has a 14thC tower. Other buildings include 17thC Fordell's Lodging and an 18thC Tolbooth (town hall). Leave on the A921 eastbound and after a mile at Dalgety Bay is the ruined 13thC **St. Bridget's Church** (HS, open access). In 3 miles is Aberdour, with a harbour and beach. Ruined **Aberdour Castle** (HS, except 0930-1300 Thu. & closed Fri., Oct.-Mar.; Inexpensive) dates mainly from the 14th-17thC and has 17thC terraced gardens. The Norman St. Fillan's Church was altered in the 16thC. Continue on the A921.

19 miles – Burntisland. TIC: 4 Kirkgate, tel. 01592 872667. This town with an important harbour was created a royal burgh in the 16thC. **Burntisland Heritage Exhibition** (1300-1600 June-Sep.; Free) includes the story of the search for *The Blessing of Burntisland*, shipwrecked in the Forth in 1633 with 800 cartloads of treasure on board, gifts to Charles I on his first visit to Scotland. **Burntisland Parish Church** (1400-1600 mid June-Aug.) of 1592 is an early post-Reformation church. **Burntisland Museum** (1000-1300, 1400-1700 Mon.-Sat.; Free) re-creates the town's annual fair in Edwardian times. **Rossend Castle** (contact TIC for access details) is a 15th-16thC tower house where Mary Queen of Scots (*see* A-Z) stayed in 1563. An admirer, French poet Pierre Chastelard, was executed after hiding in her bedchamber here. Continue on the A921. Just before Kinghorn is the monument to Alexander III, where, in 1286, the king was killed when he fell from his horse over the cliff, leaving Scotland with no heir. Carry on along the A921.

24 miles – Kirkcaldy. TIC: 19 Whyte's Causeway, tel. 01592 267775. One of Fife's major towns, Kirkcaldy now incorporates Dysart at its northeast end and the Linktown to the south, hence the nickname 'the lang toon'. By the 17thC it was a flourishing port, while the 19thC saw it become a manufacturer of linoleum, the smell of which was said to pervade the town. **Kirkcaldy Art Gallery and Museum** (1030-1700 Mon.-Sat., 1400-1700 Sun.; Free; art gallery due to re-open mid 1996, tel. 01592 260732) has displays on traditional industries, plus the Kirkcaldy Prime Gilt Box in which harbour levies were kept safe by three locks. There is also a fine collection of Scottish paintings, including many by the innovative 19thC landscape painter William McTaggart. On Sailors' Walk are 17thC houses restored by the National Trust for Scotland (*see* A-Z). On a promontory between the town centre and Dysart is **Ravenscraig Castle** (open access to exterior), a dramatic ruined castle begun in 1460 for Mary of Gueldres, James II's queen. **Dysart** has its own harbour and a 16thC Tolbooth. Among picturesque 17thC buildings restored by the National Trust for Scotland is the **John McDouall Stuart Museum** (1400-1700 June-Aug.; Free), birthplace of the first white explorer who successfully completed the south–north route through Australia. Leave Dysart on the A955. From East Wemyss (pronounced 'weems', from the Gaelic for caves), a footpath along the shore to the northeast leads to **Wemyss Caves** (access details from Wemyss Environmental Education Centre in the school, 1000-1500 Mon.-Fri.), a group of caves with Pictish symbols carved on the walls. Take great care inside the caves and use a torch if possible. There are carvings in the Court Cave, the Doo Cave and Jonathan's Cave. The Well Caves, below the ruins of Macduff's Castle, and the Sliding Cave are inaccessible. Continue on the A955. In 2 miles is Buckhaven which, like Methil a mile beyond, is industrial. **Buckhaven Museum** (1400-1700, 1730-1900 Mon., 1000-1300, 1400-1700 Tue., 1000-1300, 1400-1900 Thu., 1400-1700 Fri., 1000-1230 Sat.; Free) has displays on the town's fishing heritage. Continue through Methil.

32 miles – Leven. TIC: South St, tel. 01333 429454. The sandy beach made this a popular Edwardian resort. Just northwest is the attractive **Letham Glen** (dawn-dusk; nature centre 1200-1500 Mon.-Fri., 1400-1600 Sat., 1400-1630 Sun., April-Sep.; 1200-1500 Mon.-Fri., 1300-1500 Sat., 1300-1530 Sun., Oct.-Mar.; Free). Leave Leven on the A915 eastbound. On the right, on Lundin Links, are three impressive standing stones. Beyond is **Lower Largo**,

St. Monans

birthplace of Alexander Selkirk, the model for Daniel Defoe's *Robinson Crusoe*. A monument to Selkirk stands outside his cottage. Continue to **Upper Largo**, where the church has an early tower and chancel. The churchyard contains a Pictish stone. **Scotland's Larder** (1000-2100 April-Oct., 1000-1800 Nov.-Mar.; Inexpensive) has an exhibition on Scotland's traditional high-quality foodstuffs, plus a restaurant, shop and occasional demonstrations. Leave Upper Largo on the A917 to visit the picturesque fishing villages of the East Neuk (or corner) of Fife. Down to the right after 4 miles is Earlsferry, to the east of which is Macduff Cave, where Macduff, Thane of Fife, is said to have taken refuge when fleeing from Macbeth (*see* A-Z). Continue round into **Elie**, now a popular resort. The 18thC Lady's Tower was the private changing room of the beautiful Lady Jane Anstruther when she went bathing. The 17thC church has a later steeple. Continue on the A917 past the ruins of Ardross Castle, then Newark Castle on the right.
43 miles – St. Monans or St. Monance has attractively restored buildings round its harbour. St. Monan's Church has a choir of 1362 and an earlier square tower. King David I is said to have been cured of an arrow wound here in the 12thC. The recently restored **Windmill** (1100-1600 June-Sep.; Free) dates from the late 18thC and was used to extract salt from saltpans below. A short distance beyond St. Monans, turn left on the B942 to visit **Balcaskie House and Gardens** (1400-1800 Sat.-Wed., June-Aug.; Inexpensive; presently gardens only while house is in restoration). The architect Sir William Bruce (*see* A-Z) bought the estate in 1665 and built the fine neoclassical mansion and laid out the formal terraced gardens with views over the firth to the Bass Rock. Continue on the B942 and turn right on the B9171, for **Kellie Castle and Gardens** (NTS, house 1330-1730 Easter weekend & Mon.-Sun., May-Sep.; Fri.-Mon., Oct.; garden 0930-sunset; Inexpensive). Originally dating from the 14thC, the castle became the home of the Lorimer family, who restored it in the 19thC. It contains outstanding 17thC plaster ceilings and painted panelling, as well as furniture by the architect Sir Robert Lorimer. Outside is a Victorian garden.

Continue on the B9171 and turn first right on the minor road signposted Pittenweem.

48 miles – Pittenweem is still a fishing port with a lively new fishmarket (tel. 01333 310836) and attractive restored buildings. The church dates from 1588. **St. Fillan's Cave** (key from The Gingerbread Horse, High St), thought to have been the retreat of the 8th/9thC saint (*see* Excursion 3), became a local shrine. Leave Pittenweem by the A917, heading northeast.

50 miles – Anstruther. TIC: Scottish Fisheries Museum, tel. 01333 311073, Easter & May-Sep. Known locally as 'Anster' (pronounced 'Ainster'), this was once the busiest Scottish herring fishing port. Now it has the excellent **Scottish Fisheries Museum** (1000-1730 Mon.-Sat., 1100-1700 Sun., April-Oct.; 1000-1630 Mon.-Sat., 1400-1630 Sun., Nov.-Mar.; Inexpensive), part of which is on the site of 15thC St. Ayle's Chapel and the Abbot's Lodging. Exhibits include old fishing boats such as examples of the Fifie and Zulu herring drifters in the harbour. A stone coffin in

Anstruther Wester churchyard is said to be that of St. Adrian which floated here miraculously from the **Isle of May**. Boat trips can be made to the island (May-

Pittenweem

Sep., tel. 01333 310103) out in the Firth of
Forth. Allow 5 hr for the trip and take
food and all-weather clothing. It has the
remains of a 12thC chapel and of the first
lighthouse of 1636. Robert Louis
Stevenson's (*see* A-Z) grandfather built
its replacement in 1816. Now a National
Nature Reserve, the island has a grey seal

Anstruther

colony and thousands of seabirds, including puffins. Continue northeast on the A917. **54 miles – Crail**. TIC: Museum and Heritage Centre, Marketgate, tel. 01333 450869. A royal burgh since 1310, Crail has medieval streets, a Mercat Cross and many 17th-18thC buildings. On top of the Tolbooth is a fish weathervane. The 15th-16thC harbour recalls Crail's importance as a trading centre. **Crail Museum and Heritage Centre** (1000-1300, 1400-1700 Mon.-Sat., 1400-1700 Sun., June-Sep.; 1400-1700 Sat. & Sun., Easter & April-May; Free) gives the burgh's history. The **Church** (1000-1600 Mon.-Sat., June-Aug.) is partly 12th-13thC and has several ancient stones. Just outside the churchyard is one said to have been hurled by the Devil from the Isle of May. Further east, towards the promontory of Fife Ness, is Crail's 200-year-old golf course.

Leave Crail on the A917 and in a mile turn left on the B940, where after 3 miles is **Scotland's Secret Bunker** (1000-1700 April-Oct.; 1000-1600 Sat. & Sun., Nov.-Mar.; Moderate). This fascinating relic of the Cold War is situated 100 ft underground and was intended as a government command centre in the event of nuclear war. Return to the A917 and turn left. In a mile turn right to visit **Cambo Gardens** (1000-1600; Inexpensive), a delightful Victorian walled garden with a 'Willow-pattern' bridge. Continue north on the A917.

Crail

71 miles – St. Andrews (*see* A-Z). Leave St. Andrews on the A91 and in 4 miles turn right on the A919. At Guardbridge, the 15thC bridge over the River Eden was built for pilgrims to St. Andrews. Continue to Leuchars where there is an RAF base. **Leuchars Church** (0930-1830 Mar.-Oct.; tours and refreshments 1000-1600 Tue.) has a 12thC choir and apse considered the most beautiful examples of Norman architecture in Scotland. On the exterior are two tiers of blind arcades, while inside are richly carved arches. Continue on the A919, then at Carrick follow the A92 northbound.

81 miles – Newport-on-Tay is at the south end of the Tay Road Bridge. A car park by the bridge has views over the firth. Cross the 1.5 mile Tay Road Bridge, one of the longest in Europe, opened in 1966. To the left is the Tay Rail Bridge of 1887. It replaced the earlier rail bridge which collapsed in a storm in 1879, killing 75 people. Both the opening of the first bridge on the 'silv'ry Tay' and the Tay Bridge Disaster were immortalized in poems by Scotland's famously bad poet, William McGonagall.

83 miles – Dundee (*see* A-Z). Return to Newport across the bridge and turn right on the B946 to Wormit. At the side of the present rail bridge are the remains of the earlier one. Continue on the B946 and in 0.5 mile turn right on a minor road. To the right after 2.5 miles are the remains of **Balmerino Abbey** (NTS, open access; Donation), a Cistercian abbey founded in the early 13thC. It was burned by Henry III's troops in the 16thC and further damaged by the Reformation (*see* A-Z). Nearby is an ancient Spanish chestnut tree. From Balmerino, drive south on a minor road through Fincraigs and in 2 miles turn right on the A914. In under a mile, at Rathillet, turn left on another minor road, heading south.

98 miles – Cupar. TIC: Fluthers Car Park, tel. 01334 652874, mid June-Sep. In the centre of Fife is this fine old market town and former county town. It has a 17thC Mercat Cross and a handsome Tolbooth. Parts of the Old Parish Church date from the 15thC. Leave Cupar on the A92, then fork left on the A916. In 2 miles turn left on a minor road to visit **Hill of Tarvit** (NTS, 1330-1730, last admission 1645, Easter-mid Oct.; Moderate; garden 0930-sunset; Inexpensive), an attractive Edwardian mansion by Sir Robert Lorimer who remodelled the 17thC

house for Frederick Bonar Sharp, a Dundee industrialist and important art collector, whose collections include furniture, Chinese porcelain and bronzes, and Dutch paintings. Continue on the minor road, then veer right.

102 miles – Ceres (pronounced 'series') is one of the delights of Fife, an extremely pretty village with a number of older buildings. The 17thC weigh-house incorporated the Tolbooth and courthouse. Above the door are carved scales and attached to the wall are the 'jougs', an iron collar which held offenders by the neck. The building and others nearby now house the **Fife Folk Museum** (1400-1700 Sat.-Thu., Easter & mid May-Oct.; Inexpensive). The Bishop Bridge is said to commemorate the Episcopalian Archbishop Sharp of St. Andrews, who was murdered by Covenanters (*see* A-Z) in 1679. The Provost is a carved toby jug-like figure thought to represent a 17thC provost (mayor). Leave Ceres by the B939 west and turn right on the A916 at Craigrothie. On the left is **Scotstarvit Tower** (key from Hill of Tarvit during house opening times), an L-plan tower house which belonged to Sir John Scot, a 17thC eccentric. Continue back into Cupar and turn left on the A91. After 2 miles is the **Scottish Deer Centre** (1000-1700 Mar.-Oct.; Moderate), with several species of deer, plus falconry demonstrations. Carry on to **Auchtermuchty**, a pleasant old weaving village whose 18thC buildings include the Tolbooth. The burgh is Tannochbrae in the new TV series of *Doctor Finlay* and is the home town of The Proclaimers and of accordionist Jimmy Shand. Turn right on the B936, heading north, and in 4 miles turn left on the A913.

123 miles – Newburgh is a royal burgh which exported Tay salmon packed in ice to Billingsgate in the 18thC. The **Laing**

Museum (1100-1800 Mon.-Fri., 1400-1700 Sat. & Sun., April-Sep.; 1200-1600 Wed.-Thu., 1400-1700 Sun., Oct.-Mar.; Free) contains 19thC collections. Just east of Newburgh are the scant remains of **Lindores Abbey** (open access), founded in 1191 with Tironensian monks from Kelso (see Excursion 14). John Knox (see Reformation) visited it in 1559. Leave Newburgh on the A913 and drive 4 miles west to Abernethy, thought to have been an important Pictish centre and where, in 1072, King Malcolm Canmore met William the Conqueror and allegedly acknowledged the Norman as his overlord. **Abernethy Round Tower** (HS, details of keyholder at site; Free) probably dates from the 11thC and is one of only two towers of this type surviving on the Scottish mainland, the other being at Brechin (see Excursion 12). From the top (73 ft) are splendid views. At the bottom are a 7thC Pictish stone and the 'jougs' for village offenders. At the west end of the village take the minor road south through Abernethy Glen, and in 3 miles veer right. After a mile, cross the A91 into Strathmiglo, another old weaving village with an 18thC Tolbooth. South of the High St, by the churchyard gate, is a Pictish symbol stone. Leave Strathmiglo on the A912.

135 miles – **Falkland** is a beautiful village which grew up around the royal palace. The fine 17th and 18thC houses include the thatched Moncrief House (1610) opposite the palace. **Falkland Palace** (NTS, 1100-1730 Mon.-Sat., 1330-1730 Sun., last admission 1630, April-Oct.; Moderate) began as a royal hunting lodge. Additions during the 15th-16thC under James II, IV and V transformed it into a refined Renaissance palace. It was here that the dying James V was brought the news of the birth of his daughter, Mary, who became Queen of Scots (see A-Z) a few days later. The palace fell into

ruin after the Union of the Crowns in 1603. Restoration of the south range began in the 19thC and continued this century. Outside are attractive gardens and a 'real' (or royal) tennis court of 1539, the oldest in Britain and still in use. The early 19thC **Town Hall** (by arrangement, April-Oct., tel. 01337 857397, included in Palace ticket) has an exhibition on this royal burgh. Leave Falkland on the minor road which sweeps up over East Lomond Hill (1390 ft) with extensive views. On the summit are a Bronze Age cairn and remains of an Iron Age fort (see Prehistory). Continue downhill and turn right on the A911 at Leslie. Carry on through Auchmuirbridge. At Scotlandwell, site of an ancient well, veer right, following the A911 round Loch Leven. At Kinnesswood in 1.5 miles is **Michael Bruce's Cottage** (key from Kinnesswood Garage, 1000-1800; Donation), birthplace of the 18thC poet known as 'the gentle poet of Loch Leven'. Up to the right is Bishop Hill, with views over the loch. Carry on through Balgedie. Just before Milnathort is Burleigh Castle, a ruined 16thC tower house. At Milnathort, turn left on the A922.

153 miles – **Kinross**. TIC: Kinross Service Area, off the M90, Junction 6, tel. 01577 863680. A pleasant small town on the shores of Loch Leven. Its main attraction is **Loch Leven Castle** (HS, except closed Oct.-Mar., last boat 1530; Inexpensive) on an island in the loch, reached by a small boat. It probably dates originally from the end of the 13thC and is most famous as the castle where Mary Queen of Scots (see A-Z) was imprisoned by her nobles in 1567, and from which she escaped in 1568 with the help of boat keeper Willy Douglas. The castle was bought in the 17thC by Sir William Bruce (see A-Z), who built his own handsome **Kinross House** (house exterior only; gardens 1000-dusk, May-Sep.; Inexpensive) near

the lochside and aligned it with the castle. Around it are beautiful formal gardens. **Kinross Museum** (1300-1700 Tue.-Sat., May-Sep.; Free) has local displays. Nearby is the 17thC Tolbooth restored by Robert Adam (*see* A-Z). South of Kinross is the RSPB's **Vane Farm Nature Reserve** (1000-1700 April-Christmas, 1000-1600 Jan.-Mar.; Inexpensive), set up due to Loch Leven's importance as a freshwater site for wildfowl, especially greylag and pink-footed geese. The loch itself is a National Nature Reserve and is also famous for its species of trout. The largest island, St. Serf's Island, is associated with the 6thC Celtic saint and has remains of a later priory. Leave Kinross on the A977 west through Drum and Crook of Devon. In 7 miles turn right to **Rumbling Bridge**, where the River Devon tumbles through a gorge. Return to the A977. In another mile turn left on the A823 across the edge of the Cleish Hills which rise to 1713 ft. 5 miles further on is **Knockhill Racing Circuit**, Scotland's national motorsport centre, with events most weekends, Easter-Oct. Continue on the A823.
171 miles – Dunfermline (*see* A-Z). Leave on the A994 west, then turn left on the B9037 along the Firth of Forth.
178 miles – Culross (pronounced 'coo-ross') is one of the jewels of Scottish vernacular architecture, with many whitewashed buildings with crow-stepped gables and pantiled roofs. Its present pristine aspect is mainly due to restoration by the National Trust for Scotland. The grandest building is **Culross Palace** (NTS, 1100-1700, last admission 1615, Easter-Sep.; Moderate), built in 1597 for Sir George Bruce, who made his fortune from local coalmines, including one which extended a mile under the Forth. The interior is lined with painted woodwork. The 17thC **Town House** (1330-1700, last admission 1645,

same dates and ticket as Palace), or town hall, has material on the burgh's history. Near the Mercat Cross is **The Study** (same times and ticket as Town House) of Bishop Leighton of Dunblane (*see* Excursion 3) in a curious little turret. On the hill overlooking the burgh is **Culross Abbey** (parish church 0930-dusk), a small 13thC Cistercian monastery. Much of it fell into ruin after the Reformation, but the east end and 16thC tower of the church became the parish church of the reformed religion and were restored by Sir Robert Rowand Anderson in the early 20thC. The abbey may be on the site of a 6thC Celtic foundation by St. Serf, where St. Mungo, the patron saint of Glasgow, is believed to have been born. The ruins of the early 16thC St. Mungo's Chapel (open access) are just to the east of Culross. Continue west on the B9037 to Kincardine (on Forth), in an industrial area with two power stations. Cross Kincardine Bridge (A876), opened in 1936. Kincardine Bridge TIC, Pine 'n' Oak, Kincardine Bridge Rd, Airth, tel. 01324 417759, Easter-Sep., is signposted at the south end of the bridge. The **Dunmore Pineapple** (NTS, exterior only), an eccentric 18thC garden folly, is 2 miles west on the A905, then the B9124. Turn left on the A905. Grangemouth, an industrial town with oil refineries, is situated at the eastern end of the Forth and Clyde Canal, completed in 1790. Turn right on the A904 over the M9.
187 miles – Falkirk. TIC: The Steeple, High St, tel. 01324 620244. This industrial town is at the junction of the Forth and Clyde Canal and the Union Canal, completed in 1822. **Callendar House** (1000-1700 Mon.-Sat., 1400-1700 Sun.; last admission 1615, April-Sep.; Inexpensive), an extraordinary French château created in a 19thC remodelling of the earlier house, is being restored as a museum, and has 18thC kitchens in

Culross

which food is prepared to old recipes for tasting by visitors. **Callendar Park** (open access) has a 1300 ft stretch of the 2ndC AD Antonine Wall (*see* A-Z). Leave Falkirk on the A803 east, which runs parallel to the M90.

195 miles – Linlithgow. TIC: Burgh Halls, The Cross, tel. 01506 844600. An attractive, historical town, Linlithgow is dominated by the royal palace and the church on a hill overlooking Linlithgow Loch. **Linlithgow Palace** (HS; Inexpensive), now an extensive ruin, is undoubtedly one of the most beautiful palaces in Scotland. The present building dates from the 15th-16thC and was destroyed by fire in 1746. The east range has a fine Gothic entrance built in the reign of James I, while the west range, the chapel and the northwest tower, including the Queen's Chamber where Mary Queen of Scots (*see* A-Z) was born, were all added 1488-1506 by James IV. The palace was finished and lavishly

decorated by James V. Next to it is **St. Michael's Church** (1000-1200, 1330-1530 Mon.-Fri.), largely rebuilt after the fire which destroyed most of the town in 1424. St. Katherine's Aisle, where a ghost warned James IV of disaster at the Battle of Flodden (1513), has magnificent Gothic tracery. There is also a 15thC carved stone altarpiece and stained glass by the 19thC Pre-Raphaelite Edward Burne-Jones. The laminated timber and aluminium spire of 1964 replaced the 15thC stone crown. **Linlithgow's Story Museum** (1000-1600 Mon. & Wed.-Sat., 1300-1600 Sun., April-Sep.; Inexpensive) has local history, while **Linlithgow Union Canal Society Museum** (1400-1700 Sat. & Sun., Easter-Sep.; Free) gives the history of the canal. 30 min boat trips (half-hourly 1400-1630 Sat. & Sun., Easter-Sep.; Inexpensive) and 2.5 hr cruises (1400 Sat. & Sun., Easter-Sep.; Moderate) on the canal also start here. Leave Linlithgow north on the A706.

198 miles – Bo'ness. TIC: Union St,
tel. 01506 826626, April-Sep. Short for
Borrowstounness, Bo'ness was an
important port up to the early 19thC.
Kinneil Estate (open access) is a
fascinating journey through history. Now
a public park, it contains a section of the
Antonine Wall and behind it the remains
of a fortlet of AD 142 for 20 soldiers, the
ruin of 12thC Kinneil Church, the 16th-
17thC Kinneil House (exterior only), a
former residence of the Duke of
Hamilton, and the remains of the 1769
cottage where James Watt tested the
prototype of his steam engine. The 17thC
stable block now houses **Kinneil
Museum** (1000-1230, 1330-1700 Mon.-
Fri., 1000-1700 Sat. & Sun., May-Aug.;
1000-1700 Sat., Oct.-Mar.; Free), with
displays on the estate and the town,
including Bo'ness pottery. **Bo'ness and
Kinneil Steam Railway** (April-mid Oct.;
Moderate, tel. 01506 822298 for
timetable) runs 3.5 miles from Bo'ness
Station to **Birkhill Fireclay Mine** (tours
1155, 1325, 1440 & 1550 July-mid Aug.,
Sat. & Sun. only & May hols, April-mid
Oct.; Inexpensive). Near the station is the
Scottish Railway Exhibition (1130-1630
Sat., Sun. & May hols, April-May & Oct.;
Wed.-Sun., June-Sep.; July-mid Aug.;
Inexpensive). Leave Bo'ness on the A904.
Off to the left up the B903 is the
formidable 15thC **Blackness Castle** (HS,
except 0930-1300 Thu. & closed Fri., Oct.-
Mar.; Inexpensive). Return to the A904.
On the left is the **House of the Binns**
(1330-1730, last admission 1700, Sat.-
Thu., May-Sep.; Moderate; grounds
1000-1900, last admission 1830;
Inexpensive), the 17thC seat of the
Dalyell (pronounced 'dee-el') family,
which has important plasterwork and
fine portraits of the family, ancestors of
the MP for West Lothian. Continue along
the A904, then turn left on a minor road
to the much-restored 12thC Abercorn

Hopetoun House

Church on the site of a 5thC Celtic
church. Continue along the A904, then
turn left on a minor road for **Hopetoun
House** (1000-1730, last admission 1645,
Easter-early Oct.; Moderate; grounds;
Inexpensive), a magnificent 18thC
country house and still the home of the
Hope family, Earls of Hopetoun and
Marquesses of Linlithgow. Begun by Sir
William Bruce (*see* A-Z), then enlarged by
William Adam, it was completed by his
sons John, Robert (*see* Adam) and James.
Features include Portsoy Marble (*see*
Excursion 9) fireplaces in Bruce's rich
interior, which contrasts with the light,
rococo plasterwork of the later grand
staterooms. A rare example of Baroque
ceiling painting in Scotland was recently
uncovered in the cupola. There are also
fine 18thC paintings, furniture and

Meissen porcelain, plus 17thC tapestries. Outside are splendid views over the Forth and its bridges, especially from a rooftop viewing platform. Leave Hopetoun and take the minor road east along the shores of the Forth.

211 miles – South Queensferry is an attractive old port and former south terminal of the ferry across the Forth. It has stunning views of the Forth Bridges (*see* A-Z) and in summer a regular boat service to Inchcolm island (tel. as at North Queensferry). The High St has fine 17thC buildings, including the Hawes Inn featured in Robert Louis Stevenson's (*see* A-Z) *Kidnapped*. Leave on the B924, which climbs uphill. In a mile a minor road leads right to Dalmeny village, where **Dalmeny Church** (1400-1630 Sun. or key at house opposite) is a remarkably well-preserved example of Norman architecture, with nave, choir and apse all dating from the 12thC and with rich carving round the south door. Return to the B924 and opposite is the entrance to **Dalmeny House** (1300-1730 Sun., 1200-1730 Mon.-Tue., last admission 1645, July & Aug.; Moderate), the 19thC Tudor Gothic home of the Primrose family, Earls of Rosebery. The magnificent collections of 18thC French furniture, tapestries and porcelain were formerly in the Rothschilds' house at Mentmore in England. The Napoleon memorabilia were collected by the 5th Earl who was briefly Liberal Prime Minister. Outside are pleasant grounds by the shores of the Forth. Continue on the B924 and turn left on the A90 to Edinburgh (220 miles).

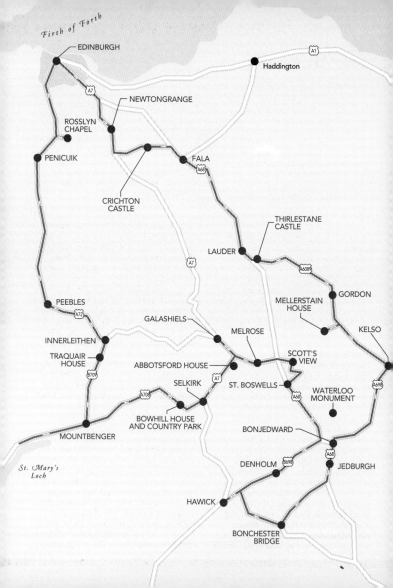

The Borders

4 –5 days

This excursion to the attractive Southern Uplands of Scotland visits the fine old Borders towns on the River Tweed and its tributaries. A number of them grew up around the important abbeys which were often attacked in Borders skirmishes. Others became rich wool towns, and several now have famous rugby teams. The area is of course also 'Scott Country', where Sir Walter Scott built his beloved Abbotsford. He also published a collection of traditional Border ballads and set works including *The Lay of the Last Minstrel* (1805) in the area. In addition to Abbotsford there are a number of impressive houses, including Mellerstain by William and Robert Adam, and castles, including Thirlestane and Floors.

Leave Edinburgh on the A7 through Lasswade to Newtongrange, 10 miles southeast of the city, where the **Scottish Mining Museum** (1000-1600, last tour 1500, Mar.-Oct.; Inexpensive) has restored the 19thC Lady Victoria Colliery and has tours and a visitor centre with displays on mining life. 2 miles south of Newtongrange, turn left on the B6372. On the right is **Vogrie Country Park** (0800-2230 or dusk, April-Oct., 0900-1630 Nov.-Mar.; Free). Turn right onto a minor road at Newlandrig, then left to visit **Crichton Castle** (HS, except closed Oct.-Mar.; Inexpensive), begun in the 14thC. The northern range of 1581-91 has an extremely unusual diamond faceting as on some Italian palaces and was commissioned by the 5th Earl of Bothwell on his return from Italy. Continue to Crichton village, where the interesting **Church** (1400-1700 Sun., May-Sep.) has a cruciform plan and tunnel vault, while the churchyard has three 19thC iron grave memorials. From Crichton, continue on the minor road and in 2 miles turn right onto the A68, heading south. Beyond Fala to the right, along the B6368, is the 12thC **Soutra Aisle** (open access), all that remains of the hospice created by Malcolm IV, while

to the south of it is the line of a Roman road, Dere Street. Continuing on the A68, the road climbs 1130 ft up Soutra Hill, from where there are views back over Edinburgh and the Firth of Forth. The road then descends into Lauderdale. **31 miles – Lauder** has a church by William Bruce (*see* A-Z) with octagonal spire and a 17thC Town Hall and former Tolbooth jail. Beyond the town, turn left to visit **Thirlestane Castle** (castle 1400-1700, last admission 1630; grounds 1200-1800 Sun.-Mon. & Wed.-Thu., Easter, May-June & Sep.; Sun.-Fri., July & Aug.; Moderate), a stunning composition of towers and turrets, largely designed by royal architect William Bruce and carried out by Robert Mylne, Charles II's master mason, for the Duke of Lauderdale, nicknamed 'King of Scotland', the most powerful man in the country as Charles's Secretary of State for Scotland. Inside are magnificent plaster ceilings by the same craftsmen as at Holyroodhouse (*see* Edinburgh). There is also an interesting collection of toys, and an exhibition on Borders country life. Turn left on the link road between the A68 and A697, then right on the A697. In 3 miles, fork right on the A6089 to Gordon, 0.5 mile west of which is **Greenknowe Tower** (HS, except details of keyholder at site Jan.-Mar.), a fine 16thC L-plan tower house still with its iron 'yett' (gate). Continue on the A6089 and 3 miles beyond Gordon turn right on a minor road for **Mellerstain House** (1230-1630 Sun.-Fri., Easter & May-Sep.; Moderate), begun in 1725 for George and Grisell Baillie, née Hume, both from famous Covenanting families (*see* Covenanters). Grisell Baillie was a songwriter and also kept a Household Book which survives as an invaluable social document. Only the two wings were completed by William Adam, while the rest of the house was carried out by Robert Adam (*see* A-Z) and contains exquisite examples of his neoclassical plasterwork as well as portraits by Ramsay (*see* A-Z) and Gainsborough, and fine furniture. Carry on south on the A6089.

50 miles – Kelso. TIC: Town House, The Square, tel. 01573 223464, April-Oct. A delightful town with cobbled streets and a wide market square, Kelso's early importance was due to **Kelso Abbey** (HS, all reasonable times; Free), the oldest and largest of the Borders abbeys, founded in 1128 by David I with Tironensian monks. The west front of its church survives with late 12thC Romanesque arches, as does the north transept, but the rest, including monastic buildings, was destroyed by the Earl of Hertford in 1545. Opposite is the attractive old Turret House containing **Kelso Museum** (1000-1200, 1300-1700 Mon.-Sat., 1400-1700 Sun., Easter-Oct.; Inexpensive), with reconstructions of a Victorian schoolroom, marketplace and skinner's workshop. The 1773 **Parish Church** (1000-1600 Mon.-Fri., May-Sep.) is of unusual octagonal plan. Beyond The Square is access to **Floors Castle** (1030-1730 Sun.-Thu., Easter, May-June & Sep.; Mon.-Sun., July & Aug.; 1030-1600 Wed. & Sun., Oct., last admission 45 min before

closing; Moderate), the huge and magnificent seat of the Duke of Roxburghe begun by William Adam in 1721 but enlarged in the 19thC by William Henry Playfair, who was also responsible for the profusion of turrets. Inside are fabulous collections of Louis XIV-XVI furniture, Brussels and Gobelins tapestries, porcelain, portraits and Post-Impressionist paintings. 5 miles northwest of Kelso on the B6397, **Smailholm Tower** (HS, except closed Oct.-Mar.; Inexpensive) is signposted. A 16thC tower set high on a rocky outcrop with views over the Cheviot, Lammermuir and Eildon Hills, it is said to have inspired the young Walter Scott (*see* A-Z), who spent part of his childhood at nearby Sandyknowe Farm. The tower now has displays of figures and tapestries relating to Scott's *Minstrelsy of the Scottish Border*. A short distance west of Kelso on the A699 are the earthwork remains of massive Roxburgh Castle (open access), destroyed in the 15thC by the Scot family. Leave Kelso on the A698 south, crossing Rennie's (*see* A-Z) bridge (1799-1803), with its elegant columns and five arches. On the hill to the right beyond Crailing is the Waterloo Monument, erected in 1815. Turn left at Bonjedward on the A68.

62 miles – Jedburgh. TIC: Murray's Green, tel. 01835 863435/688. A pleasant Borders town dominated by the ruins of the very fine **Jedburgh Abbey** (HS, Inexpensive) on a slope above the Jed Water. The abbey was begun c1138 for a community of Augustinian canons. Edward I of England stayed here at the beginning of the Wars of Independence in 1296, while its proximity to the English border meant it was frequently attacked, particularly in the 15th and early 16thC. Part of the church continued in use after the Reformation (*see* A-Z) until the late 19thC and the impressive remains show

Floors Castle

the transition in style from Norman to Gothic. Interpretive boards explain the much more ruinous monastery buildings. There is also a visitor centre, and a monastic herb garden has been re-created. **Mary Queen of Scots House** (1000-1700 Easter-mid Nov.; Inexpensive) is a good example of a bastel house, a type of fortified house, where Mary Queen of Scots (*see* A-Z) is said to have stayed when she made her exhausting ride to meet her husband Bothwell at Hermitage Castle (*see* A-Z). On the hill above the town, on the site of

the castle, is **Jedburgh Castle Jail and Museum** (closed for renovation 1995; check times with TIC), a 19thC prison with displays on prison life and the town's history. Continue south on the A68. On the left in just under 2 miles is 16thC **Ferniehirst Castle** (1330-1630 Wed., May-Oct.; Inexpensive), ancestral home of the Kerrs, one of the famous old families of the Borders. In the stable block is the Kerr Museum and an information centre on Borders families. Turn right on the B6357 and, at Bonchester Bridge, right on the A6088.

77 miles – **Hawick** (pronounced 'hoyk'). TIC: Drumlanrig's Tower, tel. 01450 372547. A major centre of the local woollen industry, Hawick is the largest of the Borders towns. Its 12thC castle survives only as a huge motte. The history of the town is presented through the latest audiovisual technology in the restored 16thC **Drumlanrig's Tower** (1000-1800 June & Sep., 1000-1900 July & Aug., 1000-1700 Oct.-May; Inexpensive). Wilton Lodge Park has 107 acres of woodland and parkland with walks by the River Teviot. It also contains the **Hawick Museum and Scott Gallery** (1000-1200, 1300-1700 Mon.-Sat., 1400-1700 Sun., April-Sep.; 1300-1600 Mon.-Fri., 1400-1600 Sun., Oct.-Mar.; Inexpensive), with displays on the town's knitwear manufacture and a collection of 19th-20thC Scottish art. There are many quality knitwear shops, while **Peter Scott's** (tours 1400 Tue. & Thu.; Free) has factory tours and **Wrights of Trowmill** (mill 0900-1600 Mon.-Thu., 0900-1200 Fri.; Free) have tours of their weaving flat. From Hawick, the B6399 leads southwest to Carlisle, passing near Hermitage Castle. Leave on the A698 heading east, through the village of Denholm, where plaques record the birthplace of James Murray, first editor of the *Oxford English Dictionary*, and John Leyden, a poet and friend of Sir Walter Scott. An obelisk also commemorates Leyden. 6 miles beyond Denholm, turn left on the A68. On the right is **Harestanes Countryside Visitor Centre** (1000-1700 April-Oct.; Free), housed in converted farm buildings where there are audiovisual presentations and exhibitions on the countryside, plus woodland walks, ranger service and indoor and outdoor play areas. Up on the hill to the right, there are more views of the Waterloo Monument. Continue north on the A68 and at St. Boswells turn right into the village with its spacious green. 2 miles beyond, on the B6404, are **Mertoun Gardens** (1400-1800, last admission 1730, Sat., Sun. & hols, April-Sep.; Inexpensive), beautiful 20 acre gardens with a walled garden and a circular doocot (dovecote). Turn left on the B6356 and take the turning for **Dryburgh Abbey** (HS; Inexpensive), a Premonstratensian abbey established in 1150 in a beautiful setting near the Tweed. Much of the surviving ruin dates from the 12th-13thC, though the west front of the church is 15thC Gothic. Sir Walter Scott is buried in St. Mary's Aisle and Field Marshall Earl Haig nearby. The remains of the monastic buildings are more extensive than is often the case in Scotland, and include the barrel-vaulted chapterhouse. Return to the B6356 and continue north uphill to Scott's View, where there are magnificent views across the Tweed to the three peaks of the Eildon Hills, the Roman Trimontium. Here Scott would come to admire his favourite

Dryburgh Abbey

Scott's View

view and it is said that his horses, when pulling the hearse containing his coffin to Dryburgh, paused at their habitual stop. Take the second minor road on the left, then left again at the A68 and first right to enter Melrose via Newstead.

103 miles – **Melrose**. TIC: Abbey House, tel. 01896 822555, April-Oct. An attractive town which grew up around its abbey, Melrose now has a number of attractions. **Melrose Abbey** (HS; Inexpensive) was founded on this site in 1136 by David I with Cistercian monks from Rievaulx in Yorkshire but was more or less destroyed by the English in the Wars of Independence. Much of the initial funding for rebuilding was given by Robert the Bruce (see A-Z), whose heart is said to

have been buried here after Sir James Douglas, 'the Black Douglas', had taken it into battle against the Muslims in Spain and it was recovered by Sir William Keith. Much of the surviving abbey dates from the 15thC and is a very fine example of decorated Gothic style with many delightful carvings, the most famous of which is the gargoyle with a pig playing bagpipes. Next to the abbey is **Priorwood Garden** (NTS, 1000-1730 Mon.-Sat., 1330-1730 Sun., April-Dec.; Inexpensive), which mainly grows plants for drying and also has an orchard showing the history of cultivation of the apple. In The Square is the **Trimontium Exhibition** (1030-1630 April-Oct.; Inexpensive), an award-winning exhibition on the important Roman fort and settlement whose site is near the town. **Teddy Melrose Teddy Bear Museum** (1000-1700; Inexpensive) will delight children of all ages, while **Melrose Motor Museum** (1030-1730 Easter-Oct.; Inexpensive) has vintage cars, motorcycles and old signs. Leave on the A6091 north.

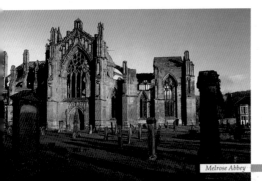

Melrose Abbey

Abbotsford House

Abbotsford House

107 miles – Galashiels (locally shortened to 'Gala'). TIC: St. John's St, tel. 01896 755551, April-Oct. A large wool town with a one-way system which may confuse first-time visitors, Galashiels is now overwhelmingly 19th and 20thC. **Old Gala House and Christopher Boyd Gallery** (1000-1600 Mon.-Sat., 1400-1600 Sun., mid Mar.-Oct.; tel. 01750 720096 for winter times; Free) has the early history

of the burgh in the former laird's house of 1583 with a 17thC painted ceiling. There are also art galleries with changing exhibitions. **Peter Anderson Cashmere Woollen Mill** (museum 0900-1700 Mon.-Sat.; also 1200-1700 Sun., June-Sep.; tours 1030, 1130, 1330 & 1430 Mon.-Thu., 1030 & 1130 Fri., April-Oct.; Inexpensive) has an interesting museum with history of the local woollen industry, plus mill tours. Backtrack on the A6091 to the large roundabout and turn right on the B7060 for **Abbotsford House** (1000-1700 Mon.-Sat., 1400-1700 Sun., mid Mar.-Oct.; Moderate), the remarkable home of Sir Walter Scott, largely rebuilt and extended for him 1818-24 and with many old architectural features collected by Scott, such as the door of Edinburgh's Tolbooth. Inside, his arms and armour and other fascinating collections reflect the historical and antiquarian interests of his novels and poems. Continue south and turn left on the A7.

115 miles – Selkirk. TIC: Halliwell's House, tel. 01750 20054, April-Oct. An ancient royal burgh overlooking the Ettrick and Yarrow valleys, Selkirk has a fine Market Square dominated by the statue of Scott. **Sir Walter Scott's Courtroom** (1000-1600 Mon.-Sat., 1400-1600 Sun., April-Oct.; Free), where he presided as Sheriff of Selkirk 1797-1832, has displays on him. **Halliwell's House Museum** (1000-1700 Mon.-Sat., 1400-1600 Sun., April-June & Sep.-Oct.; 1000-1800

Selkirk Glass

Mon.-Sat., 1400-1800 Sun., July & Aug.; 1400-1600 Nov.-mid Dec.; Free), in the town's oldest house, has local history and changing exhibitions. **Clapperton's Daylight Photographic Studio** (1400-1630 Sat. & Sun., Easter-Oct.; Inexpensive) is an 1867 photography studio with a rich photographic archive. At **Selkirk Glass** (glassmaking 0900-1630 Mon.-Fri.; Free) visitors can watch glass paperweights being made. Just outside Selkirk is 16thC **Aikwood Tower** (1400-1700 Tue., Thu. & Sun., April-Sep.; Inexpensive), which now houses an exhibition on James Hogg, 'the Ettrick Shepherd', a contemporary of Scott and fellow writer. Leave Selkirk on the A708 and in 3 miles is **Bowhill House and Country Park** (house 1300-1630 July, Moderate; park 1200-1700 Sat.-Thu., May-June & Aug.; also Fri., July; Inexpensive), the Border seat of the Dukes of Buccleuch and Queensberry, altered and extended from the original

18thC house in the 19thC. It contains an exceptionally fine collection of French furniture, porcelain, tapestries, paintings by Gainsborough, Reynolds, Canaletto and Raeburn (*see* A-Z) and portrait miniatures. The park has a visitor centre with audiovisuals, a Victorian kitchen and fire engines, plus walks and nature trails. Continue on the A708. In a short distance are the ruins of 15thC Newark Castle across the Yarrow Water. At Yarrow itself is a little church dating from 1640. 15 miles from Selkirk is **St. Mary's Loch**, a very pleasant spot with many associations with Scott and Hogg. Above it are the ruins of Dryhope Tower. The A708 continues southwest, past the Grey Mare's Tail waterfall to Moffat (*see* A-Z). Return to Mountbenger and turn left on the B709. After 7 miles is **Traquair House** (1230-1730 Easter, May-June & Sep.; 1030-1730 July & Aug., 1400-1700 Fri.-Sun., Oct., last admission 30 min before closing; Moderate), whose history goes

back 800 years and is claimed as the oldest inhabited house in Scotland. Additions and alterations were made to the original tower house in the 16th and 17thC. The Stuart family of Traquair were Jacobite supporters (*see* Jacobites) and the Bear Gates to the house have remained closed since Bonnie Prince Charlie passed through them for the last time in 1745. The house has its own 18thC brewery, still producing fine ales (tastings 1500-1600 Fri., June-Sep.), while in the grounds are crafts workshops (same hours as house, Wed.-Thu.). Carry on into **Innerleithen**, where in the High St is an interesting Victorian survival, **Robert Smail's Printing Works** (NTS, 1000-1300, 1400-1700 Mon.-Sat., 1400-1700 Sun., last admission 45 min before morning and afternoon closing, Easter-mid Oct.; Inexpensive). **St. Ronan's Wells Interpretive Centre** (1400-1700 Easter-Oct.; Free) gives the history of these mineral springs and the town's growth as a spa, helped by Sir Walter Scott's novel *St. Ronan's Well*. 2 miles east on the A72 is Walkerburn, with the **Scottish Museum of Woollen Textiles** (0900-1730 Mon.-Sat.; also 1100-1700 Sun., April-Nov.; Free) which gives the history of the industry. West of Innerleithen on the B7062 are **Kailzie Gardens** (1100-1730 April-Oct.; Inexpensive), a beautiful walled garden with herbaceous and rose borders. Leave Innerleithen on the A72 west. On the

right is the fine old Glentress Forest, with a forest drive open weekends in summer. **149 miles – Peebles**. TIC: High St, tel. 01721 720138, April-Dec. An attractive town with an old Mercat Cross and the ruins of 13thC **Cross Kirk** (HS, all reasonable times, details of keyholder at site), once a Trinitarian friary. **The Tweeddale Museum and Gallery** (1000-1300, 1400-1700 Mon.-Fri.; also 1400-1700 Sat. & Sun., Easter-Oct.; Free) has local history and art exhibitions housed in buildings given by the 19thC publisher, William Chambers, a native of the town. The **Cornice Museum** (1000-1200, 1400-1630 Mon.-Fri.; Donation) is a most unusual museum which recreates a turn-of-the-century plasterer's workshop and shows methods used in ornamental plasterwork. Hands-on experience is also encouraged. The town also has a Hydro. A mile west of Peebles on the A72 is

Traquair House

Neidpath Castle (1100-1700 Mon.-Sat., 1300-1500 Sun., Easter-Oct.; Inexpensive), a well-preserved, late 14thC tower house in a splendid setting overlooking the River Tweed. Southwest on the B712 are **Dawyck Botanic Gardens** (1000-1800 mid Mar.-Oct.; Inexpensive), part of the Royal Botanic Garden, Edinburgh, with an impressive tree collection, some over 130 ft high, plus flowering shrubs and herbaceous plants. Further west are Broughton (*see* A-Z) and Biggar (*see* A-Z). Leave Peebles on the A703, returning north, with the Moorfoot Hills on the right. The road runs parallel to the Eddleston Water. At Leadburn, continue north on the A701. **162 miles – Penicuik**. TIC: Edinburgh Crystal Visitor Centre, tel. 01968 673846, May-Oct. This former papermaking town retains some 18thC buildings. On the northern outskirts is the **Edinburgh Crystal Visitor Centre** (tours 0915-1530 Mon.-Fri.; demonstrations 1300-1430 Sat. & Sun.; Inexpensive), which has guided tours and demonstrations of glassblowing, cutting and engraving. Continue north on the A703 and in 3 miles turn right on a minor road signposted for **Rosslyn Chapel** (1000-1700 Mon.-Sat., 1200-1640 Sun., April-Oct.; Inexpensive), on the banks of the North Esk River. This former collegiate church dates from the 15th-16thC and is the most stunning example of the stonecarver's art in Scotland; every surface is covered with human and animal figures and plant motifs. Particularly outstanding is the Prentice Pillar, with four foliage twists, said to have been by an apprentice who was then killed by his jealous master. Nearby is Roslin Castle. Return to the A703 and continue to Edinburgh (176 miles).

Marischal College, Aberdeen

Aberdeen Art Gallery

Aberdeen: TIC: St. Nicholas House, Broad St, tel. 01224 632727. Now Scotland's third city with around 205,000 inhabitants, Aberdeen, at the mouth of the rivers Dee and Don, has been the major centre of the North Sea oil industry and is still one of Britain's busiest ports. Aberdeen **Fishmarket** is best visited 0700-0800 Mon.-Fri. The 'Granite City' has many handsome Georgian and later buildings of local silver-grey granite, notably in and around the 200-year-old Union St. The largest (and second-largest in the world after Spain's Escorial) is Marischal College, a 19th-early 20thC neo-Gothic building which became part of Aberdeen University. **Marischal Museum** (1000-1700 Mon.-Fri., 1400-1700 Sun.; Free) has anthropological collections and antiquities. Nearby is **Provost Skene's House** (1000-1700 Mon.-Sat.; Free), a fine early 16thC house with a rare and important series of religious paintings. The kitchen has a glass floor with a view of the cellar. The **Tolbooth** (1000-1700 Tue.-Wed. & Fri.-Sat., 1000-2000 Thu., 1400-1700 Sun., April-Sep.; Free), behind the 19thC Town House,

was the city jail. Near the 17thC Mercat Cross is **Provost Ross's House** of 1593, now a maritime museum (1000-1700 Mon.-Sat.; Free) and a National Trust for Scotland (*see* A-Z) visitor centre (1000-1700 Mon.-Sat., May-Sep.; Free). **Aberdeen Art Gallery** (1000-1700 Mon.-Wed. & Fri.-Sat., 1000-2000 Thu., 1400-1700 Sun.; Free), with an attractive Italianate courtyard, has good collections of Impressionist and modern paintings and Scottish art, including important Aberdeen artists George Jameson, Scotland's earliest portrait painter, and 19thC William Dyce and John 'Spanish' Phillip. **Satrosphere** (1000-1700 Mon. & Wed.-Sat., 1330-1730 Sun.; Moderate) has hands-on science and technology displays for all ages. North of the centre is Old Aberdeen with beautiful old cobbled streets. **St. Machar's Cathedral** (0900-1700) is now mainly 15thC and replaced earlier Norman and 6thC churches. The cathedral today consists only of the nave – the transept and choir having been destroyed when the central tower collapsed in 1688. The west front has unusual twin spires. Most remarkable, however, is the heraldic ceiling in oak of 1520 containing 48 shields of the Pope, the Holy Roman Emperor Charles V, European and Scottish royalty, and bishops and earls, thus showing Scotland's place in 16thC Christendom. Aberdeen University celebrated its quincentenary in 1995. Its story is told in **King's College Visitor Centre** (1000-1700 Mon.-Sat., 1200-1700 Sun.; Free). **King's College Chapel** (0900-

Aberdeen Harbour

1700), completed c1500, has a crown spire similar to that of St. Giles, Edinburgh, and contains fine choir stalls. Footdee (locally 'Fittie') is a perfectly preserved 19thC fishing village between the beach and the harbour. Duthie Park by the River Dee has extensive **Winter Gardens** (0930-30 min before dusk; Free). The main theatre is His Majesty's (tel. 01224 641122), while the Music Hall (same tel.) has concerts. *See* Excursions 9, 10, 11, 12.

Adam, Robert (1728-92): Robert Adam became the most important neoclassical architect and designer in 18thC Britain. Like his brothers John and James, he trained initially with his father, William Adam, who was already working in a classical style. However, his four years in Rome gave Robert direct experience of classical Roman antiquities and led him to evolve a learned yet inventive neoclassical style, examples of which are the friezes at Mellerstain (*see* Excursion 14). Also characteristic is the lightness and elegance of his interiors. Other major works in Scotland include the Italianate

Culzean Castle (*see* Excursion 1), with the stunning round drawing room and oval staircase, and the handsome north side of Charlotte Sq., Edinburgh (*see* A-Z).

Antonine Wall: This Roman wall was built c AD 142 at the order of Emperor Antonius Pius as a defence against incursions by the indigenous tribes of the North. It ran for 37 miles across the Forth and Clyde valleys of Central Scotland, from Old Kilpatrick on the Firth of Clyde to Bridgness, near Bo'ness, on the Firth of Forth. Built by legionnaires, it consisted of a turf and stone rampart, probably about 10 ft high, and was guarded by forts more or less every 2 miles along its length. Its construction indicates that the Romans intended to occupy Southern Scotland, yet the forts along the wall appear to have been abandoned only 20 years or so later. Of the 17 forts identified, the best-preserved is at Rough Castle, signposted from Bonnybridge, west of Falkirk. *See also* Excursion 3, Bearsden Roman Bath House; Excursion 13, Callendar Park, Falkirk and Kinneil Estate, Bo'ness.

Architecture: The oldest substantial remains of stone-built castles in Scotland generally date from the 13th-14thC following the introduction of a feudal system by David I. In many cases they replaced timber structures on motte and bailey sites such as at Huntly Castle (*see* Excursion 11), though at Duffus Castle (*see* Excursion 9) the new stone building was too heavy for the original motte or mound. Caerlaverock Castle (*see*

Traquair House

Excursion 1) in the southwest, with its moat and magnificent gatehouse, is a fine example of a late 13thC defensive castle, while 14thC Doune Castle (*see* Excursion 3) combined defence with a stately home. Smaller 14thC castles consisted of a square keep, as at Loch Leven Castle (*see* Excursion 13), from which developed the elegant 16th-17thC tower houses, such as Craigievar Castle (*see* Excursion 11), whose features include turrets with a decorative rather than a defensive function.

The earliest surviving church architecture also generally dates from the 12thC reign of David I and his division of Scotland into diocese. Many of the new churches and abbeys, however, were on the sites of earlier Celtic foundations, as at Iona (*see* Excursion 5). Fine examples of Norman or Romanesque architecture include Dunfermline Abbey (*see* Dunfermline) and Leuchars Church (*see* Excursion 13). Dunblane Cathedral (*see* Excursion 3) is a good example of 13thC early Gothic, while Melrose Abbey (*see* Excursion 14) shows the ornate 15thC Gothic style. Glasgow Cathedral (*see*

Glasgow) was one of the few Gothic cathedrals in Scotland to survive the Reformation (*see* A-Z) more or less intact.

Renaissance style was introduced to Scotland in the 16thC and can be seen in the royal palaces at Falkland and Linlithgow (*see* Excursion 13) and Stirling Castle (*see* Stirling). It continued into the 17thC with fine mansions such as the Argyll Lodging, Stirling. By the end of the 17thC, Sir William Bruce (*see* A-Z) and others had introduced a style based on classical and Palladian architecture. In the 18thC his pupil William Adam refined the new style at Hopetoun (*see* Excursion 13) and Duff House (*see* Excursion 9), while Adam's son, Robert (*see* A-Z), became the finest neoclassical architect and designer in Britain. His works include Charlotte Sq., part of Edinburgh's rational New Town whose grid plan and restrained Georgian architecture were typical of planned towns and villages of the late 18th and early 19thC.

The 19thC also saw a revival of Scots baronial style, notably in Queen Victoria's Balmoral Castle (*see* Excursion 11). Architects such as Alexander 'Greek'

Thomson (see A-Z) worked in a Greek Revival style, while others around the turn of the century in Glasgow created a rich eclectic style (see Glasgow Walk). The 'Glasgow style' of Charles Rennie Mackintosh (see A-Z) involved both a reinterpretation of the Scots baronial style and an extreme stylization of forms and decoration.

Vernacular buildings in Scotland range from the 'blackhouses' of the Western Isles (see Excursion 5) to the picturesque architecture of Fife towns and villages (see Excursion 13), often featuring crow-stepped gables and red pantiled roofs. The blackhouses were the typical dwellings of crofters (see Clearances) and had thick 'drystane' and clay walls with thatched roofs, and included quarters for the animals.

Arran: TIC: The Pier, Brodick, tel. 01770 302140/141; Lochranza, tel. 01770 830320 May-mid Oct.; and on Ardrossan-Brodick ferry, Easter-Oct. Arran is a large island (20 miles by 10 miles) in the Firth of Clyde. It can be reached by car ferry from Ardrossan in Ayrshire, or from Claonaig (see Excursion 4) in Argyll. It is sometimes called 'Scotland in miniature' since it contains both Highlands and Lowlands and, indeed, the Highland Fault Line passes through it. The northern, mountainous part offers good hillwalking and rock climbing. The highest point is Goat Fell (NTS), 2866 ft, reached by a footpath beginning at the bridge over the Glen Rosa Water, about a mile north of Brodick (see Walking). There are also plenty of less strenuous walks, and the pleasant resorts round the coast, such as Lamlash, Whiting Bay and Blackwaterfoot, are popular for watersports, yachting, angling and golf. The A841 runs round the coast, a total of 56 miles, while a minor road, known as 'The String', originally built by Telford

(see A-Z) in 1817, cuts across the island from Brodick to Blackwaterfoot. Just north of Brodick are the **Isle of Arran Heritage Museum** (1000-1300, 1400-1700 Mon.-Sat., April-Sep.; Inexpensive), housed in an 18thC farm, and **Brodick Castle and Gardens** (NTS, castle 1130-1700 Easter-Sep.; Moderate; gardens 0930-sunset; Inexpensive). The former seat of the Dukes of Hamilton, the castle dates in part from the 13thC, with 17th and 19thC additions, and contains outstanding collections of silver, porcelain and paintings. Lochranza, at the north end of the island, is the ferry port for Claonaig in Kintyre. Here, the **Isle of Arran Distillery** (1000-1800; Free) is Scotland's newest. Nearby is the picturesque ruin of 13th-14thC **Lochranza Castle** (HS, all reasonable times, April-Sep.; details of keyholder at site). Halfway down the west coast is Machrie Moor, where, signposted off the A841 just after Machrie Water and reached on foot, is a remarkable complex of prehistoric monuments, including six stone circles and several burial chambers. Further south at Blackwaterfoot is a 2 mile coastal walk to King's Cave, one of several said to be the site of Robert the Bruce's (see A-Z) encounter with the spider. Its walls have carvings. More prehistoric sites are at Auchagallon, near Machrie, Kilpatrick and Corriecravie to the south. At Kildonan is a much-ruined castle. Cheesemaking can be watched at Torrylinn Creamery (tel. 01770 820240), Kilmory, and at the Island Cheese Co. (tel. 01770 302788), Home Farm, Brodick. Off Lamlash on the east coast is Holy Island, an impressive, steep-sided island rising to 1030 ft, which can be reached by boat from Lamlash. It now has a Buddhist centre but in the 6thC was the retreat of the Celtic monk St. Molaise, whose cave on the west of the island contains wall carvings. See Excursion 1.

Ayr

Ayr: TIC: Burns House, Burns Statue Sq., tel. 01292 288688. The town of Ayr lies at the mouth of the river of the same name. Its extensive beach stretching round the bay has long ensured its popularity as a seaside resort. It also has many associations with Robert Burns (*see* A-Z), who was born at nearby Alloway. It is a busy and attractive town with golf courses, Scotland's principal racecourse, theatres and good shopping. It also makes an excellent base for exploring 'Burns Country'. The Tam o' Shanter Inn on the High St, where the escapade described in Burns' famous poem is believed to have started, is an attractive old building with a thatched roof. The **Auld Kirk** (1500-1600 Wed. & Sun., July & Aug.) where Burns was baptized dates from 1655 and has lofts or galleries for merchants, traders and sailors. Nearby is the 15thC Auld Brig and, beyond, the New Bridge, originally built in the 18thC – the Twa Brigs of one of Burns' poems. *See* Excursion 1.

Ben Nevis: At 4406 ft, Ben Nevis is the highest mountain in the British Isles. It lies about 5 miles southeast of Fort William, from where it appears as a great, rounded hump. To get a good view of the dramatic north face, go to Banavie (*see* Excursion 2), at the start of the Caledonian Canal. A well-maintained footpath leads from Achintee Farm in Glen Nevis (car park) to the summit, and the round trip takes about 6 hr for a fit adult. The climb should only be attempted by experienced walkers with proper hillwalking equipment; snow can remain on the summit all year round. *See* Excursion 2, Walking.

Biggar: TIC: 155 High St, tel. 01899 220166, April-Oct. A small town on the A702 and A72 in the centre of the Scottish Borders. It now has an incredible number of museums run by Biggar Museum Trust. **Moat Park Heritage Centre** (1000-1700 Mon.-Sat., 1400-1700 Sun., Easter-Oct.; Inexpensive) tells the story of the area. It also has a huge Victorian patchwork made by a local tailor during the Crimean War. **Gladstone Court Museum** (1000-1230, 1400-1700 Mon.-Sat., 1400-1700 Sun., Easter-Oct.; Inexpensive) shows Biggar in the recent past and has reconstructions of old shops. **Biggar Gasworks Museum** (1400-1700 June-Sep., also 1200-1700 Sun., July & Aug.; Free) is housed in the town's gasworks which ceased production in 1973 with the arrival of North Sea gas. **Greenhill Covenanters' House** (1400-1700 Easter-mid Oct.; Inexpensive) was originally sited 10 miles away. Now it is a museum of the troubled 17thC, the Covenanters (see A-Z) and the 'Killing Times'. **Biggar Kirk** (daylight hours), originally of 1545, is believed to have been the last collegiate church built before the Reformation (see A-Z). **Biggar Puppet Theatre** (1000-1700 Mon.-Sat., 1400-1700 Sun., Easter-Sep.; 1000-1700 Mon.-Tue. & Thu.-Sat., Oct.-Easter; Moderate, booking advisable, tel. 01899 220521) has performances by the International Purves Puppets in a Victorian puppet theatre. Just northeast is **Brownsbank Cottage** (by arrangement, tel. 01899 221050), home of the late Hugh MacDiarmid (E.M. Grieve), Scotland's major 20thC poet and a prominent Scottish Nationalist.

Broughton: A Borders village on the A701, 5 miles east of Biggar (see A-Z). The small **John Buchan Centre** (1400-1700 May-Sep.; Inexpensive) is housed in the old Free Kirk, where the novelist's father was once temporary minister. Buchan, author of The Thirty-Nine Steps and other popular novels, also spent childhood holidays in Broughton. Just north of the village is **Broughton Gallery** (1030-1800 Thu.-Tue., April-mid Oct. & mid Nov.-mid Dec.; Free), where exhibits by contemporary British artists are for sale in Broughton Place, Sir Basil Spence's

1938 Scots baronial tower house. Outside are a knot garden and a doocot (dovecote).

Bruce, Sir William (c1630-1710): A gentleman architect who did much to introduce a classical style of architecture to Scotland. In his role as surveyor and overseer to King Charles II in Scotland, he created the symmetrical, French-inspired royal palace of Holyroodhouse (see Edinburgh Attractions) in the 1670s, which incorporated the earlier tower. In his later houses, notably his own Kinross House from 1685 and the first phase of Hopetoun House, 1698-1702 (see Excursion 13), he abandoned the Scottish tower house form altogether and instead designed classical villas influenced by the Italian architect Palladio, and by his travels abroad. His garden designs too, at Balcaskie and Kinross (see Excursion 13), were also important, while the great formal garden at Pitmedden (see Excursion 11) may reflect his knowledge of French gardens.

Burns, Robert (1759-96): 'Scotland's national bard' is perhaps best-known outside Scotland for his songs, including My Love is like a Red, Red Rose and Auld Lang Syne. He was born on a small farm in Alloway (see Excursion 1) whose 7 acres had to support a family of as many children. As was common in Scotland, education was considered important, even in poor families, and the Burns children received much of their education from their father. Robert began writing poems and songs from the age of 14. A few years later, poverty and love affairs, including one with 'Highland Mary', almost forced him to leave Scotland. He planned to emigrate to Jamaica and, to raise the price of the voyage, he had a collection of his poems published in Kilmarnock in 1786. Such was the success of the now famous Kilmarnock Edition that he decided to go to Edinburgh instead, where a second edition was published. There, he became a famous literary figure and also met Mrs Agnes MacLehose (the 'Clarinda' of his poems). He returned to Ayrshire in 1788 to marry Jean Armour, with whom he already had a family. While living at Ellisland Farm near Dumfries (*see* Excursion 1), Burns wrote two of his most famous poems: *Tam o' Shanter*, the wonderful tale of witchcraft set around the Alloway of his youth, and *Auld Lang Syne*. He died at the age of 37, but left behind him a copious body of poems and songs. In them he captured the true rhythm of Scots and conveyed a sense of human worth beyond riches, while his love poems include many of outstanding beauty and tenderness. His ideas on liberty and equality have led some to see him as a revolutionary. His birthday, 25 Jan., is marked all over the world by Burns Suppers, a special dinner at which his poetry is recited, and a meal of haggis (*see* Food) is washed down with whisky.

Bute: TIC: 15 Victoria St, Rothesay, tel. 01700 502151. This island in the Firth of Clyde, below the Cowal Peninsula (*see* A-Z), is around 15 miles long and just 3 miles wide. The principal ferry route is from Wemyss Bay on the mainland Clyde coast to Rothesay, Bute's capital, tel. Caledonian Macbrayne 01475 520521 (Wemyss Bay), 01700 502707 (Rothesay). A summer ferry also operates May-Aug. between Colintraive on the Cowal Peninsula and Rhubodach, tel. Caledonian Macbrayne 01700 841235. The island became popular at the turn of the century with holidaymakers from the Glasgow area. Rothesay is a pleasantly

Rothesay

old-fashioned resort with a fine pavilion and **Winter Garden** (visitor centre 0900-1700 Mon.-Fri.; Free). **Rothesay Castle** (HS, except 0930-1300 Thu. and closed Fri., Oct.-Mar.; Inexpensive) is the impressive ruin of a 13thC castle with 16thC extension. **Bute Museum** (1030-1630 Mon.-Sat., April-Sep.; also 1430-1630 Sun., June-Sep.; 1430-1630 Tue.-Sat., Oct.-Mar.; Inexpensive) has displays relating to the island. **St. Mary's Chapel** (open access), is the ruin of a late medieval church with tombs and effigies of Walter the Steward and his wife. Just outside the town are **Ardencraig Gardens** (0930-1630 Mon.-Fri., 1300-1600 Sat. & Sun., May-Sep.; Free), famous for their fuchsias. At **Rothesay Creamery** (0800-1700 Sun.-Tue. & Thu.-Fri.; Free) cheesemaking can be viewed. To the north is the little resort of Port Bannatyne. South of Rothesay is Bute's most stunning attraction, **Mount Stuart** (house 1200-1700; gardens 1100-1700, last admission 1630, Mon., Wed. & Fri.-Sun., June-Sep.; Moderate). The house is a magnificent neo-Gothic fantasy, begun in 1897 by Sir Robert Rowand Anderson for the 3rd Marquis of Bute, and featuring astrological motifs, marble and stained glass. Outside are 18thC woodlands, a Victorian pinetum and a large winter garden. Further south are the remains of **St. Blane's Chapel** (open access) with a Norman arch.

Carnegie, Andrew (1835-1919): The famous industrialist and philanthropist Andrew Carnegie was born in a weaver's cottage in Dunfermline (*see* A-Z). The family emigrated to America where he began his working life at 13 as a bobbin boy in a textile mill in Pittsburgh. Eventually he built a vast industrial empire based on iron and steel, and became one of the richest men in the world. Having made his fortune, he spent his latter years giving away millions of dollars to worthy causes, notably libraries, education and cultural foundations in Britain and America, believing that 'the man who dies rich, dies disgraced'.

Clearances, The: This term usually applies to clearances from the Highlands and Islands and refers to the removal of tenants and their families from their homes and traditional lands during the latter part of the 18th to the mid 19thC. The reason for the upheaval was agricultural 'improvement', usually the introduction of sheep. In many cases, clearances were from inland to the coast and from communal lands to individual crofts or smallholdings. In both instances they reflected the disintegration of the traditional Highland way of life. Many of the new settlements did not succeed due to poverty, overpopulation and failure of crops, and resulted in voluntary or enforced emigration. In 1883 the Napier Commission examined crofters' grievances and eventually the Crofters' Commission was set up to protect crofters' interests.

Coatbridge: TIC: The Time Capsule, Buchanan St, tel. 01236 431133, April-Oct. 8 miles east of Glasgow off the M8, Coatbridge is a former heavy industrial town. **Summerlee Heritage Trust** (1000-1700; Free), housed in the remains of Summerlee Ironworks, has Scotland's largest collection of historic machinery operating daily. A tramway also takes visitors to a reconstructed 19thC coalmine, a row of mineworkers' cottages and an engine house with an 1810 beam engine. The **Time Capsule** (1000-2200; Moderate) is a leisure pool with flumes, cavemen, dinosaurs and space ships, while the free-form ice rink has a woolly mammoth and a video wall.

Riding the Marches, Coldstream

Coldstream: TIC: Henderson Park, tel. 01890 882607, April-Oct. On the north bank of the River Tweed which here forms the border with England, Coldstream, like Gretna Green (*see* Excursion 1), was popular with eloping couples from England who were married at the toll or marriage house at the Scottish end of the 18thC bridge.
Coldstream Museum (1000-1300, 1400-1700 Mon.-Sat., 1400-1700 Sun., Easter-Oct.; Inexpensive) has local history, including the history of the Coldstream Guards. Nearby, the **Hirsel Homestead Museum** (0900-dusk; Free; parking Inexpensive), in the estate of the Douglas-Home family, shows how a large estate functioned in the past, and includes displays on traditional tools and skills.

Coll & Tiree: TIC: Argyll Sq., Oban, tel. 01631 563122. These islands lie about 10 miles northwest of Mull (*see* Excursion 5) and can be reached by ferry from Oban, tel. Caledonian Macbrayne 01631 566688/622, or by the daily flight from Glasgow (*see* Airports) to Tiree. The islands enjoy what must be the most favourable climate in Scotland – an annual rainfall of less than 50 in and more hours of sunshine than anywhere else in the country (Tiree's weather station records an average of 220 hr of sunshine for May). The main drawback is the constant wind, from which there is no shelter, but the heavy Atlantic swell has made the islands' west coast the 'Hawaii of the North', and draws surfers and boardsailors from all over Britain. Both islands are relatively flat, but while Tiree is green and fertile, Coll is mostly moorland. The islanders survive on a combination of farming, lobster-fishing and tourism. In addition to walking, birdwatching and angling, visitors can explore the remains of a broch (*see* Prehistory) at **Dun Mor Vaul** (open access) on Tiree, and the 15thC **Breachachadh Castle** (by appointment, tel. 01879 230444) on Coll, the restored family home of Maj. Maclean-Bristol. From Ben Hynish, 462 ft, at the southwest end of Tiree, are views across 10 miles of sea to the famous Skerryvore Lighthouse, built 1838-43 by Alan Stevenson (an uncle of Robert Louis Stevenson – *see* A-Z), which stands on a rock only 10 ft above mean sea level.

Colonsay & Oronsay: TIC: Argyll Sq., Oban, tel. 01631 563122. These islands, linked by a sand spit at low water, can be reached by car ferry from Oban, tel. Caledonian Macbrayne 01631 566966/688, or from Kennacraig in Argyll, tel. Caledonian Macbrayne 01880 730253. They offer good walking and birdwatching, and there is a hotel, some holiday cottages and a few B&Bs.
Kiloran Gardens (all reasonable times; Free) on Colonsay are famous for their displays of rhododendrons in May and June, as well as azaleas, acacias and magnolias. On Colonsay's much smaller neighbour, Oronsay, named after Oran, a follower of St. Columba (*see* A-Z), are the remains of a 14thC Augustinian priory.

Covenanters: During his reign, 1625-49, Charles I tried to make the Church of

Scotland conform to principles and practice in England with the reintroduction of bishops and the 1637 *Book of Common Prayer*. In 1638 the document known as the National Covenant was drawn up and signed, first at Greyfriars, Edinburgh (*see* A-Z), and eventually in a number of copies which were said to have 300,000 signatories. It was interpreted as a rejection of episcopalianism and as a declaration of the church's independence from the king. However, the Covenanters, as they were known, became divided once civil war broke out in England. The bloodiest phase, known as the 'Killing Times', occurred in the 1680s after the restoration of Charles II who again reintroduced episcopalianism. Covenanters who left the church in protest to worship in 'coventicles' or meeting houses were persecuted. Victims included the 'Wigtown Martyrs' (*see* Excursion 1).

After the accession of William and Mary, the Covenanting period came to an end with the abolition of bishops in the Church of Scotland.

Cowal Peninsula: TIC: 7 Alexandra Parade, Dunoon, tel. 01369 703785. A beautiful area of Argyll with mountains and forests, quiet roads and superb views over the Firth of Clyde. The largest town is **Dunoon**, reached by ferry from Gourock, tel. Caledonian Macbrayne 01369 706491, Western Ferries 01369 704452, or by the A815. A seaside resort since Victorian times, it had a US naval base on the Holy Loch until 1992. The Cowal Highland Gathering (*see* Events) has major pipeband competitions. A monument to Robert Burns' (*see* A-Z) 'Highland Mary' is below the scant remains of Dunoon Castle. At **Dunoon Ceramics** (0900-1230, 1300-1630 Mon.-Fri.; Free) visitors can watch items being

Kyles of Bute

made. **Cowal Bird Garden** (1000-1800 April-Nov.; Inexpensive) has parrots, cockatoos, macaws and rare Scottish capercaillie. West of Dunoon, with stunning views from the A8003, are the Kyles of Bute, the beautiful stretch of water around the north end of the isle of Bute (*see* A-Z). From here the A8003 continues south to the little resort of Tighnabruaich. Further west is a new summer ferry crossing from Portavadie to Tarbert, tel. Caledonian Macbrayne as above. North of Dunoon on the A880 is Kilmun, where the **Arboretum** (open access) is part of the huge Argyll Forest Park on the peninsula. **Kilmun Church** (1300-1630 April-Sep.) is near the site of Celtic St. Mun's cell and has the 15thC tower of the collegiate church. The Dukes of Argyll, including the 1st Marquis, beheaded in 1661, are buried here. Puck's Glen is a spectacular gorge a short walk from the car park beyond Ardbeg on the A815. **Younger Botanic Garden** (1000-1800 mid Mar.-Oct.; Inexpensive), at the foot of beautiful Lock Eck, is an outpost of the Royal Botanic Garden, Edinburgh, and has giant redwoods planted in 1863, plus flowering trees and shrubs. **Lochgoilhead**, a popular watersports centre, is reached by the B839, which drops steeply from the A815. The Drimsynie Leisure Centre has sports facilities plus the **European Sheep and Wool Centre** (shows 1100, 1300 & 1500 Mon.-Fri., 1300 & 1500 Sat. & Sun., mid Mar.-Oct.; Moderate), a show featuring 19 breeds of sheep. An unclassified road leads down the side of Loch Goil to the ruins of 14thC **Carrick Castle** (open access).

Cumbrae: TIC: 28 Stuart St, MIllport, tel. 01475 530753. The island of Great Cumbrae in the Firth of Clyde can be reached by a 5 min ferry crossing, tel. Caledonian Macbrayne 01475 674134,

from Largs (*see* Excursion 1). Millport, the island's capital, became a busy holiday destination at the end of the 19thC and, though quieter today, remains popular, especially with day trippers, many of whom hire bicycles (*see* Bicycle Hire) in Millport and cycle round the island's 12 miles of road. The **Museum of the Cumbraes** (1100-1300, 1330-1700 Mon.-Sat., Easter, May hols & June-Sep.; Free) has local history and exhibitions in Garrison House, a former barracks. The **Marine Biological Station** (0930-1215, 1400-1645 Mon.-Thu.; also 0930-1230, 1430-1700 Sat., June-Sep.; Inexpensive) is a scientific research centre opened in 1887, with a museum and much-praised aquarium. The Episcopal **Cathedral of the Isles** (0830-1900) of 1849 is Europe's smallest cathedral. Sports facilities include a golf course and the National Watersports Centre (tel. 01475 674666).

Doon Valley: Near Dalmellington and the A73 in Ayrshire is one of Scotland's newest industrial heritage complexes. **Doon Valley Heritage** (1100-1600 May-Oct.; Inexpensive, tel. 01292 313579/531144) is in the former Dalmellington Iron Co. works. Nearby is a reconstructed ironworker's cottage. The **Scottish Industrial Railway Centre** (Sat., June-Sep.; Inexpensive) has a collection of locomotives, including steam engines.

Drinks: Scotland is world-famous for its whisky (the name comes from the Gaelic *uisge beatha*, meaning 'water of life'), of which there are more than 2000 brands. Over 100 of these are single malts, distilled purely from malted barley and aged in wooden casks. The malts are classified according to geographical area. Thus there are Lowland and Highland malts, the latter including Speyside and

Island malts. Each single malt has its own individual character but, within the broad geographical classifications, some generalizations can be made. For example, Islay malts have a very distinctive peaty flavour, while Speyside ones, which include some of the most famous malt whiskies, are described as mellow and subtle. Many distilleries are open for tours and sampling. Other whiskies are blends, mixtures of 15 to 50 grain whiskies (distilled from a mix of malted barley and other, unmalted cereals), with a smaller amount of malt whisky. Whisky liqueurs include Drambuie and Glayva. There are also some excellent Scottish draught beers, including Belhaven, Maclay's, Caledonian, Greenmantle, Calder's, Gillespie's and McEwan's 80/-. They are often classified in the traditional manner as 60/-, 70/- or 80/- according to strength and roughly equivalent to English mild, bitter and best. Distinctive bottled beers include the organic Golden Promise from Caledonian, and Traquair Ale, brewed in the Earl of Traquair's private 18thC brew house (see Excursion 14). Traditional oatmeal stouts have also made a reappearance. Many distilleries and breweries are open for visits (see Excursion 11, Borve Brew House; Dunbar). The country's most popular nonalcoholic drink is, of course, tea, available, as are coffee and soft drinks, in countless tearooms and cafés all over Scotland. Bottled, pure Scottish spring water includes Highland Spring and Strathmore. **Lovat Mineral Water** has a visitor centre (0930-1630 Mon.-Fri., April-Oct.; Free) and viewing gallery at its bottling plant at Fanellan, west of Inverness.

Dumbarton: TIC: Milton, A82 Northbound, tel. 01389 742306. A royal burgh in 1222, Dumbarton, to the west of Glasgow, owed much of its early importance to the amazing natural fortress of Dumbarton Rock, a 240 ft basalt volcanic plug jutting out into the Firth of Clyde. It was the site of the ancient capital of Strathclyde.
Dumbarton Castle (HS, except 0930-1300 Thu. and closed Fri., Oct.-Mar.; Inexpensive) was the last place of refuge in Scotland to which Mary Queen of Scots (see A-Z) was taken as a child and from here she was sent to France and safety. In the 18th-20thC, Dumbarton was famous for its shipbuilding yards, now all closed. The **Denny Ship Model Experiment Tank** (1000-1600 Mon.-Sat.; also 1200-1600 Sun., April-Sep.; Inexpensive), now part of the Scottish Maritime Museum (see Excursion 1), dates from 1833 and is the oldest in the world. Visitors are shown the process of making wax hulls for experiment.

Dumfries: TIC: Whitesands, tel. 01387 253862. The oldest burgh in southwest Scotland, created in 1186, Dumfries (locally 'drumfreesh') straddles the River Nith. In the High St is the 17thC Midsteeple or tolbooth (town hall). A plaque in Castle St, opposite the present Greyfriars Church, marks the site of the friary where in 1306 Robert the Bruce (see A-Z) murdered his rival, John Comyn. The old 15thC bridge, now a footbridge, is still known as Devorgilla's Bridge and recalls the earlier one erected by Devorgilla Balliol (see Excursion 1, Sweetheart Abbey). The oldest house in Dumfries (1660) is at the far side and now houses the **Old Bridge House Museum** (1000-1300, 1400-1700 Mon.-Sat., 1400-1700 Sun., April-Sep.; Free), with a Victorian nursery and a 1900 dental laboratory. Robert Burns (see A-Z) lived in the town in his later years at **Burns House** (1000-1300, 1400-1700 Mon.-Sat., 1400-1700 Sun., April-Sep.; 1000-1300,

Burns Mausoleum, Dumfries

Burns Statue, Dumfries

1400-1700 Tue.-Sat., Oct.-Mar.; Inexpensive), now a museum, while the **Robert Burns Centre** (1000-2000 Mon.-Sat., 1400-1700 Sun., April-Sep.; 1000-1300, 1400-1700 Tue.-Sat., Oct.-Mar.; Free; audiovisual Inexpensive) is in a converted 18thC mill. The town still has a number of its old inns, including the Hole in the Wall (1620), and the Globe Inn, Burns' local. **St. Michael's Church** (1000-1600 Mon.-Fri., May-Sep.) has the Burns family pew, while in the churchyard is the poet's mausoleum. **Dumfries Museum and Camera Obscura** (1000-1300, 1400-1700 Mon.-Sat., 1400-1700 Sun., April-Sep.; museum closed Mon., Oct.-Mar.; camera obscura closed Oct.-Mar.; museum Free, camera obscura Inexpensive), with local displays, is housed in an 18thC windmill tower on Corbelly Hill, with the camera obscura on top. A mile north on the A701, **Gracefield Arts Centre** (1000-1700 Tue.-Fri., 1000-1200, 1400-1700 Sat., 1200-1700 Sun.; Free) has contemporary Scottish paintings. **Dumfries and Galloway Aviation Museum** (1000-1700 Sat. & Sun., Easter-Oct.; Inexpensive), 3 miles north on the A701, has a Spitfire and the first British-built helicopter. Just outside town on the A76 are the ruins of

Lincluden Collegiate Church (HS, daylight hours; details of keyholder at site), founded in 1389, with a fine chancel and the monumental tomb of Princess Margaret, daughter of King Robert III and wife of Archibald the Grim, 3rd Earl of Douglas. **Ellisland Farm** (tel. 01387 740426), 6 miles north on the A76, was where Burns unsuccessfully tried new farming methods 1788-91 but wrote some of his best poems.

Dunbar: TIC: 143 High St, tel. 01368 863353. A royal burgh from the 15thC, Dunbar later became a major herring port and remains a popular holiday resort. The Town House (town hall) dates from the 17thC. **John Muir House** (1100-1730 Mon.-Tue. & Thu.-Sat., 1400-1730 Sun., late May-late Sep.; Free) was the birthplace of John Muir, the 19thC conservationist who helped found the US National Parks. Dunbar's **John Muir Country Park** (open access), with 8.5 miles of cliffs, dunes, saltmarsh and woodland, attracts a wide variety of wildlife, including migratory and breeding birds, and starts from the ruins of **Dunbar Castle** (open access), successfully defended against the English in the 14thC by 'Black Agnes',

Countess of Dunbar, but destroyed in the 16thC because of its associations with Mary Queen of Scots (*see* A-Z) and her husband, Bothwell. Real ale fans will want to take the opportunity of a tour of **Belhaven Brewery** (1030 & 1430 Tue.-Thu.; Inexpensive. Adults only, booking essential, tel. 01368 864488).

Dundee: TIC: 4 City Sq., tel. 01382 434664. Now Scotland's fourth-largest city, with a population of 175,000, Dundee grew rapidly in the 19thC and became known for jute, jam and journalism. Jam-making has disappeared, while jute production has fallen drastically. Verdant Works (tel. 01382 226659 or contact TIC for times), a 19thC flax and jute mill, reopens summer 1996 as a museum of Dundee's textile industries.

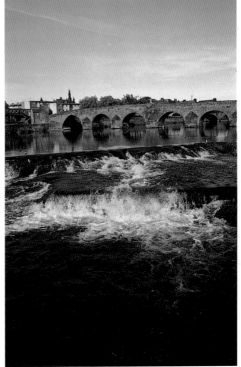

The Old Bridge, Dumfries

Shaw's Sweet Factory (1130-1600 Mon.-Fri., June-Sep.; 1330-1600 Wed., Oct.-May; Inexpensive) is in the old Keiller's jam factory and has viewing of sweets being made to traditional recipes. The city also has an important maritime history, including shipbuilding and whaling. Capt. Scott's RSS *Discovery*, launched here in 1901, is moored at **Discovery Point** (1000-1700 Mon.-Sat., 1100-1700 Sun., April-Oct.; 1000-1600 Mon.-Sat., 1100-1600 Sun., Nov.-Mar.; Moderate), a visitor centre from where there are visits aboard the polar exploration ship. At Victoria Dock are the frigate **Unicorn** (1000-1700; Moderate) of 1824, the oldest British-built ship afloat, and the **North Carr Lightship** (contact TIC or tel. 01382 224121 for times), formerly stationed off Fife Ness, the easternmost point of Fife. **Dundee Parish Church** (1000-1200 Mon.-Tue., Thu.-Sat.)

Caird Hall, Dundee

is the site of St. Mary's Church, founded in 1190. Only the 15thC tower remains of its successor, destroyed by fire in 1841. The present church has fine stained glass. The Howff, once the garden of Greyfriars Monastery, was given to the people of Dundee by Mary Queen of Scots (*see* A-Z). As well as a burial ground, it became the 'howff' or meeting place of Dundee's Nine Trades, many of whose guild symbols are on the gravestones. The **McManus Galleries** (1100-1700 Mon., 1000-1700 Tue.-Sat.; Free) have local history, archaeology, applied arts and a good collection of 19thC and Scottish paintings, housed in an attractive neo-Gothic building by George Gilbert-Scott. The **Barrack Street Museum** (1000-1700 Mon.-Sat.; Free) has natural history, including the skeleton of a humpback whale which swam up the Tay in 1883. **St. Andrew's Church** (1000-1200 Tue. & Thu.; Free) of 1772 was built for the Nine Trades' Guild and has fine stained glass with trades emblems. Next to it is the former **Glasite Chapel** (same times as St. Andrew's) of 1777 for a breakaway religious sect. Nearby is the

Wishart Arch, where Protestant reformer George Wishart (*see* Reformation) is said to have preached during the plague of 1544. In High St, **St. Paul's Episcopal Cathedral** (1000-1600 Mon.-Fri.) is another Gilbert-Scott building. Theatres include Dundee Rep (tel. 01382 223530) and the main concert hall is Caird Hall (tel. 01382 434940). The city's highest point is Dundee Law, 571 ft, a volcanic plug from where there are spectacular views of the city, the Firth of Tay and Tay Bridges. **Camperdown Country Park** (open access), around the neoclassical Camperdown House, has **Camperdown Wildlife Centre** (1000-1630, last admission 1545, April-Sep.; 1000-1530, last admission 1445, Oct.-Mar.; Inexpensive), with animals such as bears, wolves and wildcats. To the east is Broughty Ferry, once a separate village, now a pleasant suburb. **Broughty Castle** (1100-1300, 1400-1700 Mon.; 1000-1300, 1400-1700 Tue.-Thu. & Sat.; also 1400-1700 Sun., July & Sep.; Free), a 15thC fort on the Tay besieged by the English in the 16thC and by Cromwell's troops in the 17thC, now has displays on whaling and military and local history. To the west is **Mills Observatory** (1000-1700 Tue.-Fri., 1400-1700 Sat., April-Sep.; 1500-2200 Tue.-Fri., 1400-1700 Sat., Oct.-Mar.; Free) on 480 ft Balgay Hill. *See* Excursion 13.

Dunfermline: TIC: 13-15 Maygate, tel. 01383 720999. A fine historic town, Dunfermline has many associations with Malcolm Canmore and his queen, St.

Margaret (*see* A-Z), who were married here. She is believed to have founded a priory here, predecessor to **Dunfermline Abbey** (HS, except 0930-1300 Thu. and closed Fri., Oct.-Mar.; Inexpensive). The nave of the great abbey church was begun c1128 under Margaret's son, David I, and is a very important example of Norman architecture in Scotland. Its huge piers with zigzag and

Manderston

spiral patterns are similar to those at Durham Cathedral. Robert the Bruce (*see* A-Z) was buried here, minus his heart (*see* Excursion 14, Melrose Abbey). Outside are the ruins of the Benedictine monastery, the royal apartments of the abbey guesthouse, and the once magnificent Royal Palace of Anne of Denmark, who gave birth to Charles I here in 1600. Nearby **Abbot House** (1000-1700; ground floor Free, upper floors Inexpensive) is a heritage centre in the former abbot's house of the monastery. It has the history of the house and of the people associated with it, as well as the history of the town. In Pittencrieff Park is Malcolm Canmore's Tower (11thC) and **Pittencrieff House Museum** (1100-1700 Wed.-Mon., April-Sep.; Free), with displays in a 17thC mansion. The park also has peacocks and an Art Deco pavilion. It was given to the people of the town by Andrew Carnegie (*see* A-Z), whose **Birthplace Museum** (1100-1700 Mon.-Sat., 1400-1700 Sun., April-Oct.; 1400-1700 Nov.-Mar.; Inexpensive) tells his story. **Dunfermline District Museum and Small Gallery** (1100-1700 Mon.-Sat.;

Free) has local history, art exhibitions and displays on Damask linen for which the town was famous in the 19thC. Below Glen Bridge car park is **St. Margaret's Cave** (1100-1700 Wed.-Mon., April-Sep.; Free), now a Holy Shrine. The town's sports facilities include the Scottish National Waterski Centre (tel. 01383 620123). *See* Excursion 13.

Duns: In the southeast of Scotland, at the junction of the A6105 and the A6112, is this pleasant little market town and former county town of Berwickshire. It may have been the birthplace of the famous medieval scholar, Duns Scotus, whose statue is in the park. The **Jim Clark Room** (1000-1300, 1400-1700 Mon.-Sat., 1400-1700 Sun.; Inexpensive) displays over 200 of the world motor racing champion's trophies and awards. 2 miles east is **Manderston** (1400-1730 Thu. & Sun., mid May-Sep.; Moderate), a beautiful Edwardian classical house, set in extensive formal and woodland gardens. Extravagant features include a unique silver staircase and a superb marble dairy.

Edinburgh: TIC: Waverley Centre, 3 Princes St, tel. 0131 557-1700. Scotland's capital and one of the most beautiful cities in the world, Edinburgh is rich in history, architecture and culture and is a must for any visitor to Scotland. The city is dominated by its Castle Rock, a volcanic plug and naturally defensive site on which there is evidence of settlement from prehistoric times. Edinburgh Castle now consists of buildings of many dates, the oldest surviving being St. Margaret's Chapel (*see* St. Margaret), a small 12thC Norman church. The Great Hall, begun c1503, has a splendid hammerbeam roof, and in the palace are displayed the 15th-16thC Scottish Crown Jewels, rescued from Cromwell in the 17thC (*see* Excursion 12, Dunnottar Castle). The early walled city developed down the hill from the Castle on what is now the Royal Mile (*see* Edinburgh Walk). Halfway down is the church of St. Giles. This mainly 15thC

church replaced an earlier one and was itself largely reconstructed in the 19thC, although the central piers date from the 12thC. Inside are many memorials and tombs, and towards the south of the nave an inscription on the floor marks the spot where Jenny Geddes supposedly threw her stool at the preacher in protest at the introduction of a book of prayer. 19thC stained glass includes a window on the west wall by Pre-Raphaelite Burne-Jones. The new main west window commemorates Robert Burns (*see* A-Z). In the southeast corner is the Thistle Chapel for the Knights of the Order of the Thistle, with fine vaulted roofs, heraldic windows and carved oak stalls.

The cramped and overcrowded Old Town contrasts with the rational grid plan and neoclassical elegance of the 18th-19thC New Town extending to the north. It begins at Princes St, one of the world's most famous and scenic shopping streets. The New Town has a

National Gallery of Scotland, The Mound

number of impressive squares and circuses, including Charlotte Sq., designed by Robert Adam (*see* A-Z), where the **Georgian House** (1000-1700 Mon.-Sat., 1400-1700 Sun., last admission 1630, April-Oct.; Moderate) has been restored by the National Trust for Scotland. The many classical monuments on Calton Hill, and William Playfair's Greek temple designs for the National Gallery of Scotland and the **Royal Scottish Academy** (1000-1700 Mon.-Sat., 1400-1700 Sun. during exhibitions; Variable) on Princes St earned the city the description of the 'Athens of the North'.

Edinburgh University was founded in 1583, Scotland's fourth and the first after the Reformation (*see* A-Z). Its Old College on South Bridge, begun in 1789, is by Robert Adam and William Playfair. The university became renowned worldwide for its medical faculty. The present Medical School is in Bristo Pl. Nearby on Candlemaker Row is 17thC Greyfriars Church, in whose churchyard in 1638 the National Covenant (*see* Covenanters) was signed. There are many interesting gravestones but the most photographed is the one nearest the gate, commemorating Greyfriars Bobby, the dog who was said to have kept vigil by his master's grave for 14 years. A little statue of the dog is outside.

The Edinburgh International Festival (*see* Festivals) has helped put Scotland on the world cultural map. Theatres include Edinburgh Festival Theatre (tel. 0131 662-1199), with an elegant new glass front, and the Traverse Theatre (tel. 0131 228-3223), a well-known repertory theatre. The Usher Hall (tel. 0131 228-8616) is the main concert hall. The festival has also meant that the number, range and quality of eating places has improved greatly. Where pubs are concerned, Edinburgh has always had plenty with lots of atmosphere, including those in Rose St,

which is Edinburgh's street of pubs.

Away from the centre, there is Holyrood Park with craggy Arthur's Seat, 823 ft, and there are many attractive villages, including Dean Village, Duddingston and Cramond, which are all now part of Edinburgh. Attractions within a short distance of the city include the **Scottish Agricultural Museum** (1000-1700 April-Sep., 1000-1600 Mon.-Fri., Oct.-Mar.; Free). *See* Edinburgh.

Elgin: TIC: 17 High St, tel. 01343 542666. Elgin is an attractive town, though a busy main road now separates the centre and the magnificent ruined cathedral. **Elgin Cathedral** (HS, except 0930-1300 Thu., and closed Fri., Oct.-Mar.; Inexpensive), the 'Lantern of the North', was begun in the 1220s and is considered to have been the most beautiful medieval cathedral in Scotland. Rebuilt after it was burned by the Wolf of Badenoch (*see* A-Z) in 1390, it gradually fell into ruin after the Reformation (*see* A-Z). Sufficient remains to give an idea of its great size and quality. Best preserved are the 13thC east end and the chapterhouse, with elaborate vaulting and fascinating carvings. On the River Lossie, beyond Cooper Park, **Old Mills** (1000-1700 Tue.-Sun., May-Sep.; Inexpensive) have a restored, water-powered meal mill. Returning to the High St, past the 19thC neoclassical Gray's Hospital with cupola, the centre has St. Giles' Church, also neoclassical, though nearby buildings give an idea of the medieval town here. The Italianate **Elgin Museum** (1000-1700 Mon.-Fri., 1100-1600 Sat., 1400-1700 Sun., April-Oct.; Inexpensive) has an extremely important collection of fossils, plus archaeology and natural history. **Moray Motor Museum** (1100-1700 April-Oct.; Inexpensive) has veteran, vintage and classic cars and motorbikes. On the outskirts, Johnston's of Elgin have a **Cashmere Visitor Centre** (0900-1730 Mon.-Sat.; Free) which tells the story of cashmere. 6 miles southwest of the town, off the B9010 and in a beautiful wooded setting in a wide valley, is **Pluscarden Abbey** (0530-2030), which was originally founded in 1230 and ruined after the Reformation. Benedictine monks returned this century and have rebuilt it. *See* Excursion 9.

Eyemouth

Enlightenment: Scotland played an important part in the 18thC rationalist movement known as the Enlightenment. Within Scotland its main focus was Edinburgh, which enjoyed a tremendous flowering of intellectual activity, including art and literature, although other centres were Glasgow and Aberdeen, also university towns. Major figures included David Hume (1711-76), the great rationalist philosopher, author of *An Enquiry Concerning Human Understanding*, historian and a famous atheist. His friend Adam Smith (1723-90) was born in Kirkcaldy and became professor of moral philosophy at Glasgow University. Smith's *Wealth of Nations* has been interpreted this century as favouring individualism and an expanding economy. The painter Allan Ramsay (*see* A-Z) and the architect and designer Robert Adam (*see* A-Z) can both be seen as reflecting Enlightenment ideas, while the rational grid plan and restrained elegance of Edinburgh New Town may also be interpreted as an expression of it.

Eyemouth: TIC: Auld Kirk, Manse Rd, tel. 01890 750678, April-Oct. On the east coast near the English border is this pleasant little seaside resort and busy fishing port. **Eyemouth Museum** (1000-1700 Mon.-Sat., 1400-1600 Sun., April-May; 1000-1730 Mon.-Sat., 1400-1600 Sun., June & Sep.; 0930-1800 Mon.-Sat., 1300-1800 Sun., July & Aug.; 1000-1230, 1330-1630 Mon.-Sat., Oct.; Inexpensive), housed in the Auld Kirk, includes displays on fishing and the massive Eyemouth Tapestry (1981), commemorating the disaster of 1881 when 189 local fishermen were drowned. Southwest on the B6355, **Ayton Castle** (1400-1700 Sun., May-Sep.; Inexpensive) is a fine Victorian castle which replaced two earlier ones. North, at Coldingham, is the **John Wood Collection** (0900-1700 Mon.-Fri., 0800-1200 Sat.; Free), a fascinating photographic archive showing life here at the turn of the century. The prints are from glass negatives found in a garage. Nearby are the remains of a 13thC priory. **St. Abb's Head** (open access; Free; parking and centre Inexpensive), a National Nature Reserve, is a spectacular headland with 300 ft cliffs on which nest southeast Scotland's largest colonies of seabirds.

Street performer, Edinburgh Festival Fringe

Festivals: The Scottish calendar is full of interesting festivals. Some are international in both character and importance, most notably the Edinburgh International Festival held each year in the last three weeks of Aug. As well as the official festival, there is the famous Military Tattoo, plus the Jazz, Film and Book festivals and the huge Festival Fringe, particularly famed for experimental theatre and, in recent years, stand-up comedy. Glasgow's much younger Mayfest has also achieved international status. Other annual festivals include many of folk and traditional music. Recent years have also seen the revival of the *fèis* or Gaelic festival, now with an emphasis on workshops in language, music, song and dance. The many held each year include those in Portree, Skye, in April, Fort William in May, and Barra, North and South Uist, Harris and Lewis in July to early Aug. There is also the National Mod or competitive Gaelic music festival in a different town in Oct. each year. The best-known festivals of traditional culture are the Highland Games held in many places throughout Scotland between May and Sep. The most famous is the Braemar Royal Highland Gathering (*see* Excursion 11), though others including Cowal Highland Games (*see* Cowal Peninsula) are also important. They consist of competitions in sporting events, the most famous of which is 'tossing the caber' (throwing a tree trunk), as well as in bagpiping and Highland dancing (solo dances such as the Highland Fling and the Sword Dance, originally for men but now usually performed by young girls). The Borders, and particularly Dumfries and Galloway, have a very different type of traditional summer festival usually called the Riding of the Marches or the Common Ridings. These are spectacular horseback processions dating back to the times when borders had to be protected against raiders. There are many other local galas or summer festivals throughout Scotland. In winter, a number of ancient, pagan fire festivals survive, of which the Viking Up-Helly-Aa in Shetland is the most famous. Others are at Stonehaven (*see* Excursion 12), Burghead (*see* Excursion 9), Comrie (*see* Excursion 3), Biggar (*see* A-Z) and Grantown-on-Spey (*see* Excursion 11). The Scottish Tourist Board's *Events in Scotland* lists more festivals, while the regional tourist guides available from local TICs give details of festivals in their areas. *See* Events, What's On.

Braemar Royal Highland Gathering

Food: Scotland's high-quality foods are world-famous, from meats such as prime Aberdeen Angus beef and Scotch lamb to game, including venison from red deer and of course grouse. Fish includes salmon and trout from well-known fishing rivers, while seafood ranges from lobsters, crayfish, crabs and prawns to mussels, scallops and oysters. The favourite white fish in Scotland is haddock, though sole, cod, whiting and ling also appear on menus. Herring is Scotland's other favourite fish and may be offered fried or grilled in oatmeal, 'soused' or pickled, or smoked as kippers, the most famous being from Loch Fyne. Haddock is also smoked in different ways, including Finnan haddie, smoked over peat, or Arbroath smokies, smoked round over oak or beech. Scottish salmon is most famous smoked but is also delicious poached or baked. Among many hearty soups are Scotch broth, made with barley, vegetables and stock, cock-a-leekie, made with chicken and leeks (and originally prunes), partan bree (crab soup), and Cullen skink, with smoked haddock, potatoes and milk or cream. Vegetable accompaniments to fish or meat dishes include Ayrshire potatoes and Scotch tomatoes often grown around Lanark (*see* A-Z). Haggis is the most famous Scottish dish of all, made from the minced liver, heart and lungs of a sheep, mixed with oatmeal, onion and seasoning, all stuffed into a sheep's stomach and cooked. It tastes much better than it sounds and there are also vegetarian versions now. It is traditionally eaten with 'bashed neeps and tatties' (mashed turnip and potato) on Burns Night (*see* Burns), 25 Jan. Desserts include berry fruits when in season, such as strawberries and raspberries, many of which are grown in Strathmore (*see* Excursion 12), and brambles (blackberries). Athole brose is a rich mixture of cream, whisky and oatmeal, while cranachan is similar but also has soft fruits such as raspberries. Clootie dumpling, a delicious pudding steamed in a 'clootie' or muslin cloth, has become enormously popular again. Cheeses include crowdie, an old-fashioned cream cheese, while Dunlop and Orkney are Cheddar-like cheeses. Hand-made farm cheeses have also been revived. Oatcakes are the traditional accompaniment to cheese. Local specialities are always worth trying; for example, butteries in the Northeast, a type of morning roll eaten warm for breakfast, or Forfar bridies, savoury pastries filled with a meat and onion mixture.

Forth Bridges: These two spectacular bridges span the Firth of Forth between South Queensferry, about 8 miles west of Edinburgh, and North Queensferry in Fife. There was a ferry crossing here, believed to have been initiated by St. Margaret (*see* A-Z) in the 11thC, which offered free passage to pilgrims to St. Andrew's (*see* A-Z). In 1890 the Forth rail bridge was completed at an estimated cost of £3.2 million. At the time it was the largest bridge in the world – 55,000 tons of steel were said to have been used in its construction – and painting its 45 acre surface was a never-ending task. The neighbouring Forth road bridge, which stretches 1.4 miles across the firth, was opened in 1964 at a cost of £19.5 million. Its 512 ft towers support two steel cables, each 6 ft thick, from which a four-lane highway and a cycle/footpath are suspended. *See* Excursion 13.

Fort William: TIC: Cameron Sq., tel. 01397 703781. The principal town of the western Highlands, and a centre for road and rail transport, Fort William is situated beneath Ben Nevis (*see* A-Z) at the southern end of the Caledonian Canal (*see* Great Glen). It is a major tourist centre with a wide range of facilities. In Cameron Sq. is the **West Highland Museum** (1000-1700 Mon.-Sat., June & Sep.; 0930-1730 Mon.-Sat., 1400-1700 Sun., July & Aug.; 1000-1300, 1400-1700 Mon.-Sat., Oct.-May; Inexpensive), with local collections and good Jacobite (*see* A-Z) material, including a famous secret portrait of Bonnie Prince Charlie. From the town pier, Seal Island Cruises (tel. 01397 705589) do boat trips on Loch Linnhe (pronounced 'linnie') to see seals and other wildlife. Also on the pier is the award-winning Crannog Seafood Restaurant. For railway enthusiasts, a steam locomotive runs four times a week, June and Sep., and five times July and Aug. on the scenic West Highland Line between Fort William and Mallaig; for further information, tel. 01379 707752. The town is an important base for all-year-round outdoor activities. In addition to the Nevis Range Ski Centre (*see* Excursion 2) at Aonach Mor, facilities and instruction in various sports are available at Snowgoose Activities, tel. 01397 772467. *See* Excursion 2.

Forth Road Bridge

Forth Rail Bridge

Glasgow: TIC: 35 St. Vincent Pl., tel. 0141 204-4400; Glasgow Airport, tel. 0141 848-4440. Glasgow is Scotland's largest city, and one of its growing tourist attractions. Over recent years much effort has gone into improving the city's image and dispelling its reputation as a violent, hard-drinking city of slums. The campaign has been a great success, for although social problems remain as in any large city, Glasgow's appearance and, perhaps more importantly, its confidence, have improved enormously. The event which altered the world's perception of Glasgow was the opening of the prestigious Burrell Collection in 1983.In addition, almost all of the blackened buildings have been cleaned and the centre has many fashionable new shops, shopping centres, restaurants and café-bars. The most elegant of the new shopping centres is Princes Square (*see* Glasgow Walk). Much more downmarket but an authentic and colourful survival of an older Glasgow are The Barras (barrows), a covered market open at weekends (best in the morning).

Glasgow School of Art

Glasgow's beginnings can be traced to the 7thC, when the Celtic monk St. Mungo (also known as St. Kentigern) buried a holy man, Fergus, at a spot called Glas-cu or 'dear green place'. Glasgow Cathedral is believed to have been founded over the graves of Fergus and Mungo in the 12thC. The present church dates mainly from the 13thC and is a fine example of Gothic style. Glasgow University was originally founded nearby in 1451, the second in Scotland, when Glasgow was growing in importance. Across from the cathedral is the new **St. Mungo Museum of Religious Life and Art** (1000-1700 Mon.-Sat., 1100-1700 Sun.; Free), housing Salvador Dali's *Christ of St. John of the Cross*, one of the world's most famous paintings. Opposite is **Provand's Lordship** (1000-

1700 Mon.-Sat., 1100-1700 Sun.; Free), Glasgow's oldest house (1471). The centre of the city progressively moved west during expansion in the 18th-19thC. In the 18thC Glasgow became a major port for transatlantic trade, with rich and powerful Tobacco Lords, while in the 19thC Glasgow became the 'Second City of the Empire', whose ships, locomotives and other manufactures were exported all over the world. Art and architecture also flourished, although Charles Rennie Mackintosh (*see* A-Z) received little recognition at the time, while industrialists like Burrell formed the art collections which later enriched the city's museums. Glasgow's 20thC decline followed that of heavy industry. However, the renaissance is now well under way, helped by the annual Mayfest and the fact that Glasgow was European City of Culture in 1990. Theatres include the Theatre Royal (tel. 0141 332-3321) and the Citizens' Theatre (tel. 0141 429-5561) with a famous repertory company, while Glasgow Royal Concert Hall (tel. 0141 353-4134) opened in 1990. The **Gallery of Modern Art** (1000-1700 Mon.-Sat., 1100-1700 Sun.; Free) opened in March 1996 in Royal Exchange Sq. and in 1999 Glasgow becomes UK City of Architecture and Design. *See* Glasgow.

Glasgow Boys: These were a group of artists who came together in Glasgow in the 1880s, with James Guthrie as their unofficial leader. Other members included E.A. Walton, Englishman Joseph Crawhall, Irishman John Lavery, and George Henry and E.A. Hornel who visited Japan together. Their unromanticized landscapes and unsentimental figures of country people showed a new realist approach to subject matter and they also experimented with the new French technique of painting in the open air *(plein air)*. They gained much from the work of the French Realists and the American artist James McNeill Whistler. Examples of their work include Guthrie's *A Hind's Daughter* (1883), National Gallery of Scotland, Edinburgh; Lavery's *The Tennis Party* (1885), Aberdeen Art Gallery; and Henry's *A Galloway Landscape* (1889), Glasgow Art Gallery and Museum.

Glen Affric: This is one of the most beautiful glens in Scotland and is reached by the A831 to Cannich from Drumnadrochit *(see* Excursion 2) or Beauly *(see* Excursion 8), thereafter by a minor road, then a track. It contains one of the largest surviving areas of natural woodland in Scotland, including Scots pine and birch, part of the ancient Caledonian forest which covered the country 4000 years ago. There are a number of fine walks, details of which are available at the visitor centre (open access). Leaflets can be obtained from the Forestry Commission office, Fort Augustus *(see* Excursion 2).

Glencoe Massacre (1692): When William of Orange came to the British throne in 1689, he sought proof of the allegiance of the clans, and so demanded that each clan chief swear an oath of loyalty to him. The deadline was midnight, 31 Dec. 1691. Macdonald of Glencoe was reluctant but did set out to sign the oath. After confusion as to where this had to take place, his oath was accepted late at Inveraray, but in Edinburgh his lateness was regarded as suspicious. The decision to make an example of the troublesome Macdonalds was taken by Secretary of State for Scotland, John Dalrymple. The Campbell of Argyll regiment was chosen to carry out the task, led by Campbell of Glenlyon. He and 128 of his soldiers lodged with the Macdonalds for two weeks and won their confidence. Then, in the early hours of 13 Feb. 1692, the Campbells turned on their hosts, carrying out government orders to put all Macdonalds under 70 to the sword. 38 clan members were slain, including the chief and his wife; women, children and invalids were not spared. Others perished in the snow attempting to escape. A commemorative plaque is near the Clachaig Hotel *(see* Excursion 2).

Great Glen: Also called Glen Mor or Glen Albyn, this runs southwest to northeast between Fort William and Inverness and was formed by the Great Glen Fault, the second major geological fault in Scotland after the Highland Fault which divides the Highlands and the Lowlands. Filling it are Loch Lochy, Loch Oich and Loch Ness, the last of which is by far the largest, 23 miles long by about a mile wide. It is believed to be up to 1000 ft deep and contains the largest volume of freshwater in the British Isles, more than all the lakes and reservoirs together in England and Wales. Sightings of the Loch Ness Monster or 'Nessie' are said to date back to St. Columba's *(see* A-Z) time when the saint saved some followers by calming the monster. No other sightings

Haddington

are documented until this century. Many scientific techniques have been brought in to try to establish or disprove the monster's existence, so far unsuccessfully. The Caledonian Canal, opened in 1822, utilized the three lochs by linking them by canal with Loch Linnhe sea loch and the Moray Firth, thus providing a waterway between the North Sea and the Atlantic avoiding the treacherous Pentland Firth in the north. *See* Excursion 2, Telford.

Haddington: This beautiful and well-preserved town to the east of Edinburgh retains its medieval street plan and contains nearly 300 buildings of historical or architectural interest. 14thC **St. Mary's Church** (1000-1600 Mon.-Sat., 1300-1600 Sun.), where John Knox (*see* Reformation) worshipped as a boy, is an impressive building on the banks of the River Tyne. Nearby is **Lennoxlove House** (1400-1700 Wed., Sat. & Sun.,

Easter & May-Sep.; Inexpensive), whose name commemorated the Duchess of Lennox's love for her husband. It has a fine collection of porcelain, portraits and furniture, plus gardens. **Jane Welsh Carlyle House** (1400-1700 Wed.-Sat., April-Sep.; Inexpensive) is now a museum with material relating to Jane Welsh and her husband, the great 19thC historian, Thomas Carlyle. 2 miles east is **Stevenson House** (1400-1730 Thu., Sat. & Sun., July-mid Aug.; gardens all year; Inexpensive) of 1624.

Hamilton: TIC: Road Chef Services, M74 Northbound, tel. 01698 285590. Off the M74, Junction 6, is this former mining town, named after the Hamilton family, marquises and later dukes of the area, whose magnificent palace here was destroyed in the early 20thC. The 18thC **Old Parish Church** (call at church hall 0900-1600 Mon.-Fri., 1000-1200 Sat., 1200 Sun.) is by William Adam. Beside it is the

Celtic Netherton Cross, while the Heads Memorial tells the gory story of Covenanters (*see* A-Z) executed in 1666. Part of the Muir Street Museum or **Museum of South Lanarkshire** (1000-1700 Mon.-Sat., 1200-1700 Sun.; Free) is housed in a 17thC coaching inn and 18thC assembly room with fine plasterwork and musicians' gallery. The museum complex also includes the **Cameronians (Scottish Rifles) Museum** (same hours; Free). In **Chatelherault Country Park** (locally 'shatt-le-row') (same times as museum; Free) is the stunning 1730s hunting lodge designed by William Adam for the 5th Duke of Hamilton. The park also has a unique herd of white cattle descended from an ancient wild British species and the 500-year-old oaks of Cadzow Forest. On the other side of the M74 is Strathclyde Country Park with an artificial loch and international rowing centre. In the park but west of the M74 is the 19thC **Hamilton Mausoleum** (tours 1500 Easter-Sep.; also 1900 Sat. & Sun., July & Aug.; 1400 Sat. & Sun., Oct.-Mar.; Free), with a stunning marble floor and doors based on the famous ones of the Florence Baptistry.

Hebrides: This name refers to the islands off Scotland's west coast and is said to come from the Norse *Havbredey*, 'islands on the edge of the sea'. The islands are divided into two groups: the Outer Hebrides (Lewis and Harris, the Uists, Benbecula and Barra), which form a 130 mile-long chain across The Minch from the northwest mainland, and the Inner Hebrides (Skye, the Small Isles – *see* A-Z, Coll and Tiree – *see* A-Z, Mull, Islay and Jura – *see* A-Z) which lie closer to the mainland. Of over 200 islands in the Outer Hebrides, only 13 are inhabited, and 80% of the 31,000 population live on the largest islands, Lewis and Harris. The

Hill House, Helensburgh

predominantly Gaelic-speaking islanders make a living from crofting (smallholdings), supplemented by fishing and cottage industries like the weaving of Harris tweed. Lewis, Harris and North Uist form the stronghold of the Free Church and Free Presbyterian Church, which practise strict Sabbath observance (*see* Customs). The extraordinary, ancient sound of Gaelic psalm-singing may be heard when passing their churches on Sun. South Uist and Barra are predominantly Roman Catholic. In the Inner Hebrides, Skye is the largest and most populated of all Scotland's islands. Much of the land is still given over to crofting. Although Gaelic is not as widely spoken there as in the Outer Hebrides, there are many efforts to revive it. *See* Excursion 5.

Helensburgh: TIC: The Clock Tower, tel. 01436 672642, April-Oct. A fine seaside town at the entrance to Gare Loch on the

Firth of Clyde, Helensburgh can be reached by road or rail, or by ferry from Gourock via Kilcreggan, tel. Caledonian Macbrayne 01475 650100. Its major attraction is **The Hill House** (NTS, 1330-1730, last admission 1700, April-Dec.; Moderate) of 1904, a remarkable adaptation of Scots baronial style (*see* Architecture) by Charles Rennie

Inverness Castle

Mackintosh (*see* A-Z) for the publisher Walter Blackie and considered the architect's finest house. Decorative schemes, furniture and fittings were all by Mackintosh too, while his wife, Margaret Macdonald, designed the fabrics and painted a gesso panel. The gardens are currently being restored and also reflect Mackintosh's design ideas.

Hermitage Castle: HS, except 0930-1630 Sat., 1400-1630 Sun. only, Oct.-Mar.; Inexpensive. In Liddesdale near the English border is this imposing stronghold in a desolate landscape. It passed from the Douglas family to the Hepburns, Earls of Bothwell, in the 15thC and in 1566 was visited by Mary Queen of Scots (*see* A-Z), who rode the 40 miles from Jedburgh and back in a day to see her husband, the 5th Earl of Bothwell. 5 miles south, at Newcastleton, is the **Clan Armstrong Trust Centre** (1330-1630 Tue.-Sat., Easter & late May-Sep.; Inexpensive), with memorabilia and archives on Armstrongs from the medieval Border reivers (raiders) to the astronaut. Also, **Liddesdale Heritage Centre** (1330-1630 Wed.-Mon., Easter-

Sep.; Inexpensive) in the old church has local history. *See* Excursion 14.

Inverness: TIC: Castle Wynd, tel. 01463 234353. An ancient burgh and 'capital of the Highlands', Inverness is now a busy modern town, one of the fastest-growing in Scotland. To the right of the TIC on High St is the Town House (town hall) of 1880, and the Mercat Cross whose base incorporates the Clach-na-Cudainn stone or 'stone of the tubs', on which women rested their washtubs when coming from the river. **Inverness Museum and Art Gallery** (0900-1700 Mon.-Sat., Sep.-June; 0900-1800 Mon.-Sat., July & Aug.; Free) has displays on Highland culture, archaeology, local and natural history, plus paintings. On the hill behind is 19thC Inverness Castle (exterior only), housing law courts and local government offices. Across the River Ness is **St. Andrew's Episcopalian Cathedral** (0830-1800) of 1869, the first new cathedral completed in Britain after the Reformation (*see* A-Z). Next to it is the modern Eden Court Theatre (tel. 01463 221718), with music, drama and dance, plus a cinema and a riverside restaurant. Further upstream, Ness Islands have pleasant walks and waterbirds. On the west bank is Bught Park, at the far end of which is **Floral Hall** (1000-2000 Mon.-Fri., 1000-1800 Sat. & Sun., April-Sep.; 1000-1630 Oct.-Mar.; Free), an attractive winter garden with waterfall, fountain and grotto. Downstream in Huntly St is **Balnain House** (1000-1700 Tue.-Sat.; also Sun. & Mon., July & Aug.; Inexpensive), a beautiful neoclassical house of 1722, where, through audiovisuals and interactive compact disc, the visitor learns about Highland music from its origins to the present. Bagpipes, clarsach (harp), fiddle and other instruments can also be tried. The **Scottish Kiltmaker Centre** (0900-2000 Mon.-Sat., 1000-1800 Sun., mid May-mid Sep.; 0900-1730 Mon.-Sat., mid Sep.-mid May; Free) at Hector Russell House has a visitor centre devoted to the history of the kilt and kiltmaking. Across in Church St is the High Church, rebuilt 1770-72, but with a vaulted 14thC tower from which a curfew bell is still rung each night at 2000, though it no longer means people have to stay indoors! The **Amazon Museum Ship** (1000-1700 April-Dec.; Inexpensive), at Clachnaharry, was built in 1885 and formerly belonged to the actor Arthur Lowe. Jacobite Cruises (tel. 01463 233999) on the Caledonian Canal and Loch Ness (*see* Great Glen) sail from Tomnahurich Bridge, while Moray Firth Cruises (tel. 01463 242881/232120) go in search of dolphins and seabirds in the firth. *See* Excursions 2, 8, 9.

Islay & Jura: TIC: Bowmore, Islay, tel. 01496 810254. Islay (pronounced 'ay-la') is served by ferry, tel. Caledonian Macbrayne 01880 730253, from Kennacraig (*see* Excursion 4), West Loch Tarbert to Port Askaig, and Jura by the short ferry crossing, tel. Western Ferries

01496 840681, from Port Askaig to Feolin Ferry. Islay has three main centres: Port Ellen, Port Askaig and Bowmore. The landscape is a mix of farmland and moors, and offers excellent walking and birdwatching. Off the A846 to the right, between Port Askaig and Bowmore, the **Finlaggan Centre** (1430-1700 Thu. & Sun., April; 1430-1700 Tue., Thu. & Sun., May-Sep.; 1400-1600 Thu. & Sun., Oct.; Inexpensive) has interpretive material on the 14th-15thC buildings and administrative centre of the Lords of the Isles on the islands on Loch Finlaggan, to which there is access by boat. Bowmore is a fine 18thC planned village with circular-plan church of 1767. Further east, at Port Charlotte, is the **Museum of Islay Life** (1000-1700 Mon.-Sat., 1400-1700 Sun., April-Oct.; 1400-1700 Sun., Nov.-Mar.; Inexpensive), with displays of traditional crafts, prehistory and a collection of carved stones. From Port Wemyss are good views of the lighthouse (1824-5) by Robert Stevenson, grandfather of Robert Louis Stevenson (*see* A-Z), on Orsay. On a minor road 7 miles northeast of Port Ellen is 12th-13thC **Kildalton Church** (open access), with the Kildalton Cross, thought to date from the 9th-10thC and the finest carved Celtic cross in Scotland. Islay's distilleries, which produce distinctive peaty malts, are also major visitor attractions. Laphroaig (tel. 01496 302418/393), Bunnahabhain (tel. 01496 840646), Caol Ila (tel. 01496 840207) and Bowmore (tel. 01698 747226) can all be visited by prior appointment.

Jura is very different from its close neighbour: a wild and mountainous place, given over mainly to deerstalking. The Paps of Jura, rising to 2576 ft, provide rugged hillwalking, and at the northern end of the island, in the narrow strait between Jura and Scarba, is the famous Corryvreckan whirlpool. Spring tides rush through this gap at up to 10 knots, and underwater ledges force the swirling water into dangerous rips and overfalls. When the east-going tide meets a westerly gale, the roar of the whirlpool can be heard on the mainland, several miles away. 5 miles from the ferry, **Jura House Walled Garden** (0900-1700 Mon.-Sat.; Inexpensive) has an organic garden, plus attractive woodland and cliff walks. Further round the A846, after Craighouse, is **Keils** (open access), a fascinating old crofting township.

Jacobites: These were the supporters of the Stewart king James VII of Scotland and II of England and his son, James Francis Edward Stewart or Stuart, 'the Old Pretender'. James VII, a Roman Catholic, was forced into exile by English Protestants in 1688 and succeeded by William of Orange, grandson of King Charles I, who was married to Mary, James VII's daughter. The first Jacobite strike was the Battle of Killiecrankie (*see* Excursion 2) where the Jacobites, almost exclusively Highlanders, won but their leader, Viscount Dundee ('Bonnie Dundee' or 'Bluidy Clavers'), was killed. The union of the Scottish and English parliaments in 1707 attracted more Scottish sympathizers to the Jacobite cause in addition to the Highlanders, Episcopalians and Roman Catholics who already supported it. In 1708 a small fleet, led by a French commander and with the Old Pretender on board, reached the Fife coast but turned back on the arrival of English ships. The 1715 Jacobite Rebellion occurred soon after the accession of the first Hanoverian king, George I, and was led by the Earl of Mar. It was also unsuccessful after the indecisive Battle of Sheriffmuir (*see* Excursion 3) and was followed by the government's roadbuilding scheme in the Highlands, directed by Gen. Wade,

and the erection of barracks such as Ruthven near Kingussie (*see* Excursion 2) to discourage or quickly put down any further rebellion. The 1745 Jacobite Rebellion was led by the Old Pretender's son, Charles Edward Stewart (1720-88), 'the Young Pretender' or 'Bonnie Prince Charlie' who, born in exile in France, arrived in Scotland for the first time in 1745 and raised the Jacobite standard at Glenfinnan (*see* Excursion 5). French promises of help never really materialized yet the charismatic new leader gathered sufficient Scottish support to march south, taking Perth and setting up court at the Palace of Holyroodhouse (*see* Edinburgh Attractions), before defeating Hanoverian forces at the Battle of Prestonpans. His campaign reached as far south as Derby, only 130 miles from London, but he retreated into Scotland and was finally routed on 16 April 1746, at the bloody Battle of Culloden (*see* Excursion 9). The prince escaped into the mountains and spent several months in hiding while Hanoverian soldiers tried to hunt him down. Despite a price of £30,000 on his head, not one Highlander betrayed him. His most famous escape was from South Uist to Skye, when he was helped by Flora Macdonald, who disguised him as her maidservant. He finally took ship back to France on 20 Sep. 1746, never to return. He remains a romantic figure in the minds of many Scots and is the subject of songs such as *Will ye no' come back again* and the *Skye Boat Song*. The Jacobite defeat was followed in Scotland by the confiscation of supporters' lands, the building of Fort George (*see* Excursion 9) near Culloden and the banning of much Highland culture, including bagpipes and tartan.

Kirriemuir: TIC: Cumberland Close, tel. 01575 574097, April-Sep. This is a pleasant little town built of red sandstone on two hills above Strathmore in Angus. **Barrie's Birthplace** (NTS, 1100-1730 Mon.-Sat., 1330-1730 Sun., Easter-Sep.; 1100-1730 Sat., 1330-1730 Sun., Oct.; Inexpensive) is where the writer J.M. Barrie, creator of Peter Pan, was born. The **RAF Museum** (1000-1700 Mon.-Thu. & Sat., 1100-1700 Fri. & Sun., April-Sep.; Donation) has wartime memorabilia. From Kirriemuir roads lead west and north to the popular and attractive glens, Glen Clova and Glen Prosen.

Lanark: TIC: Horsemarket, Ladyacre Rd, tel. 01555 661661. A pleasant market town, Lanark is the centre of a soft fruit and tomato growing area and has a regular agricultural market. The town has associations with William Wallace (see A-Z) who is said to have lived at Castlegate and to have begun his campaign against the English here after his wife was killed. A 19thC statue of him is above the door of the belltower of the 18thC Church of St. Nicholas. Nearby is the fascinating village of **New Lanark**, internationally important in the history of the Industrial Revolution and of social reform. It began in 1783-5 with a partnership between Glasgow banker David Dale and English cotton-spinning pioneer, Richard Arkwright. Their cotton mills utilized the water power of the spectacular Falls of Clyde nearby, while the village became a model industrial community, with pioneering educational provision and conditions of work and housing. Dale's son-in-law, Robert Owen, introduced a cooperative shop and a crèche and increased the emphasis on education. The visitor centre (1100-1700; Inexpensive) gives an insight into the daily life of an 1820s mill girl. Owen's village store and a mill worker's house can also be visited, as well as the classic car collection and model railway. There

are walks to the Falls of Clyde at Corra Linn, now a nature reserve with a **Scottish Wildlife Trust Visitor Centre** (1100-1700 Easter-Oct., 1300-1700 Sat. & Sun., Oct.-Easter; Free). 5.5 miles northeast is 16thC **Craignethan Castle** (HS, except closed Oct.-Mar.; Inexpensive), a ruin with gun ports visible and a vaulted artillery chamber or caponier. Cartland Bridge (1822), west of Lanark on the A73, is by Thomas Telford (see A-Z) and crosses a spectacular gorge.

Languages: Although English is the official language of Scotland, about 65,000 people also speak Gaelic (pronounced 'gaa-lic', as opposed to Irish 'gay-lic'), the Celtic language brought by the Scots (see A-Z) from Ireland in the 5thC AD. It was the first language of the Highlands and Islands but began to die out with the introduction of schools in the 19thC, where teaching was in English and Gaelic speaking was disapproved of. The revival in interest in Gaelic language and culture began about ten years ago and includes television, arts projects and the beginnings of education through the Gaelic medium. There are also an increasing number of courses for learners. A Gaelic tourism brochure which includes details of courses, attractions and festivals featuring Gaelic culture is available from: Comunn na Gàidhlig, 5 Mitchell's Lane, Inverness IV2 3HZ, tel. 01463 234138. Scots, from the same Anglo-Saxon root as English, is now a dialect but was once the written and spoken language of Lowland Scotland, and the language of parliament and court. Strong regional dialects survive, notably in the Northeast and Shetland, in the latter case containing many Norse words. The Northeast dialect is known as 'the Doric' and includes a rich oral and written tradition. It is also undergoing a revival.

Lismore: This long, thin island, 10 miles by 1.5, is at the bottom of Loch Linnhe, northeast of Oban (*see* A-Z). It is accessible by passenger ferry, tel. 01631 730217, from Port Appin or car ferry, tel. Caledonian Macbrayne 01631 566688, from Oban. It offers pleasant, quiet walking and was once an important Christian site. The present parish church is in the choir of the 14thC cathedral, which in turn was believed to have been the site of Celtic St. Moluag's 6thC church. There are also the remains of Achanduin Castle and Coeffin Castle, both 13thC, and Tirefour Broch.

Loch Lomond: TIC: Balloch Rd, Balloch, tel. 01389 753535, Mar.-Nov.; The Square, Drymen, tel. 01360 660068, May-Sep. This loch has the largest surface area of any Scottish loch and measures 26.5 miles from south to north and 5 miles across at its widest point. It is also one of the most famous, because of the song *The Bonnie Banks o' Loch Lomond*. The Highland Fault Line passes through the loch, hence the difference between the narrow northern half and the wider southern one. It was once a sea loch, and among its rich wildlife is the powan, a type of herring. Loch Lomond lies within a 30 min drive from Glasgow city centre, by the A82 to the west side or the A809 to Drymen, then the B837 along the east side to Balmaha, a popular mooring for yachts, and an unclassified road to Rowardennan, where there is a hotel. Above it rises the distinctive peak of Ben Lomond, 3194 ft. The West Highland Way (*see* Walking) goes through Drymen and Rowardennan. Drymen, near the southeast corner of the loch, is a pretty village, popular with day trippers from Glasgow. The predecessor of the 1771 church was one of Rob Roy's (*see* A-Z) favoured collecting points for his protection rackets. At Balloch, on the

Loch Lomond and Ben Lomond

southwest corner on the A811, **Balloch Castle Country Park** (visitor centre 1000-1800 Easter-Sep.; park dawn-dusk; Free) has woodland, parkland and gardens. Nearby is **Antartex Village Visitor Centre** (1000-1800; Free), with factory tours showing the manufacture of sheepskin goods and a British Antarctic Survey exhibition. The tiny village of Luss, off the A82, is an extremely picturesque conservation village, featured in the Scottish Television soap, *High Road*. In St. Kessog's churchyard are early sculptured stones and a 10thC sarcophagus. **Thistle Bagpipe Works** (0900-1700) is by the main A82. Sweeney's Cruises (tel. 01389 752376/751610) at Balloch, Cruise Loch Lomond (tel. 01301 702356/636) at Tarbet and Luss, and Macfarlane & Son (tel. 01360 870214) at Balmaha operate cruises throughout the year. Passenger ferries operate in summer between Rowardennan and Inverbeg, Luss and Tarbet, tel. Loch Lomond Ferry Service, 01360 870273, and to and from the largest island, Inchmurrin, tel. Inchmurrin Island Co., 01389 850245. *See* Excursion 2; Excursion 3, Inversnaid.

Macbeth (c1005-1057): The real-life Macbeth was not the villain depicted in Shakespeare's famous Scottish play. He did kill Duncan, but in battle, and had a prosperous and stable reign from 1040 till his death at the hands of Duncan's son, Malcolm Canmore. Macbeth was the son of a ruler of Moray but his castle there is unlikely to have been at Cawdor (*see* Excursion 9). *See also* Excursion 2, Birnam; Excursion 12, Glamis.

Macdonald, James Ramsay (1866-1937): Born in Lossiemouth (*see* Excursion 8), Ramsay Macdonald formed his first (minority) Labour government in 1923 but failed to bring about the social revolution that many of the party's supporters had hoped for. In 1929 he again led the party to power but in 1931 he resigned, in the face of opposition from the Independent Labour Party, to form a coalition National government. The new National government again went to the country in 1931 and was voted back, with a large majority, just prior to the Depression.

Mackintosh, Charles Rennie (1868-1928): Glasgow's most famous architect was born in the city and began his professional training in 1884. He also attended evening classes at the Glasgow School of Art. Together with Herbert MacNair and the sisters, Frances and Margaret Macdonald, 'The Four' became the major exponents of the 'Glasgow Style', related to other forms of Art Nouveau, but characterized, particularly

in Mackintosh's case, by elongations of form, geometric decoration and the extreme stylization of natural forms, as in his famous rose. Mackintosh married Margaret Macdonald, while MacNair and Frances also wed. In 1896 Mackintosh won the competition for the design of the new Glasgow School of Art building. Completed in 1909, it is considered his masterpiece and has often been claimed as a pioneering work of the Modern Movement. Other commissions included several tearooms, of which the Willow Tearoom (*see* Glasgow Walk) is the only survivor. His major private commission was The Hill House (*see* Helensburgh), while The Mackintosh House, part of the Hunterian Art Gallery (*see* Glasgow Attractions), contains the interiors of the Mackintoshes' own house. They left Glasgow in 1914 and eventually moved to France, where Mackintosh devoted himself to watercolours.

Mary Queen of Scots (1542-87): Mary was the daughter of James V of Scotland and his French queen, Mary of Guise, a marriage which continued the 'Auld Alliance' between Scotland and France against England. She became queen when only six days old but, for safety, spent most of her childhood in France during Henry VIII's 'Rough Wooing' of Scotland and the young queen. In 1558 she married the French Dauphin and was briefly queen of France (1559-60), but returned to Scotland in 1561 after the death of her husband, Francis II. She came back to a Protestant country. She retained her own Roman Catholic religion but accepted the Reformation (*see* A-Z) of the Church of Scotland. In 1565 she married her first cousin, Lord Darnley. Both had a claim to the English throne to which Elizabeth I had succeeded in 1558. Darnley was involved in the murder of the queen's secretary, Rizzio, in 1566, and was himself murdered in 1567. Mary's third husband, the Earl of Bothwell, was believed to have been involved in Darnley's murder and the new marriage was disastrous in alienating many of her supporters. After imprisonment at Loch Leven Castle (*see* Excursion 13) by her nobles and defeat at the Battle of Langside in 1568, Mary fled to England and sought the protection of her cousin, Elizabeth. Fearing Roman Catholic plots, the English queen had her imprisoned and eventually executed. Mary has become the most romantic and tragic figure in Scottish history. *See also* Excursion 3, Inchmahome Priory; Excursion 14, Jedburgh; Dumbarton, Dunbar, Hermitage Castle.

Moffat: TIC: Churchgate, tel. 01683 220620, Easter-Oct. In the Borders off the A74 and at the western end of the A708, Moffat has been a burgh since 1648, while its sulphur springs made it a popular spa town in the 18thC. **Moffat Museum** (1030-1300, 1430-1700 Mon.-Tue. & Thu.-Sat., 1430-1700 Sun., Easter & late May-Sep.; Inexpensive) is in an old bakehouse in the older part of town and has a Scotch oven. **Craigieburn Woodland Garden** (1230-2000 Wed.-Sun., Easter-Oct.; Inexpensive) has the UK's largest collection of Himalayan plants, while **Tweedhope Sheepdogs Centre** (1030-1630 Mon.-Fri., demonstrations 1100 & 1500 Easter-Oct.; weekends & Nov.-Mar. by arrangement, tel. 01683 221471) shows the skills of working Border Collie sheepdogs. **Moffat Woollen Mill** (0900-1730 April-Sep., 0930-1600 Oct.-Mar.; Free) has the story of wool. 6 miles north on the A701 is the Devil's Beef Tub, a great hollow in the hills near the source of the River Annan, where beef cattle were often hidden after Border raids. 10 miles northeast off the A708 is the

Grey Mare's Tail (NTS), a stunning 200 ft waterfall from Loch Skeen above. Keep to the paths and take great care.

Music: Bagpipes are the instrument most commonly associated with Scotland. Pipe music can be heard at Highland Games, the Edinburgh Military Tattoo and other festivals (*see* Festivals), while some of the history is given at the piping museum in Skye (*see* Excursion 5). Traditional Scottish music, typically consisting of reels, jigs, strathspeys and hornpipes, is also played on a number of other instruments, notably the fiddle. Shetland fiddle music and fiddlers are among the most famous but many towns throughout Scotland have accordion and fiddle societies with regular programmes of events. Song is a major element of Gaelic music. Particularly fascinating is the unaccompanied 'mouth music', some of it consisting of strong rhythms and nonsense words to accompany the pounding of cloth ('waulking' songs). Gaelic singing can be heard at the National Mod and at the concerts associated with each *feis* or Gaelic festival. The 'bothy ballads' of Aberdeenshire, Border ballads, Burns' songs and many others make up a huge repertoire of traditional song which may be heard at the many festivals of folk and traditional music, or performed by local singers and bands in pubs. Balnain House, Inverness (*see* A-Z) provides an introduction to Scottish music and visitors can try playing traditional instruments. *See* Events, Festivals, Hebrides.

North Berwick: TIC: Quality St, tel. 01620 892197. A traditional and attractive resort on the shores of the Forth, east of Edinburgh. Set in the rocks beside the pleasant harbour is a heated open-air pool, while the **Museum** (1000-1300, 1400-1700 Mon. & Sat., 1400-1700 Fri. &

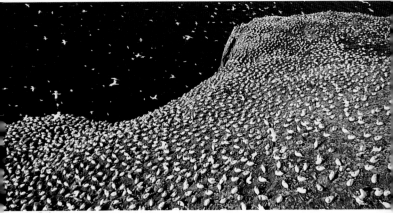

Bass Rock

Sun., Easter-May & mid Sep.-Oct.; 1000-1300, 1400-1700 Mon.-Sat., 1400-1700 Sun., June-mid Sep.; Free) on School St has local and natural history. The Bass Rock lies offshore, a 350 ft island with thousands of seabirds, including the world's third-biggest colony of gannets. For boat trips, tel. 01620 892838. Just beyond the town off the A198 is Berwick Law, a 613 ft volcanic plug with a watch tower from Napoleonic times and a whalebone arch. From here are spectacular views across the firth. Further east is **Tantallon Castle** (HS, except 0930-1300 Thu. and closed Fri., Oct.-Mar.; Inexpensive), on shoreline cliffs, built in 1375 and finally destroyed by Gen. Monk in 1651. To the west of North Berwick is the pretty village of Dirleton, with a village green and the splendid ruin of **Dirleton Castle** (HS; Inexpensive), dating back to 1225 and with an early 'donjon' tower. 4 miles south at East Fortune is the **Museum of Flight** (1030-1630 April-Sep.; Inexpensive), with a collection of aircraft, aero engines and even rockets.

Oban: TIC: Argyll Sq., tel. 01631 563122. Oban is an important railway terminus and ferry port, and a lively centre for tourism and yachting. It has been a popular resort since Victorian times, and now has sports facilities and outdoor activities. It is also a good base from which to explore the surrounding area and islands. Caledonian Macbrayne, Railway Pier (reservations: tel. 01631 562285, enquiries: tel. 01631 566688) runs car ferries to Mull, Lismore, Coll, Tiree, Colonsay, Barra and South Uist, and also offers cruises to many islands, including Iona and Staffa. There is a sandy beach at Ganavan, 2 miles north of the town, beyond the remains of 13thC Dunollie Castle, once a MacDougall stronghold. Prominent on the skyline above the town centre is McCaig's Folly, a 19thC circular 'ruin' reminiscent of the Colosseum in Rome and the brainchild of local banker, John Stuart McCaig, partly to ease unemployment in the area. It can be reached on foot up Craigard St, towards the north end of George St (the main street along the harbour front). Another good viewpoint is Pulpit Hill, above the south end of the harbour, and reached from Argyll Sq. via Albany St. Both look over to Mull (*see* Excursion 5) and Kerrera, the island 4 miles long which protects the entrance to Oban harbour and accessible by passenger ferry from 2 miles south of the town (*see* Excursion 4). It contains the ruins of 16thC Gylen Castle, another MacDougall stronghold. In the town itself, **Oban Distillery** (0930-1700 Mon.-Fri.; also Sat., Easter-Oct., last tour 1600; Inexpensive) produces a classic malt. An exhibition gives the history of this 1794 distillery built as a brewery. **A World in Miniature** (1000-1800 April-Oct.; Inexpensive) on nearby North Pier houses an unusual exhibition of British miniaturists, with displays of tiny rooms, models, dioramas, etc. 10 miles north on the A838, **Oban Sealife Centre** (0900-1800 Feb.-June & Sep.-Nov.; 0900-1900 July & Aug.; 0900-1800 Sat. & Sun., Dec. & Jan.; Moderate) has sharks, seals and rays. *See* Excursions 4, 5.

Orkney: This group of islands off the north coast of Scotland is mainly low-lying with much good agricultural land, though there are also spectacular cliffs and formations such as the Old Man of Hoy. Not only have more ancient monuments survived here than on the British mainland, but the monuments themselves, including the prehistoric village of Skara Brae, the stone circle Ring of Brodgar, and Maes Howe chambered cairn, are of outstanding quality. The islands were settled by Vikings in the 9thC AD and passed to the Scottish Crown only when the Danish King Christian I pledged them as security for part of his daughter's dowry in her marriage to James III in 1468. Viking influences remain strong in the culture. In both World Wars the British

fleet was anchored in Scapa Flow. In recent decades Orkney has benefited from North Sea oil. It has a very lively arts scene, partly due to the writer, George Mackay Brown, and the composer, Sir Peter Maxwell Davies, and includes the St. Magnus Festival in June. *See* Excursion 7.

Paisley: TIC: Town Hall, Abbey Close, tel. 0141 889-0711. Though only 7 miles southwest of central Glasgow, this large, mainly industrial town retains its independent character. **Paisley Abbey** (1000-1500 Mon.-Sat.) was founded with Cluniac monks c1163 by Walter Fitzalan, steward of King David I, and replaced the Celtic foundation of St. Mirren (now the name of Paisley's football team). Burned by the English in 1307, it was largely rebuilt in the 15thC. The 1499 chapel of St. Mirren has a carved wall frieze with scenes from the life of the saint, an unusual survival in Protestant Scotland. Tombs include one possibly that of Marjory Bruce, daughter of Robert the Bruce (*see* A-Z) and mother of the first Stewart king. The Barochan Cross may date from the 8thC. The so-called Place or Palace of Paisley was originally part of the abbey's monastic buildings. Paisley is also synonymous with shawls and thread. In the 19thC the Coats company was responsible for much of the town's thread manufacture and the family is commemorated by the **Thomas Coats Memorial Church** (1400-1600 Mon., Wed. & Fri., April-Sep.) of 1894, and **Coats Observatory** (1400-2000 Mon., Tue. & Thu., 1000-1700 Wed., Fri. & Sat.; Free), with meteorological and seismological as well as astronomical instruments. **Paisley Museum and Art Galleries** (1000-1700 Mon.-Sat.; Free) has the internationally important collection of Paisley shawls, as well as displays on their manufacture. The Kashmiri origins of the Paisley pattern are also explained. There are also good 19thC Scottish paintings, modern ceramics and local and natural history.

Paxton House: 1200-last tour 1615 Easter-Oct.; Moderate. Situated on the southeastern border of Scotland, off the A1 and A6105, is this fine 18thC Palladian country house with Adam (*see* A-Z) interiors, Chippendale furniture and a magnificent picture gallery with paintings from the National Galleries of Scotland.

Perth: TIC: 45 High St, tel. 01738 638353; Inveralmond, A9 City Bypass, tel. 01738 638481, April-Oct. Built on the banks of the River Tay, the 'Fair City' of Perth and ancient capital of Scotland became the Roman 'Bertha'. Until the Reformation, it was 'St. John's Toun', a name which survives in the local football club, St. Johnstone. **St. John's Kirk** (1000-1200, 1400-1600 Mon.-Wed. & Fri.-Sat.; also 1400-1600 Sun., June-Sep.) is mainly 15thC and was restored as a war memorial this century. It was here that John Knox (*see* Reformation) denounced the 'idolatry' of the Roman Catholic Church in 1559. The Fair Maid's House is a much-restored building on the site of Glover's Hall and was where Catherine Glover lived in Sir Walter Scott's (*see* A-Z) *The Fair Maid of Perth*. Nearby, **Perth Art Gallery and Museum** (1000-1700 Mon.-Sat.; Free), in an attractive classical-style building, has interesting local and natural history, archaeology and a good collection of mainly Scottish paintings and applied art. There are many fine Georgian buildings, notably Perth Waterworks (1832), a neoclassical rotunda which now houses the important **Fergusson Gallery** (1000-1700 Mon.-Sat.; Free), containing works by Scottish Colourist (*see* A-Z) J.D.

Branklyn Garden, Perth

Fergusson given to the city by the Fergusson Foundation. Balhousie Castle, originally 15thC but rebuilt, houses the **Black Watch Regimental Museum** (1000-1630 Mon.-Sat., May-Sep.; 1000-1530 Mon.-Fri., Oct.-April; Free), with displays on this famous Highland regiment. **Branklyn Garden** (0930-sunset, Mar.-Oct.; Inexpensive), off Dundee Rd in town, is a small 2 acre garden created earlier this century. It has such an outstanding collection of rhododendrons, alpines, herbaceous and peat-garden plants that it is visited by gardeners and botanists from all over the world. **Lower City Mills** (1000-1700 Mon.-Sat., April-Aug.; Inexpensive) have a working water-powered oatmeal mill. Towards the outskirts on Glasgow Rd are **Bell's Cherrybank Gardens** (0900-1700 May-mid Oct.; Inexpensive), with 18 acres of landscaped gardens, including the Bell's National Heather Collection. 2 miles west off the A85, **Huntingtower Castle** (HS, except 0930-1300 Thu. and closed Fri., Oct.-Mar.; Inexpensive) has two 15th-16thC towers linked by a 17thC range and contains fine painted decoration. 3 miles southeast is **Elcho Castle** (HS, exterior only), a 16thC fortified mansion with its original wrought-iron grilles. At Inveralmond, **Caithness Glass** (0930-1630 Mon.-Fri.; Free) has factory viewing of glass-making. 7 miles east on the A90,

Fairways Heavy Horse Centre (1000-1800 April-Sep.; Inexpensive) has Clydesdale horses. *See* Excursions 3, 12.

Picts: The Picts were the descendants of the Iron Age tribes of Scotland. They were first referred to as Picti or 'painted people' in a Latin poem of AD 297. A custom of painting or tattooing their bodies is not recorded elsewhere. They harassed the Romans through their frequent raids around and beyond Hadrian's Wall in the 3rd and 4thC AD. The kingdoms of the Scots and the Picts appear to have been united in the middle of the 9thC under Kenneth MacAlpine who was proclaimed king at Scone (*see* Excursion 12). Sueno's Stone, Forres (*see* Excursion 9) depicts a Pictish battle perhaps against the Vikings or the Scots. The meaning of many of the symbols on their fine carved stones is not always clear. Their largest known fort was at Burghead (*see* Excursion 9). *See also* Excursion 12, St. Vigeans & Meigle.

Prehistory: Scotland's visible prehistoric remains date from as early as the 4th millennium BC. Many of the best surviving monuments are in relatively remote areas such as the far north and the islands. The Callanish Standing Stones, Isle of Lewis (*see* Excursion 5), with their unique cross pattern, and the huge diameter (nearly 340 ft) of the Ring of Brodgar in Orkney (*see* Excursion 7), make these the most outstanding stone circles in Scotland and date from around the 3rd millennium BC. An unusual recumbent stone circle type also survives in the northeast of Scotland (*see* Excursion 11) where a Stone Circle Trail leaflet is available from local TICs. The precise significance of such monuments is not known, though they clearly had a ceremonial function, perhaps related to nearby burial sites. Burial monuments include round and chambered cairns, most of which are thought to date from the 3rd millennium BC. Good examples are Maes Howe, Orkney, the Grey Cairns of Camster (*see* Excursion 8), Caithness, and Clava Cairns (*see* Excursion 9), near Inverness. There are many sites of Iron Age hill forts, the most impressive perhaps being Tap o' Noth, Rhynie, near Huntly in the northeast. Brochs are a type of tower structure unique to Scotland, circular in plan with extremely thick double walls of stone, only one door and no windows. Dating from the 1st millennium BC to the first centuries AD, they were certainly defensive structures, perhaps for use by farming communities in times of attack. The best preserved is at Mousa, Shetland (*see* Excursion 10), and other remains are found, often near the sea, throughout the islands of the north and west, and the Highlands. Crannogs were another type of defensive structure, this time in lochs, notably Lochs Tay, Ness, Awe and Venachar and Lake of Menteith. They were artificial islands of timber and stone, possibly for dwellings and were linked to the shore by an underwater causeway. The finest surviving prehistoric settlement is of course Skara Brae, Orkney, dating from the 3rd-4th millennium BC, while Jarlshof in Shetland dates from the Bronze Age up to the 9thC AD and later. A number of earthhouses or souterrains, underground stores built in the form of stone passages, survive in the north and on Tayside. Fine examples include Culsh (*see* Excursion 11), at Tarland on Deeside, Ardestie and Carlungie off the A92 between Dundee and Arbroath, and Tealing, off the A929 north of Dundee. They date from the early centuries AD.

Raeburn, Sir Henry (1756-1823): Along with Ramsay (*see* A-Z), Raeburn is one of Scotland's most important portrait painters. Born in Edinburgh, he began his painting career as a miniaturist. After a brief visit to Italy in 1784, his distinctive rich and bold style began to emerge. By contrast with Ramsay's, his compositions were much sketchier, his paint handling much broader and his colouring and tones much warmer. His portraits of Sir Walter Scott (see A–Z) used dramatic light and shade to suggest his sitter's qualities of imagination and genius, while compositions such as *Col. Alasdair McDonnell of Glengarry* (National Gallery of Scotland, Edinburgh) also used light to create powerful images. His portraits of the fiddler Neil Gow (Scottish National Portrait Gallery) and of the Rev. Thomas Walker skating on Duddingston Loch (National Gallery of Scotland) have tremendous naturalism.

Ramsay, Allan (1713–84): One of Scotland's greatest portrait painters. He studied in London under the Swedish portrait painter Hans Hysing and in 1736 visited Rome and Paris. He practised successfully as a portrait painter in both London and Edinburgh but although he painted many of the fashionable figures of his day, his works were much more than mere society portraits. His paintings of women, notably the one of his second wife, Margaret Lindsay, in the Scottish National Portrait Gallery, Edinburgh, show his sensitivity to character and his ability to convey intelligence. The cool lighting, assured draughtsmanship and frank observation of his portraits perfectly reflected the ideas of the Enlightenment (see A–Z) in Scotland. Other important portraits are of Dr William Hunter, the scientist and founder of the Hunterian Museum, Glasgow (in the Hunterian Art Gallery) and David Hume, leading Enlightenment philosopher (Scottish National Portrait Gallery).

Reformation, The: The religious revolution which swept through Europe in the 16thC challenged the authority of the Roman Catholic Church and led to the establishment of the Protestant Church. Its influence was first felt in Scotland through individuals who had contact abroad with the ideas of Luther and Calvin. Early martyrs were Patrick Hamilton (1528) and George Wishart (1546) (see St. Andrews). But it was John Knox (c1513–72) who was most instrumental in changing Scotland into a Calvinist country. He had trained as a priest in the Roman Catholic Church but supported George Wishart and became one of the Reformers who avenged Wishart's death with that of Cardinal Beaton and the occupation of St. Andrews Castle. For this he served as a prisoner on the galleys in 1547-8. Later, in Geneva, he developed his Calvinist principles and eventually rejected Episcopalian ideas in favour of Presbyterianism. In 1557, members of the Scottish nobility who called themselves the 'Lords of the Congregation' began the process of reforming the Church. Knox returned in 1559. He preached against 'idolatry' in Perth (see A–Z) but criticized the destruction of churches and monasteries which followed. He was ordained as minister of St. Giles, Edinburgh, where there is now a bronze statue to him. He is also remembered for his pamphlet, *The First Blast of the Trumpet Against the Monstrous Regiment of Women*, and for his uncompromising attitude towards Mary Queen of Scots (see A–Z). In 1560, Parliament abolished the authority of the Pope and established the Protestant religion. Thereafter the Church of Scotland was organized along Presbyterian lines. The reform process was continued by Andrew Melville (1545-1622), who argued for the complete separation of Church and State.

Rennie, John (1761-1821): Born at Phantassie in East Lothian, Rennie studied at Edinburgh University and became one of the most famous and sought-after engineers of his day. His most admired bridge is at Kelso, built 1799-1808 (*see* Excursion 14). He was also the engineer of the Crinan Canal (*see* Excursion 4) in Argyll, constructed 1793-1801, and of part of Leith Docks from 1799. In England he designed many of the bridges over the Thames in London, including Waterloo Bridge and London Bridge. He is buried in Westminster Abbey.

Robert the Bruce (1274-1329): Robert I or Robert the Bruce is regarded as one of Scotland's greatest heroes for his decisive defeat of the English at Bannockburn (*see* Stirling) which assured the continuation of the nation's independence at least for the duration of Bruce's reign. After Wallace's (*see* A-Z) death, while Scotland was still in the grip of Edward I of England ('the Hammer of the Scots'), Bruce stabbed to death John Comyn, a rival claimant to the Scottish throne, at Greyfriars Friary, Dumfries (*see* A-Z) in 1306, then had himself crowned King of Scots at Scone (*see* Excursion 12). He was excommunicated by the Pope and the campaign to regain Scotland's independence went badly at first. Whether or not he saw a spider in any one of a number of caves off Scotland or Ireland, he returned to try again in 1307-8. He won a series of victories and his support increased: he was now backed by the Church, the French king and many of the clans. His greatest victory came in June 1314, at Bannockburn, when his army, although outnumbered at least two to one, defeated a force of 15,000-20,000 soldiers sent by Edward II. A widespread sense of nationhood in Scotland was part of Bruce's achievement, as witnessed by the extraordinary Declaration of Arbroath (*see* Excursion 12) of 1320, while in 1328 Edward III formally recognized Scottish independence under the Treaty of Northampton. Bruce died in 1329 and was buried in Dunfermline Abbey (*see* Excursion 13), but his heart was said to have been carried into battle against the Muslims in Spain by Sir James Douglas and is now thought to be buried at Melrose (*see* Excursion 14).

Rob Roy (1671-1734): Robert Macgregor, popularly known as Rob Roy (Red Robert) because of his red hair, was an outlaw and cattle thief, but has tended to be regarded as a folk hero, partly due to the romanticization by Sir Walter Scott (*see* A-Z) in his novel *Rob Roy* of 1818. The recent film with Liam Neeson has not greatly altered this image. His home territory was the Trossachs, where he began as a cattle dealer but was declared an outlaw after an employee of his stole letters of credit regarding a loan from the Duke of Montrose. He turned to sheep and cattle stealing and 'blackmail' or protection rackets involving black cattle once it was no longer possible to continue legitimate cattle dealing. He escaped from custody twice but eventually gave himself up in 1725 and received a royal pardon. His grave is believed to be at Balquhidder. *See also* Excursion 3; Loch Lomond.

St. Andrew: The adoption of the disciple St. Andrew as patron saint of Scotland appears to have been due to the 8thC Pictish King Angus, who is credited with establishing the first church dedicated to St. Andrew at Kinrymont, now St. Andrews. Part of the legend states that he devoted himself to the saint after the St. Andrew's Cross formed in the sky before a battle. It was also believed that relics of the saint had been brought to St. Andrews from the Greek island of Patras by St. Rule or Regulus. The saint's shrine at St. Andrews became an important place of pilgrimage in medieval times, encouraged by St. Margaret (*see* A-Z) who, in the 11thC, is believed to have established the ferry across the Forth which gave pilgrims free passage.

St. Andrews: TIC: 70 Market St, tel. 01334 472021. A bustling town and seaside resort, St. Andrews owed its early importance to the pilgrimage to the shrine of St. Andrew (*see* A-Z). It also has Scotland's oldest university and, as the home of golf, attracts golfers from all over the world. The town repays exploration on foot, as there are many interesting and attractive old buildings to visit. **St. Andrews Cathedral** (HS; Inexpensive; ticket includes entrance to Cathedral Museum, St. Rule's Tower and St. Andrews Castle) comprises the ruins of Scotland's largest cathedral, begun in 1160. The most complete areas are at the east and west ends. Little remains of the priory, while the tall tower is all that stands of the earlier church of St. Rule. The museum in the Prior's House contains monuments and other material from the site, including the 8th-9thC St. Andrews Sarcophagus, which has exceptionally fine carvings. Nearby are the scant remains of the Celtic or Culdee Church of St. Mary of the Rock. **St. Andrews Castle** (same times and ticket as cathedral), at the edge of the rocky shore, originally dates from 1200, though the existing ruin is mainly 16thC. Built as the residence of the bishops, later archbishops, it witnessed many of the dramatic scenes of the Reformation (*see* A-Z). The bottle dungeon survives in which the Reformer George Wishart was imprisoned before he was burned, watched from the castle by Cardinal Beaton. The Cardinal was himself killed when Wishart's supporters, including

John Knox, took the castle. A mine and countermine survive of the siege techniques employed in 1546-7. St. Andrews University (contact TIC for details of tours) was created in 1410-14. Its first college, St. Salvator's, North St, was founded in 1450 by Bishop Kennedy whose very fine French tomb of c1460 is in the chapel, while a magnificent mace of 1461 is in the vestry. Outside in the cobbles, the initials 'PH' commemorate the burning here of Patrick Hamilton in 1528, which signalled the beginning of the Reformation in Scotland. Other early colleges were St. Leonard's (1512), near the cathedral, now a prestigious girls' school, and in South St, St. Mary's (1539), remodelled in the 19thC. **St. Andrews Preservation Trust Museum** (1400-1700 June-Sep.; Inexpensive) by the cathedral has local history, including reconstructed 19thC shops, in a fine merchant's house. Down on the links is the Royal and Ancient Golf Club, founded in 1754 and the headquarters of the world game. There are six courses, including the Old Course (advance reservations, all courses, tel. 01334 475757; *see* Sport). Nearby is the **British Golf Museum** (1000-1700 Thu.-Tue., Mar. & April; 1000-1730 May-Oct.; 1100-1500 Thu.-Mon., Nov.-Feb.; Moderate), which has the history of the game. **St. Andrews Sea Life Centre** (1000-1800; till 2100 July & Aug.; Moderate) has native marine species, including stingrays, sharks and conger eels. In the **Crawford Arts Centre** (1000-1700 Mon.-Sat., 1400-1700 Sun.; gallery Free) are changing art exhibitions and a studio theatre. The Byre Theatre (tel. 01334 476288) has repertory in the summer months. At the end of South St is the West Port, one of the few surviving city gates in Scotland. **St. Andrews Museum** (1000-1700 April-Sep.; Free) is in Kinburn Park and includes the history of the town. *See* Excursion 13.

Royal & Ancient Golf Club, St. Andrews

Students' Sunday Walk, St. Andrews

St. Andrews Beach

St. Andrews Castle

St. Columba (c521-597): Columba was an Irish monk of royal birth who was exiled with 12 companions to the island of Iona (*see* Excursion 5) in AD 563, where he founded the church and monastery which became the centre of Celtic Christianity. From there, he and his missionaries evangelized the Picts (*see* A-Z) of northern Scotland and founded a number of churches and religious communities.

St. Margaret (c1046-93): A Saxon princess born in Hungary. Her family fled the Norman Conquest in England and their ship, blown off course by gales, landed in Scotland. They were given sanctuary by the king, Malcolm Canmore, whom Margaret married c1070 at Dunfermline (*see* A-Z). Margaret is believed to have established the queen's ferry across the Firth of Forth which gave free passage to pilgrims on their way to St. Andrews (*see* A-Z). Norman influence in Scotland is thought to have increased due to her, and she is also credited with having brought the Celtic or Culdee Church into line with the Roman Church. She was buried at Dunfermline Abbey and canonized in 1250. Dunfermline has many places associated with her, while St. Margaret's Chapel at Edinburgh Castle (*see* Edinburgh) was perhaps built by her son, David I.

St. Ninian (c360-c432): By tradition, St. Ninian was a Briton whose family was converted to Christianity, possibly by invading Roman soldiers. He is believed to have been a Roman-trained bishop and to have returned to found a church and religious school – the first Christian foundations in Scotland – at Whithorn (*see* Excursion 1) in Galloway (the name comes from the ancient English *hwit aerne*, meaning 'white building'). He was the first recorded Christian missionary in Scotland.

Sanquhar: TIC: Tolbooth, tel. 01659 50185, Easter-Sep. On the A76, 26 miles northwest of Dumfries, Sanquhar is a small burgh whose **Post Office** (0900-1730 Mon.-Wed. & Fri., 0900-1230 Thu. & Sat.; Free) of 1783 is the oldest working post office in the world. The William Adam **Tolbooth** of 1735 contains a museum (1000-1700 Tue.-Sat., 1400-1700 Sun., April-Sep.; Free), with displays on local industries such as mining and crafts, including Sanquhar gloves. The site of the Mercat Cross commemorates Covenanters (*see* A-Z) who, in 1680 and 1685, affixed to the cross the Declarations of Sanquhar, renouncing allegiance to King Charles II. **Sanquhar Castle** (open access), now ruined, was the home of the Dukes of Queensberry before Drumlanrig Castle (*see* Thornhill).

Scots: The Scots are thought to have arrived in Argyll from Ireland around AD 400-500. Their kingdom was known as Dalriada and their kings are believed to have been proclaimed at Dunadd (*see* Excursion 4). St. Columba (*see* A-Z) was supported by the Scots of Dalriada, notably Aidan, who was proclaimed king by Columba. Their centre moved to Scone (*see* Excursion 11) with the union of the Scots and the Picts under Kenneth MacAlpine.

Scott, Sir Walter (1771-1832): Sir Walter Scott, one of Scotland's most famous and influential writers, was born and educated in Edinburgh. He became an advocate in 1792 and was appointed Sheriff of Selkirk in 1799. He had fallen in love with the Borders and its rich ballad tradition when, as a child, he was sent to his grandfather's farm at Sandyknowe, near Smailholm (*see* Excursion 14). His collection of Border ballads appeared in 1802-3 and he became famous for his Romantic narrative poems such as *The*

Scott's View

Lay of the Last Minstrel (1805) and *The Lady of the Lake* (1810). Now most famous as the author of the Waverley novels, including *Rob Roy* (1818), *Ivanhoe* (1819) and *Redgauntlet* (1824), his authorship of them was kept secret for many years since novels were not considered a particularly respectable form of literature. He was made a baronet in 1820 and in 1822-4 was involved in the most ambitious phases of the creation of his 'country seat' at Abbotsford (*see* Excursion 14). His health suffered after a financial crisis of 1826. He has had a tremendous influence on Romantic and historical novels, narrative poetry, painting and opera throughout Europe and North America. This century, however, he has been accused of obscuring much of Scottish history through his romanticizations. The fact that most Scots now accept the kilt and tartan as national rather than Highland dress is a measure of Scott's influence.

Scottish Colourists: This term is used to group together four Scottish artists: S.J. Peploe, Leslie Hunter, F.C.B. Cadell and J.D. Fergusson, whose styles were all formed in the early years of the 20thC, when they had contact with French art, notably Post-Impressionists such as Matisse and the so-called Fauves or 'wild beasts', Picasso and Cézanne. Their work is characterized by distinctive, bright colour and had strong design qualities. Common subjects were still life, landscape, interiors such as *The Orange Blind* (Glasgow Art Gallery and Museum) in the case of Cadell, and nudes in the case of Fergusson, many of whose works can now be seen at the Fergusson Gallery, Perth (*see* Perth).

Shetland: The Romans called these northern islands Ultima Thule, or 'the final frontier', yet Shetland was not so remote as to discourage early settlers. On the contrary, there are remains dating back beyond the 3rd millennium BC. For the Vikings, who colonized the islands from the 9thC AD, Shetland was at the geographical centre of their world. The islands only became part of Scotland in 1469 when Christian I of Denmark, who had already pledged Orkney (*see* A-Z) to Scotland as security for part of the dowry of his daughter Margaret in her marriage to James III, failed to raise enough money for the rest of the dowry and pledged Shetland instead. The Viking influence remains strong, as illustrated by the place names, the annual festival of Up-Helly-Aa, and also by the Shetland dialect which contains many Norse words. The traditional occupations of crofting, fishing and knitting using Shetland wool and intricate Fair Isle patterns, still remain, although the islands' economy was radically improved by the construction of the Sullom Voe North Sea oil terminal in the 1970s. The Shetlanders are lively and outgoing people whose spirit is reflected in their famous Shetland fiddle music. *See* Excursion 10.

Small Isles: The Small Isles are the Inner Hebridean islands of Eigg, Muck, Rum and Canna which lie a short distance to the south of Skye. They can be reached by passenger ferry from Mallaig, tel. Caledonian Macbrayne 01687 462403. The largest is Rum, formerly spelt Rhum, with an area of 64 sq. miles, a wild and mountainous island rising to 2659 ft, of great interest to naturalists, birdwatchers, geologists and hillwalkers. It is a National Nature Reserve and anyone planning to stay overnight must seek permission to camp from the Reserve Office, The Whitehouse, Rum PH43 4RR, tel. 01687 462026. Luxury accommodation is available at Kinloch Castle, near the ferry landing, a magnificent residence built in 1901 by Sir George Bullough, then owner of the island, and now run by Scottish Natural Heritage, tel. 01687 462037. Eigg (5 miles by 2.5 miles) has a distinctive, rocky hill, the Scuir of Eigg. The Singing Sands of Camus Sgiolaig on the beach in the northwest of the island squeak or 'sing' when walked on, or sometimes even when blown by the wind. Muck and Canna are smaller and flatter, with sparse populations and no services, but provide pleasant and secluded walking.

Staffa: The tiny island of Staffa lies off the west coast of Mull, and can be reached by boat from Oban, tel. Caledonian Macbrayne 01631 566688, or from Ulva Ferry (Turus Mara, tel. 01688 400242; Staffa Trips, tel. 01681 700358), or Fionnphort (Gordon Grant Marine, tel. 01681 700338) on Mull (see Excursion 5). It is composed of basalt lava, which on the south and west coasts can be seen in spectacular cliffs of hexagonal columns, formed by the contraction of the lava as it cooled. The island is famous for Fingal's Cave, a sea-filled cavern which penetrates almost 230 ft into the cliffs, with a roof 65 ft high. The composer Mendelssohn visited the cave in 1820 and was inspired to write his famous *Hebrides Overture*.

Stevenson, Robert Louis (1850-94): This world-famous writer was born in Edinburgh, into a family of famed engineers and designers of lighthouses (see Excursion 12, Bell Rock; Coll & Tiree). He lived with his family at 17 Heriot Row, in the city's New Town. He qualified as an advocate at Edinburgh University in 1867, but made his name as a writer with such works as *A Child's Garden of Verse*, *Treasure Island*, *Kidnapped* and *The Strange Case of Dr Jekyll and Mr Hyde*. His own life was full of adventure despite being the sickly child glimpsed in 'The Lamplighter' in *A Child's Garden of Verse*. He felt constricted by Edinburgh society and fell in love with Fanny Vandegrift Osbourne, an American older than himself and estranged from her husband. They were eventually married in 1880. In 1888 they set sail for the South Seas. He died in Samoa in the South Pacific and is buried there. A monument to him is in St. Giles.

Stirling: TIC: Dumbarton Rd, tel. 01786 475019; Visitor Centre, Castle Esplanade, tel. 01786 479901; Pirnhall Service Area, Junction 9, M9, tel. 01786 814111, Mar.-Nov. Dominated by its castle with its superb defensive position overlooking the Forth valley, Stirling was of great strategic importance in the past and was known as the 'Key to the Kingdom'. Battles fought around Stirling included Stirling Bridge in 1297, William Wallace's (see A-Z) great victory, and Bannockburn in 1314, where Robert the Bruce (see A-Z) triumphed. The present 15thC Stirling Old Bridge may be the site of the battle. **Bannockburn Heritage Centre** (NTS, 1100-1500 Mar. & Nov.-Dec., 1000-1730 April-Oct.; Inexpensive), signposted from motorway Junction 9, has an exhibition and audiovisual presentation on the battle, while a rotunda incorporates fragments of the Borestone,

Stirling Castle

said to have been Bruce's command post. The **Royal Burgh of Stirling Visitor Centre** (0930-1830 April-June & Sep.-Oct., 0900-1830, till 2100 Tue., July & Aug., 0930-1700 Nov.-Mar.; Free) on Castle Esplanade provides a good introduction to this historic town through audiovisuals, film and viewing windows with commentary. **Stirling Castle** (HS, 0930-1715 April-Sep., 0930-1615 Oct.-Mar.; Moderate) combines military fortress and royal palace. The Great Hall (c1500) with magnificent hammerbeam roof is under restoration, while work continues on the Chapel Royal, which has rare 17thC illusionistic painted decoration. The 16thC Palace is an important early example of Renaissance architecture in Britain. **The Regimental Museum of the Argyll and Sutherland Highlanders** (1000-1730 Mon.-Sat., 1100-1630 Sun., Easter-Sep.; 1000-1600 Mon.- Sat., Oct.-Easter; Free) is also at the castle. On the left coming from the castle is the **Argyll Lodging** (HS, tel. 0131 668-8600), considered one of the finest Renaissance mansions in Scotland. Part of it, including the newly restored High Dining Room and living quarters of the 1680s, opens in June 1996. On the

right, Mar's Wark (c1570) is another splendid Renaissance building, though unfinished. Beyond it is the **Church of the Holy Rude** (1000-1700 Mon.-Fri., May-Sep.), where the infant King James VI was crowned in 1567. Further on to the right is the Guildhall (1649), formerly an almshouse for 'decayed' merchants. Down Spittal St are many interesting buildings, including 17thC Spittal's Hospital, incorporating an earlier panel with scissors and the inscription of the founder, Robert Spittal, King James IV's tailor. Down Broad St is the Tolbooth (town hall) and former jail, now a theatre (tel. 01786 451142). **The Smith Art Gallery and Museum** (1030-1700 Tue.-Sat., 1400-1700 Sun.; Free) has local and social history. A mile east are the ruins of Cambuskenneth Abbey, where Robert the Bruce held a parliament in 1326. 1.5 miles northeast off the A907, the 19thC **National Wallace Monument** (1000-1700 Mar.-May & Oct., 1000-1800 June & Sep., 0930-1830 July & Aug., 1000-1600 Sat. & Sun., Feb. & Nov.; Inexpensive), the 220 ft tower on top of Abbey Craig, has a multimedia presentation on Wallace and superb views. *See* Excursion 3.

Telford, Thomas (1757-1834): Born in Dumfriesshire, Telford became one of Britain's most famous civil engineers. He began his career as a stonemason but became an engineer on major public projects with the help of his patron, William Pulteney MP. He was responsible for the layout of Ullapool (*see* Excursion 6) for the British Fisheries Society and designed the Caledonian Canal (*see* Excursion 2; Great Glen), opened in 1822. His bridges include Dean Bridge, Edinburgh and Craigellachie Bridge (*see* Excursion 11).

Thomson, Alexander 'Greek' (1817-75): Glasgow's other great architect who, unlike Charles Rennie Mackintosh (*see* A-Z) in recent years, has not yet received full recognition for his remarkable buildings which drew on Greek and Egyptian forms in a most innovative and imaginative way. Surprisingly, he never travelled abroad and instead assimilated his influences through books on architecture and the work of other Greek Revival architects. St. Vincent St Church, completed in 1859, has a dramatic hill site and features rich detail at the top of its tall tower and strange Egyptian-inspired doorways. Other buildings in the centre of Glasgow, such as the Grecian Chambers (1865), Sauchiehall St, and Egyptian Halls (1871), Union St, have a more subtle horizontal emphasis and incorporate unusual dwarf columns. *See* Glasgow Walk.

Thornhill: This pleasant village on the A76 14 miles northwest of Dumfries has the Queensberry monument of 1714. At Nith Bridge is a 9 ft Anglian cross-shaft thought to be 10thC. 3 miles north on the right off the A76 are the ruins of 14thC Morton Castle. **Drumlanrig Castle and Country Park** (castle 1100-1700 Fri.-Wed., Moderate; grounds 1100-1800;

Inexpensive, early May-late Aug.) is a 17thC Scottish Renaissance castle with square towers topped with turrets. Inside is exceptionally fine French furniture, plus paintings by Rembrandt, Holbein and Murillo, and even a Leonardo da Vinci, all part of the collections of the Duke of Buccleuch and Queensberry (*see* Excursion 14, Bowhill). Outside are gardens, woodland walks and a bicycle museum commemorating Kirkpatrick Macmillan (1813-78), inventor of the pedal bicycle. Northeast on the A702 is **Durisdeer Church** (open access), whose Queensberry aisle has an extraordinary Baroque baldacchino and the superb black and white marble tomb of the 2nd Duke of Queensberry by John Van Nost. Southwest on the A702 is **Maxwelton House** (1030-1730 Easter-Sep.; Inexpensive), birthplace of Annie Laurie, immortalized by the famous ballad.

Wallace, William (c1270-1305): Wallace was the first great hero of Scotland's struggle for independence from England after Alexander III's death in 1286. Wallace's campaign began when he murdered the English Sheriff of Lanark, perhaps to avenge his wife's murder, and was declared an outlaw. Thereafter he and his supporters made surprise attacks

Wallace Monument, Stirling

on English-held castles and barracks. The uprising culminated in Wallace's great victory at the Battle of Stirling Bridge in 1297, where, though the Scots were heavily outnumbered, they succeeded through tactics. He ruled as Guardian of Scotland for a year before Edward I, 'the Hammer of the Scots', sent an army north which defeated the Scots at the Battle of Falkirk. After it, Wallace went into hiding. In 1305 he was betrayed to the English and taken to London, where he was hanged, disembowelled, drawn and quartered. His head was placed on a pike on London Bridge, and his severed limbs were displayed in Scottish towns as a warning to other patriots. Wallace's campaign led the way for that of Robert the Bruce (*see* A-Z). Mel Gibson's recent film has aroused new interest in Wallace.

Wanlockhead: Scotland's highest village, at 1380 ft, lies not in the Highlands, but just 9 miles southwest of the M74 at Junction 13 and about the same distance from Sanquhar (*see* A-Z) and the A76. Mining of lead, silver and gold has gone on here and at nearby Leadhills since the 16thC or earlier, and the crowns of James V and his queen incorporated gold from the area. The lead mines have ceased production but the **Museum of Lead Mining** (1100-1630; tour Easter-Oct.) includes a guided tour down one of them, while miners' cottages show life here in the past. Nearby is the **Wanlockhead Beam Engine** (open access), a 19thC wooden water-balance pump, thought to be the only one still intact. 2 miles away, in Leadhills, the **Allan Ramsay Library** (1400-1600 Wed. & Sat.-Sun.; Inexpensive) is a fascinating survival, a subscription library founded in 1741 for the lead miners and named after the poet Allan Ramsay, whose father was an overseer at the mines. **Lowther's Railway** (1100-1700 Sat. &

Sun., Easter & May-Sep.; Moderate) was Britain's highest narrow-gauge adhesion railway. It has locomotives and rolling stock related to the local leadmining.

Wick: TIC: Whitechapel Rd (off High St), tel. 01955 602596. Wick is a pleasant fishing port ranged around the bay that gives it its name (*vik* is Old Norse for 'bay'). Places of interest include the award-winning **Wick Heritage Centre** (1000-1700 Mon.-Sat., June-Sep.; Inexpensive) at Bank Row, which is housed in several buildings. It has the largest museum collections in the north, with displays on themes ranging from prehistory to local industries, including the history of the world's largest herring-fishing port. On the south side of the town is the **Caithness Glass Factory**, which offers self-guided tours of the glassworks (0900-1700 Mon.-Fri.; Free). A few miles further south on the coast is the Castle of Old Wick, the ruin of an early Norse tower house on a spectacular site reached by a 10 min clifftop walk on which great care is needed. North of the town, near the lighthouse on Noss Head, are two more ruined castles – Castle Girnigoe and Castle Sinclair. *See* Excursion 8.

Wolf of Badenoch (d c1394): The nickname of Alexander Stewart, Earl of Buchan, the violent natural son of King Robert II, who had lands in Badenoch, around Kingussie. He was excommunicated by the Bishop of Moray in 1390 for leaving his lawful wife for another woman. In revenge, he destroyed Elgin and its cathedral (*see* Excursion 9), though he later did penance at Elgin's Mercat Cross for his atrocious deeds. An armoured effigy in Dunkeld Cathedral (*see* Excursion 2) may be of him.

Accidents & Breakdowns: If you are involved in an accident where no one has been hurt, exchange name, address and insurance details with the other driver, and take the names and addresses of any witnesses. Inform your insurance company or car rental firm as soon as possible. If there are any injuries, an ambulance should be called and the police must be informed. In the event of a breakdown, there are emergency telephones at regular intervals along motorways and major roads. In remote areas you may have to seek help from the nearest farm or village. Visitors who are members of motoring organizations belonging to the International Touring Alliance can summon assistance free of charge from the AA (Automobile Association) 24 hr breakdown service, tel. 0800 887766, or the RAC (Royal Automobile Club) 24 hr rescue service, tel. 0800 550550. *See* Consulates, Driving.

Accommodation: Scotland offers a huge range of holiday accommodation, from self-catering cottages to luxury hotels. Hotels range from intimate, family-run establishments to romantic castles and country houses, while the ubiquitous bed and breakfast offers excellent value. The B&B is usually a private home where a bedroom costs from as little as £12 per night. The bathroom is often shared, and a hearty cooked breakfast is included in the price. A hotel room with en suite bathroom will cost around £25-£80 per night, while self-catering accommodation (usually booked in advance) ranges from £80-£400 per week, depending on location, season, size and degree of luxury. The Scottish Tourist Board (STB) has a two-tier system for classifying hotels, guesthouses, B&Bs and self-catering accommodation. The range of facilities provided by an establishment is indicated by the classification, from 'Listed' for basic accommodation to five crowns for a luxury suite in hotels, guesthouses and B&Bs, and from one to five crowns for self-catering. Quality of service is shown by the Quality Assurance Grading, which may be Approved, Commended, Highly Commended or Deluxe. Hotel room prices must, by law, be prominently displayed. Regional lists of hotel, guesthouse, B&B and self-catering accommodation can be obtained free from the STB or local TICs (*see* Tourist Information). Also available from the STB and from bookshops are the following annual guides: *Scotland: Hotels and Guesthouses* (£6.99); *Scotland: Bed and Breakfast* (£4.99); and *Scotland: Self-Catering* (£5.50). Advance booking of accommodation is recommended for Easter weekend and July and Aug. The STB runs a free booking service called Book-a-Bed-Ahead. Simply ask at any TIC and they will reserve a room for you anywhere in Scotland. A small deposit is charged but will be deducted from your accommodation bill. Other cheaper forms of accommodation such as tourist hostels in cities and bunkhouses in rural areas are also available and are popular with backpackers, walkers, etc. The *Budget Accommodation Scotland* booklet is available free from the STB, while TICs have details of what is available locally. Climbers and walkers may also wish to contact the Mountain Bothies Association, tel. 01698 813258. *See* Camping & Caravanning, Youth Hostels.

Airports: Scotland has four international airports. These are siuated at Glasgow, Edinburgh, Aberdeen and Prestwick. Regular shuttle services operate from London to Glasgow, Edinburgh and Aberdeen. These three principal airports also have some regular scheduled flights to and from European airports. Most transatlantic flights now land at Glasgow, though some still fly to Prestwick. British Airways has many internal flights connecting the main cities to smaller outlying airfields. All four airports have modern terminals with tourist information, accommodation, bank, currency exchange, post office, restaurants and shops. Glasgow Airport has recently been extended and is now by far the largest. It is 9 miles west of the city centre, about 20 min by bus or taxi. Prestwick Airport is about 31 miles south of Glasgow, 1 hr away by bus or train, and about 80 miles from Edinburgh, around 2 hr by bus. Edinburgh Airport is 6 miles west of the city centre, about 30 min by bus or taxi. Aberdeen Airport is 7 miles northwest of the city centre, about 30 min by bus or taxi. British Airways offers a special Highland Rover ticket for five flights, with a special budget price for additional flights up to a maximum of 12. It is valid for any BA flights within Scotland and Northern Ireland, though each flight can only be taken once. Scottish airports covered by the ticket include Barra, Benbecula, Stornoway, Wick, Kirkwall (Orkney) and Lerwick (Shetland), as well as Inverness, Aberdeen, Edinburgh and Glasgow. Flights must be taken in a minimum of seven days, maximum three months. The ticket must be purchased at least seven days in advance. Information from British Airways, tel. 0345 222111. Flight information: Aberdeen, tel. 01224 722331; Edinburgh, 0131 333-1000; Glasgow, 0141 887-1111; Prestwick, 01292 479822.

Banks: Note that in a number of small towns and villages, banks may have only limited opening hours. In many parts of the Highlands and Islands, there are no permanent banks at all. Instead, mobile banks call at many places once or twice a week, usually for about 2 hr in the morning or afternoon. *See* Currency.

Best Buys: The high-quality products made in Scotland make good souvenirs. They include Harris tweed, hand-woven in the Outer Hebrides (*see* Hebrides), a hard-wearing woollen cloth coloured with natural dyes, which can be bought by the metre or made up into garments. A finer type is also becoming available. Scotland is also famous for quality woollens from the Borders and Shetland, including intricate Fair Isle patterns and fine wool shawls, all available at the many mill shops. If you can afford it, cashmere, though the wool itself is mainly imported, has traditionally been made in Scotland and is considered of unbeatable quality. Then, of course, there is tartan, produced in a wide variety of colour combinations, most of them associated with particular Scottish clans. Specialist shops can match Scottish-derived surnames to specific tartans. Tartan items range from ties, scarves, kilts and other garments to rugs and even pottery. There are many craft shops and workshops with handcrafted goods made from traditional materials. Silver jewellery in Celtic designs or, as in Orkney, using motifs derived from archaeological finds, will appeal to most tastes. Stones such as semi-precious cairngorms, either set in jewellery or uncut, make attractive souvenirs. Edinburgh Crystal and Caithness Glass produce high-quality crystal and glassware. Cassettes or CDs of traditional music are a good way of remembering a holiday. A taste of Scotland is also popular, from traditional shortbread (rich butter biscuits) or oatcakes to preserves, heather honey or sweets, including Edinburgh Rock. Some traditional foods such as smoked salmon and haggis (*see* Food) can be delivered for you all over the world or are available by mail order – ask at the shop. Finally, there is a vast selection of single-malt whiskies (*see* Drinks).

Bicycle Hire: Bicycles can be rented all over Scotland. TICs have the addresses of local hirers. Prices range from £4-£8 per day for a touring bike to £10-£12 per day for a 21-speed mountain bike. A returnable cash deposit of around £20 is usually required.

Boat Trips: Many local companies offer day, half-day and even shorter cruises around the coast of the mainland and the islands or on the busier lochs such as Loch Lomond (*see* A-Z) and Loch Ness. Types of boat can range from beautiful old steamers, the most famous of which is the *Waverley* (tel. 0141 221-8152), the world's last sea-going paddle steamer, with cruises on the Firth of Clyde in high season, to converted fishing boats which take visitors to see seals and seabirds. Caledonian Macbrayne and P&O also have special day trips (*see* Ferries). Details are available from TICs or enquire at harbours. A number of tour companies do cruises of several days using Caledonian Macbrayne or P&O ferries (details in the ferry brochures), with prices from around £250. The *Hebridean Princess* is a luxury cruise ship with prices from £700 to over £4,000. Details from Hebridean Island Cruises Ltd, Acorn Park, Skipton, North Yorks, BD23 2UE.

Buses: Scottish Citylink operates frequent coach services from Glasgow and Edinburgh to destinations all over Scotland. Prices are very reasonable compared to trains. Sample journey times are: Glasgow-Inverness 3 hr 25 min express; Edinburgh-Ullapool 9 hr 5 min. Tickets can be bought at bus stations or

through travel agents. Advance booking is available for some busy services. Timetables and fares are obtainable from St. Andrew's Bus Station, Edinburgh, tel. 0131 558-1616, or Buchanan Bus Station, Glasgow, tel. 0141 332-9191. The Tourist Trail Pass is valid on Scottish Citylink or National Express coach journeys throughout Britain. Tel. 0990 808080 for details. The Travelpass is also valid on selected bus routes (*see* Transport). In the Highlands and Islands, tiny postbuses are often the only public transport; details from local post offices or TICs.

Camping & Caravanning: This is a popular form of accommodation for summer visitors to Scotland, and there are many sites to choose from. The Scottish Tourist Board (*see* Tourist Information) issues an annual guidebook, *Scotland: Camping & Caravan Parks* (£3.99), which lists details and prices of over 400 parks throughout the country. Sites are also listed in the regional accommodation brochures available free from local TICs. They are inspected under the British Graded Holiday Parks Scheme and are graded from one tick for acceptable to five ticks for excellent, according to facilities and, especially, cleanliness. In Scotland, the Thistle Award may be made to individual luxury caravans. Note that caravans are not permitted to park overnight in car parks or lay-bys. For backpackers and hillwalkers, wild camping is possible in the more remote areas of the country. Wild camping is free; no official permits are required, but always try to get permission from the landowner first, and never leave litter.

Car Hire: Cars can be rented in most towns. You must be over 21 and in possession of a full driving licence with at least 12 months' experience. A large cash deposit will be required unless you are paying by credit card. Prices and systems of charging vary considerably among rental companies, so make sure you are aware of the full cost, including insurance, VAT and any mileage charge or other surcharges. Small, local firms often charge much lower prices than the nationwide chains, so it may be worth telephoning round and comparing quotes. Many companies have special weekend deals.

Edinburgh: Avis, 100 Dalry Rd, tel. 0131 337-6363; Arnold Clark, Lochrin Pl., tel. 0131 228-4747; Hertz, 10 Picardy Pl., tel. 0131 556-8311.

Glasgow: Avis, 161 North St, tel. 0141 221-2827; Arnold Clark, St. George's Rd, tel. 0141 334-9501; Hertz, 106 Waterloo St, tel. 0141 248-7736. *See* Driving.

Climate: Scotland has a reputation for wet and miserable weather. This is perhaps a little unfair as most visitors come in July and Aug., the two wettest months of the year. One of the best times to visit Scotland is in the spring, between mid-April and the end of June. Average temperatures are only 7-13°C but rainfall is at its lowest then. There are many sunny days and in the north in June it is dark for only 4-5 hrs out of 24. The scenery is particularly good there too, with rhododendrons and bluebells in bloom, while snow patches linger on higher mountains. July and Aug. are slightly warmer (average temperature 14-15°C) but much wetter. Note that the north and west are noticeably wetter than the south and east. Autumn (Sep. & Oct.) is another wonderful time to visit, when it is often dry and sunny, the hills are purple with heather, and trees are golden, red and brown. Winter (Nov.-Mar.) sees snow and rain and long, dark nights, but is popular with skiers, climbers and hillwalkers, and of course there is the traditional Scottish Hogmanay to celebrate.

Consulates: Embassies are located in London. Consuls in Scotland include:
Australia: Hobart House, 80 Hanover St, Edinburgh, tel. 0131 226-6271.
Canada: 3 George St, Edinburgh, tel. 0131 220-4333.
USA: 3 Regent Terr., Edinburgh, tel. 0131 556-8315.

Crime & Theft: Although crimes against visitors to Scotland are relatively rare, it is sensible to take the usual precautions against theft. Leave any valuables in the hotel safe and not in your room. Beware of pickpockets in crowded areas such as shopping centres and city railway stations. Always lock your car and keep any items of value locked out of sight in the boot. Report any theft to the police immediately, and if your passport has been lost or stolen, contact your consulate too. *See* Consulates, Police.

Currency: The British unit of currency is the pound sterling (£), equal to 100 pence (p). Banknotes come in denominations of £50 (red), £20 (purple), £10 (brown), £5 (blue) and £1 (green). The coins are £1, 50p, 20p, 10p, 5p, 2p and 1p. Note that the three Scottish banks – Bank of Scotland, Royal Bank of Scotland and Clydesdale Bank – all issue their own distinctive banknotes which are different in appearance (but not in value) from their English equivalents. Only Royal Bank £1 notes remain in circulation. Scottish banknotes are now widely accepted elsewhere in Britain but many people prefer to exchange them at a bank for Bank of England notes to avoid difficulty. Outside Britain, Scottish banknotes can almost never be exchanged. *See* Banks.

Customs: Visitors to the far northwest of Scotland, and especially to Lewis, Harris and North Uist (*see* Hebrides), should be aware that there is a strong tradition of Sabbath observance in this area. Everything is closed on Sun., including shops, pubs, ferries and public transport, and this should be taken into account when planning a trip.

Disabilities: The Scottish Tourist Board publishes a booklet, *Practical Information for Visitors with Disabilities to Scotland*, (50p), available from main TICs or by post from the STB (*see* Tourist Information). This gives information and advice on travel, accommodation, Artlink (access to arts venues), Shopmobility, sports, toilets, etc. It also lists access guides obtainable for different parts of Scotland and has a list of useful addresses. Almost all major attractions in Scotland have at least some kind of provision for wheelchair access. The National Trust for Scotland has made further provision at some of its sites, through interpretive material for a range of disabilities. This may include induction loops for hearing difficulties, tapes and Braille sheets for the visually impaired, and basic language tapes, as well as wheelchairs and wheelchair access. A detailed leaflet on these can be obtained at main sites or by post from the Trust (*see* National Trust for Scotland).

Driving: Driving in Britain is on the left-hand side of the road. The wearing of seat belts is compulsory for the driver and front-seat passenger, and also for back-seat passengers where seat belts are fitted. Most road signs conform to international standards. Speed limits are 30-40 mph/48-64 kph in built-up areas, 60 mph/96 kph on single-carriageway main roads and 70 mph/112 kph on dual carriageways and motorways. Driving conditions are generally good, though congestion in the city centres of Glasgow and Edinburgh can be frustrating, especially during the weekday peak hours 0800-0900 and 1700-1800. In addition, the centre of Glasgow has a one-way system which may confuse visitors. In the remote areas of Scotland many of the roads are single-track with passing places. They are wide enough for only one vehicle at a time, so drive carefully and use the passing places, usually marked with a striped pole, to allow oncoming traffic to pass. These passing places should also be used to allow following traffic to overtake you – local people are often frustrated by tourists who drive slowly but refuse to allow them to pass. Never park in a passing place. Many roads in the Highlands and Islands are unfenced, so be on the lookout for sheep, cattle and deer that have strayed onto the road. Also, petrol stations can be few and far between in the Highlands and they may close early and all day Sun. Fill up before starting your journey or check details of petrol stations with local TICs. *See* Accidents & Breakdowns, Car Hire.

Eating Out: The number, range and quality of eating places in Scotland have improved greatly in the last 20 years or so. Perhaps the most encouraging sign is the increased use of fresh, local produce. Other improvements include more imaginative food preparation and presentation, the revival of traditional dishes, healthier food and more provision for vegetarians. Taste of Scotland is a scheme supported by the Scottish Tourist Board, Scottish Enterprise and a number of Scottish food producers which selects around 400 eating establishments each year and publishes them in a guide, price £4.50, available from TICs, bookshops and

Taste of Scotland, 33 Melville St, Edinburgh EH3 7JF, tel. 0131 220-1900. Criteria for inclusion are use of fresh, local produce and good food preparation, presentation and service. Towns and cities have a wide range of eating places. Chinese, Indian, Italian and French cuisine are all widely available. Scottish cooking is still often harder to find. Some of the best restaurants are in rural areas, many with beautiful settings in country houses, castles, cottages, farmhouses and converted barns. Bar meals, sometimes only available at lunchtime, offer good value. Lunch is usually served 1200-1400 or 1430 and dinner 1800 or 1900-2200. *See* Edinburgh Restaurants, Glasgow Restaurants, Drinks, Food.

Events: The following is a selection of the annual events and festivals in Scotland:
January: Ba' Game (massive game of street football), Kirkwall, Orkney; Burning the Clavie (fire festival), Burghead; Up-Helly-Aa (Viking festival), Lerwick, Shetland; Celtic Connections (folk festival), Glasgow.
March: International Folk Music Festival, Edinburgh.
April: International Science Festival, Edinburgh; Links Market (Europe's largest street fair), Kirkcaldy; Festival of Traditional Music, Tobermory, Isle of Mull; Scottish Grand National, Ayr Racecourse; Shetland Folk Festival.
May: International Gathering of the Clans, Inverness; Mayfest (cultural festival), Glasgow; Scottish International Children's Festival, Edinburgh; River Tweed Festival, Borders towns; Blair Atholl International Highland Games; Jazz Festival, Isle of Bute.
June: Arran Folk Festival; International Jazz Festival, Glasgow; Lanimer Day (historic festival), Lanark; Royal Highland Show (Scotland's main

agricultural show), Edinburgh; St. Magnus Festival (arts festival), Orkney; Eyemouth Seafood Festival.
July-September: Highland Games, various locations.
July: International Highland Games, Aviemore; Riding of the Marches, Annan; Common Riding (riding the borders), Langholm; Shopping Week (music, dancing and events), Stromness, Orkney.
August: International Youth Festival, Aberdeen; Folk Music Festival, Isle of Skye; Aboyne Highland Games; Military Tattoo, International Festival, Festival Fringe, Film Festival, Jazz Festival, Edinburgh; Glenfinnan Gathering and Highland Games; Cowal Highland Gathering, Dunoon; World Pipe Band Championships, Glasgow.
September: Braemar Royal Highland Gathering; Ben Nevis Race (fell runners compete on the UK's highest mountain), Fort William; Kirriemuir Traditional Music Festival; Leuchars Air Show; Northlands Festival (celebrating arts links with other northern lands), Thurso and Wick; Burns Festival, Dumfries area.
October: National Mod (Gaelic music festival), at different venue each year; Aberdeen Alternative Festival.
30 November: St. Andrew's Day Celebrations, St. Andrews.
31 December: Fireball Ceremony, Stonehaven; Flambeaux Procession, Comrie; Edinburgh's Hogmanay; New Year Spectacular, Aberdeen.
More details and events are listed in the Scottish Tourist Board's free booklet, *Events in Scotland* (*see* Tourist Information). *See* Festivals, What's On.

Ferries: There are numerous ferries serving Scotland's many islands. The great majority of these are run by two large companies: Caledonian Macbrayne serves the Firth of Clyde and the Western

Isles, while P&O Scottish Ferries serves Orkney and Shetland. Services are frequent in summer (May-Sep.), less so in winter. Note that some ferries in the Western Isles do not operate on Sun. (*see* Customs). If you plan to take your car to the islands during the high season (July & Aug.), advance reservation is recommended, either through a travel agent or direct with the ferry companies (see telephone numbers below). If you intend to use a number of Caledonian Macbrayne ferry services, there are special Island Rover tickets which work out cheaper than buying individual tickets for each ferry. Island Hopscotch tickets are available for 23 routes among the Hebrides. They are valid for a month and can be used for one trip on each leg of the route. For the northern isles, special day trip fares to Orkney and round trips to Orkney and Shetland offer the best value. Information is available from main TICs or from the ferry companies: Caledonian Macbrayne, The Ferry Terminal, Gourock PA19 1QP, tel. 01475 650100; P&O Scottish Ferries, PO Box 5, Jameson's Quay, Aberdeen AB9 8DL, tel. 01224 572615. *See* Boat Trips.

Guides: Guided coach tours and walking tours are available for all popular tourist areas: ask at TICs or travel agents. If you would like your own qualified, 'blue badge' guide, write for information to the Scottish Tourist Guides Association (STGA), 6 Springfield Ave, Uddingston, Glasgow G71 7LY or contact local branches: 32 Henderson Dr., Aberdeen AB31 6RA, tel. 01224 741314; 23 Mains Terr., Dundee DD4 7BZ, tel. 01382 462228; 14 East Court, Thistle Foundation, Niddrie Mains Rd, Edinburgh EH16 4ED, tel. 0131 661-7977; 3 Myrtle Ave, Lenzie, Glasgow G66 4HW, tel. 0141 776-1052; Wester Knockfarrie, Pitlochry PH16 5DN, tel. 01796 472020.

Health: Under Britain's National Health Service, overseas visitors are eligible for free emergency treatment at hospital accident and emergency departments. Nevertheless, you are strongly recommended to take out adequate medical insurance before your trip. EU nationals can take advantage of reciprocal health care arrangements by filling out form E111 before the trip. Contact your own health service for details. In a medical emergency, tel. 999 and ask for an ambulance. There are 24 hr accident and emergency departments at hospitals in the main cities of Edinburgh, Glasgow, Dundee and Aberdeen. In the Highlands and Islands, the main hospitals are in Inverness and Fort William, and emergency cases in remote areas are often airlifted to one of these by helicopter. For less serious complaints, make an appointment to see a local doctor. Your hotel or the local police station will have a list of doctors and dentists. *See* Midges.

Historic Scotland: This organization looks after Scotland's ancient monuments, as well as many historic buildings, totalling well over 300 sites in all, on behalf of the Secretary of State for Scotland. Most of the staffed sites under the care of HS have the following standard opening times: 0930-1830 Mon.-Sat., 1400-1830 Sun., April-Sep.; 0930-1600 Mon.-Sat., 1400-1630 Sun., Oct.-Mar. Last admission is 30 min before closing. Some smaller sites close for lunch and a number have limited opening or are closed completely in winter. Principal sites charge a small admission fee and guidebooks can be purchased. Many smaller sites are free, unattended and open at all reasonable times. Annual membership gives free access to all sites. Explorer Tickets are also available. For details contact Historic Scotland,

Longmore House, Salisbury Pl., Edinburgh EH9 1SH, tel. 0131 668-8600.

Midges: These tiny biting insects are the bane of Scottish summers. They appear in their thousands on open ground between June and Sep. and tend to be worst in the West Highlands. Fortunately, their bite is irritating rather than dangerous in all but a few very rare instances. However, a good insect repellant is an absolute must for all outdoor activities in the west and north in summer.

National Trust for Scotland (NTS): This organization was founded in 1931, with the aim of preserving places of historic interest and natural beauty in Scotland. It is a registered charity supported by members' subscriptions, admission fees and voluntary contributions. It cares for over 100 sites, as different in character as Glencoe (see Excursion 2) and Culzean Castle (see Excursion 1) or Inverewe Garden (see Excursion 6) and the Tenement House (see Glasgow Walk). Membership gives free admission to all NTS properties, and also to a further 300 National Trust properties in the rest of the UK. For further information contact the NTS head office at 5 Charlotte Sq., Edinburgh EH2 4DU, tel. 0131 226-5922.

Newspapers: Scotland's national newspapers are the broadsheet *Scotsman* and *Herald*, and the tabloid *Daily Record*. UK national dailies are usually available throughout Scotland, but in the far north and west morning editions do not arrive in the shops until the afternoon. There are also a number of regional dailies, including the Aberdeen *Press & Journal*, sometimes the only daily obtainable in the north, the *Dundee Courier* and the *Oban Times*. These and the local weekly newspapers are good sources of information on local events. Scottish Sunday newspapers are the broadsheet *Scotland on Sunday*, and the tabloid *Sunday Mail* and *Sunday Post*. *See* What's On.

Police: Scottish police wear a dark uniform and black peaked cap with a chequered band. They are not armed and are generally friendly and helpful in their dealings with visitors. In an emergency, tel. 999 and ask for the police. *See* Crime & Theft.

Post Offices: These are indicated by a red sign with yellow lettering. In small towns and villages the post office is often in the village store. An increasing number of post offices are now found in supermarkets and shopping centres. Letter boxes are painted bright red and display the times of collections. Post offices sell stamps for letters and parcels, and there is often a vending machine outside where stamps can be bought. They are also available from many newsagents and other shops. Within the UK, letters can be sent either first or second class: first class is slightly more expensive but should guarantee next-day delivery; second-class mail may take several days to arrive. You can receive mail addressed c/o Poste Restante at the post office in any town provided you have its address. You will need your passport or other identification when you go to collect anything. The city centre post office in Edinburgh is in the St. James Centre EH1, while central offices in Glasgow include one at 85 Bothwell St, G2. Post office core opening times are 0900-1730 Mon.-Fri., 0900-1230 Sat. Some central post offices in large towns and cities stay open till 1900 on Sat. and those in supermarkets have the same hours as the store itself. Many small offices close one weekday afternoon.

Public Holidays: 1-2 Jan. (New Year); Good Fri.; 1st Mon. in May (May Day bank holiday); last Mon. in May (Spring bank holiday); 1st Mon. in Aug. (August bank holiday); 25 Dec. (Christmas Day); 26 Dec. (Boxing Day). Bank holidays are observed by banks but many shops and offices remain open. Note that there are also some local Mon. holidays in Scotland when shops may be closed and banks have limited opening hours in one town or area. Local TICs have details.

Railways: ScotRail services connect Glasgow and Edinburgh to London and all principal mainland towns in Scotland. The main lines north from Glasgow and Edinburgh run through Perth and on to Inverness, one via Aviemore, the other via Aberdeen. Branch lines continue to Kyle of Lochalsh (for Skye), and to Wick and Thurso (for Orkney). From Glasgow, a line runs southwest through Ayr to Stranraer (for Northern Ireland), and the scenic West Highland Line (*see* Fort William) runs through the mountains to termini at Oban (for Mull and the Outer Hebrides) and Mallaig (for Skye and the Small Isles). The long-distance InterCity services have buffet/restaurant cars and sleeper facilities. London to Edinburgh takes about 4.5 hr. If you plan to do a lot of travelling by rail, you might consider buying a ScotRail Rover ticket. These tickets are available from major railway stations in Scotland and England, and from travel agents, and are valid for travel on selected ScotRail services from Berwick and Carlisle in the south to Wick and Thurso in the north. Details can be obtained from information desks at main railway stations. Travelpass tickets (*see* Transport) are valid on ScotRail services. For details of ScotRail timetables and fares from Edinburgh, tel. 0131 556-2451; and from Glasgow, tel. 0345 212282.

Sports: Scotland is the home of golf and has more golf courses per head of population than anywhere else in the world. While many visitors wish to try the world-famous courses at St. Andrews, Turnberry and Gleneagles, there are more than 400 others to choose from, many in very scenic locations. Booking for the Old Course at St. Andrews begins in Oct. for the following year. A round there costs £50 and admission is by letter of approval from a golf club and handicap certificate. Most other courses are relatively uncrowded and remarkably cheap. *Scotland: Home of Golf* (£3.95) is available from the STB (*see* Tourist Information). Angling for trout and salmon is excellent. Although salmon fishing on famous rivers like the Tweed and the Tay can be extortionate, at many other places it costs very little, and occasionally it is free. Permits are often obtainable at local TICs, or information is available there on where to get them. More details are included in *Scotland for Game, Sea and Coarse Fishing* (£3.95), available from the Scottish Tourist Board. Other outdoor pursuits which can be enjoyed at many locations in Scotland include horse riding (around £7.50-£10 per hr), mountain biking (*see* Bicycle Hire) and sailing. Scapa Flow, Orkney and the waters off the west coast of Scotland attract many scuba divers. There are beginners' courses at schools in Oban, Fort William and elsewhere. Windsurfing is also popular.

In winter the ski slopes at Aviemore, Glenshee, the Lecht, Glencoe and Aonach Mor draw skiers from all over Britain: instruction and equipment hire are available. Scotland's traditional winter sport is curling. It can now be tried all year round in many indoor ice rinks where skating is available too. Activity holidays where one or more sports are taught are increasingly popular. The STB publishes *Scotland: Activity Holidays* (£3.95). *See* Walking.

Tourist Information: The Scottish Tourist Board (STB) runs more than 170 Tourist Information Centres (TICs) all over the country, many of which are mentioned in this book. They can reserve accommodation (*see* A-Z), issue free maps and leaflets, and offer help with any enquiry you may have. Opening hours are generally 0900-1700 Mon.-Sat., but they may be open shorter hours Mon.-Fri. only during the low season and longer hours seven days in July and Aug. Most are open only April-Oct., but main centres are open all year round. Information and special publications can be obtained from the STB head office, 23 Ravelston Terr., Edinburgh EH4 3EU, tel. 0131 332-2433 (postal and telephone enquiries only). There is an STB office at 19 Cockspur St, London SW1Y 5BL, tel. 0171 930-3661, while the TIC at the ferry terminal, North Shields, tel. 0191 257-9800, also has full information on Scotland. For the 24 hr STB Information Line, tel. 01891 666465.

Transport: A comprehensive network of air, bus, train and ferry routes serves most of Scotland, making public transport a viable means of seeing much of the country. All services are comfortable and easy to use. Buses are slower than trains over long distances, but are considerably cheaper and cover a much wider area. For visitors planning to travel extensively on public transport, the Freedom of Scotland Travelpass offers excellent value. It is valid for unlimited travel on ScotRail trains, the Glasgow Underground and most Caledonian Macbrayne ferries. It also gives a 20-33% discount on P&O ferries and 33% off selected bus services. Also included are timetables, an information

pack and discounts for some attractions. It is available from staffed ScotRail stations, rail-appointed travel agents and main stations in London, Carlisle, Newcastle and Birmingham. *See* Airports, Buses, Ferries, Railways.

Walking: Scotland's beautiful countryside provides excellent walking for all levels of ability, from short strolls along well-marked footpaths, through hillwalking, to expeditions of several days into some of Britain's wildest mountains. There are a few signposted long-distance footpaths, notably the West Highland Way, from Glasgow to Fort William (95 miles), and the Southern Upland Way, from Portpatrick in the southwest to Cockburnspath in the southeast (212 miles). TICs have details of local walks. The STB publishes a free booklet, *Scotland: Walking*, available by post (*see* Tourist Information), while the *Official Guide to the West Highland Way* (£11.95) and *Official Guide to the Southern Upland Way* (£17.50), including guidebooks and maps, are published by HMSO, and are available from TICs and bookshops. Hillwalking has become extremely popular in Scotland and includes 'Munro-bagging' – going to the top of all 277 Munros or Scottish mountains over 3000 ft. The Scottish Mountaineering Club has a hillwalking guide to the Munros (£14.95 from bookshops). Scotland's hills can be very dangerous. Weather conditions can change very quickly and snow can fall on the high summits at any time of year. Anyone planning a walking trip above valley level should be fully equipped with proper walking boots, all-weather clothing, map, compass, first-aid kit, whistle and plenty of food. Leave a note describing your proposed route and expected time of return with a responsible person. Free leaflets on winter walking safety are available from the Scottish Sports Council, Caledonia House, South Gyle, Edinburgh EH12 9DC. Hillwalking courses are available at Glen More Lodge, Cairngorms, tel. 01479 861256. *See* Edinburgh Walk, Glasgow Walk.

What's On: There are separate monthly listings brochures published in each Scottish Tourist Board region. They are generally titled *What's On in ...* and can be picked up free at TICs, hotels, etc. There is also a free national listing, *Events in Scotland*, covering up to six months. An annual listing is also available. The Sat. editions of the *Scotsman* and the *Herald* give weekly listings of exhibitions, music, theatre, cinema, events and museums, while local papers cover what is happening in their area. *The List* (£1.50 from newsagents) is a fortnightly magazine for cinema, music, theatre, art, events, etc., mainly in Glasgow and Edinburgh. *See* Events, Festivals, Newspapers.

Youth Hostels: The Scottish Youth Hostels Association (SYHA) has over 80 youth hostels all over Scotland, ranging from large, modern establishments to small cottages with only a handful of beds, several miles' walk from the nearest road. Facilities and prices vary considerably. You must be a member of the SYHA or your own national Youth Hostels Association. For further information contact the SYHA head office at 7 Glebe Cres., Stirling FK8 2JA, tel. 01786 451181. Membership costs £6 per year and you can join at most hostels; a passport-size photo is required.

Kirkcudbright

Selective Index of Places and People

Numbers in **bold** indicate a main entry

Abbotsford House 186, 235
Aberdeen 190-1
Aberfeldy 66-7
Aberfoyle 71-2
Achiltibuie 113
Adam, Robert 33, 38, 48, 52, 178, 182, **191**, 193, 207, 208, 227
Affric, Glen 215
Ailsa Craig 46
Alford 150
Alloway 50
Anstruther 168
Antonine Wall 71, 81, 177, 178, **191**
Aonach Mor 59
Applecross 110
Arbroath 160
Arbuthnott 158
Ardnamurchan Point 96
Ardrishaig 85
Ardrossan 52
Armadale 97
Arran 52, 88, **193**
Arrochar 83
Auchterarder 67
Auchtermuchty 174
Aviemore 62
Ayr 51, **194**

Ballachulish **58**, 89
Ballantrae 46
Ballater 151
Balmedie 141
Balmoral Castle **151**, 192
Balquhidder 73
Banchory 149
Banff 139
Bannockburn 10, 86, **230**, 236

Barra 102
Bearsden 71
Beauly 132
Benbecula 102
Bettyhill 115
Biggar 194-5
Birsay 120
Blair Atholl 64-5
Blairgowrie 162
Bo'ness 178
Boat of Garten 61
Bonnie Prince Charlie 10, 17, 63, 96, 103, 135, 213, 220; see also Jacobites
Braco 76
Braemar 151-2
Brechin 158
Bridge of Orchy 55
Brig o' Turk 73
Broadford 97
Brodick 193
Brora 128
Broughton 195
Bruar 64
Bruce, Robert the; see Robert the Bruce
Bruce, Sir William 175, 178, 181, 192, **195**
Buckhaven 166
Buckie 138
Burghead 137
Burns, Robert 22, 50, 194, **195-6**, 199, 201-2, 212
Burntisland 165
Bute 196-7

Caerlaverock Castle **41**, 192
Cairnbaan 88
Callander 79
Callanish 10, **105**, 228

Campbeltown 86
Canna 236
Cape Wrath 114
Carinish 101
Carnegie, Andrew 197, **205**
Carradale 88
Carrbridge 61
Castle Douglas 43
Cawdor Castle 135
Ceres 174
Clachan of Campsie 80
Claonaig 88
Clearances, The 115, **197**
Coatbridge 197
Coldstream 198
Coll 95, **198**
Colonsay 198
Comrie 74
Corpach 59
Corrieshalloch Gorge 112
Couper Angus 162
Covenanters 10, 44, 87, 136, 157, 182, **198-9**, 207, 217, 234
Cowal Peninsula 83, **199-200**
Craigievar Castle **150**, 192
Crail 172
Crathes Castle 149
Crathie 151
Creetown 43-4
Crieff 76
Cromarty 132
Cruden Bay 141
Cuillins, The 97, 98
Cullen 138
Culloden 10, 61, 88, 96, 135, **220**
Culross 176
Culzean Castle 10, **48**, 191
Cumbrae 52, **200**
Cupar 174

Dalwhinnie 64
Dingwall 130
Dirleton 225
Doon Valley 200

Dornoch 129
Doune 78
Drumnadrochit 60
Dufftown 153
Duffus 137
Dumbarton 55, **201**
Dumfries 41, **201-2**
Dunbar 202-3
Dunblane 67, **78**
Dundee 174, **203-4**
Dunfermline 176, **204-5**, 234
Dunkeld **67**, 239
Dunnet Head 125
Dunnottar Castle 157
Dunoon 199
Dunrobin Castle 128-9
Duns 205
Dunvegan Castle 98
Durness 114

East Fortune 225
Edinburgh 10, **16-27**, **206-7**
Edzell 158
Eigg 236
Eilean Donan Castle 109
Elgin 138, **207-8**, 238
Elgol 97
Elie 167
Enlightenment, The **208**, 229
Eriskay 103
Eyemouth 208-9

Fair Isle 143
Falkirk 176
Falkland 175
Fettercairn 158
Findhorn 137
Fintry 80
Fochabers 138
Fordyce 138
Forfar 160
Forres 136
Fort Augustus 60
Fort George 135

Forth Bridges 165, 179, **212**
Fortingall 66
Fortrose 132
Fort William 58, 96, **212-13**
Fraserburgh 140

Gairloch 112
Galashiels 186
Gigha 86
Girvan 46
Glamis 160-1
Glasgow 10, **29-39**, **213-14**
Glasgow Boys 215
Glencoe 55-7
Glencoe Massacre 215
Gleneagles 67
Glenelg 109
Glenfinnan Monument **96**, 220
Golspie 129
Grantown-on-Spey 61
Great Glen 215-16
Gretna Green 41

Haddington 216-17
Hamilton 216
Harris 103
Hawick 184
Hebrides 217
Helensburgh 55, **217-18**
Helmsdale 128
Hermitage Castle 183, **218**
Hopetoun House 178-9
Huntly 154

Innerleithen 188
Inveraray 84-5
Inverewe Gardens 112
Inverkeithing 165
Inverness 61, **218-19**
Inversnaid 72
Inverurie 154
Iona **94-5**, 234
Irvine 51
Islay 86, **219**

Jacobites 109, 152, 188, 213, 220; see also
    Bonnie Prince Charlie
Jedburgh 182-3
John o' Groats 125
Jura 86, **219-20**

Keith 154
Kelso 182, 230
Kilbarchan 52
Kilbirnie 52
Killin 73
Kilmahog 73
Kilmartin 88
Kilmuir 99
Kilmun 199
Kilphedder 101
Kilwinning 51
Kingussie 63
Kinlochbervie 114
Kinlochleven 58
Kinross 175
Kippen 80
Kippford 43
Kirkcaldy 166
Kirkcudbright 43
Kirkoswald 47
Kirkwall 122
Kirriemuir 220-1
Knox, John; see Reformation
Kyle of Lochalsh 60, **109**
Kylerhea 109

Lanark 221
Largo, Upper and Lower 166-7
Largs 52
Latheron 126
Lauder 181
Leadhills 239
Lerwick 143
Leven 166
Leven, Loch 175-6
Lewis 104
Linlithgow 177
Lismore 222

Lochaline 96
Lochboisdale 102
Lochearnhead 73
Lochgilphead **85**, 88
Lochgoilhead 199-200
Lochinver 1113
Lochmaddy 101
Lochranza 193
Lochwinnoch 52
Lomond, Ben 55, **222**
Lomond, Loch 55, 72, 83, **222-3**
Lossiemouth 138

Macbeth 67, 94, 135, 137, 167, **223**
Macdonald, James Ramsay 223
Macduff 139
Macgregor, Robert; *see* Rob Roy
Mackintosh, Charles Rennie 10, 29, 33, 35, 36, 37, 193, 214, 218, **223**, 238
Maes Howe 120
Mallaig 97
Manderston 205
Mary Queen of Scots 10, 17, 43, 65, 79, 166, 175, 182, 203, 204, 217, **223-4**, 229
May, Isle of 168-9
Meigle 161
Melrose 185
Millport 200
Milngavie 71
Moffat 224
Montrose 159
Muck 236
Mull 93
Mull of Galloway 46
Mull of Kintyre 87
Muthill 76

Nairn 135-6
Ness, Loch 60, **215-16**, 219
Nevis, Ben 58, **194**, 212
New Abbey 41
Newburgh (Tayside) 174-5
Newport-on-Tay 174

Newtonmore 63
Newton Stewart 44
North Berwick 224-5
North Queensferry 165

Oban 89, 93, **225-6**
Old Pretender; *see* Jacobites
Orkney 119-123, **226**
Oronsay 198

Paisley 226-7
Paxton House 227
Peebles 189
Penicuik 189
Pennan 139
Perth 67, **227-8**, 229
Peterhead 140
Pitlochry 65
Pittenweem 168
Plockton 110
Port of Menteith 79
Portpatrick 46
Portree 98
Portsoy 138-9
Prestwick 51

Raasay 98
Raeburn, Henry 187, **228-9**
Ramsay, Allan 182, 208, **229**
Redpoint 111
Reformation, The 10, 23, 25, 17, 67, 79, 163, 182, 204, 207, 216, 220, 223, 227, **229**, 231
Rennie, John 182, **230**
Robert the Bruce 11, 44, 86, 90, 149, 185, 192, 200, 205, 226, **230**, 236, 237, 239
Rob Roy 11, 72, 73, 149, 222, **230**
Rockcliffe 43
Rodel 103
Rosehearty 140
Rosemarkie 132
Rothesay 196-7
Rum 97, **236**
Ruthwell 41

St. Andrew 230-1
St. Andrews 172, 229, **231**, 234
St. Columba 67, 87, 94, 198, 215, **234**
St. Fillans 74
St. Margaret 160, 205, 206, 212, 231, **234**
St. Monans 167
St. Ninian 45, **234**
Saltcoats 51
Sandwood Bay 114
Sandyhills 43
Sanquhar 234
Scalloway 144
Scone Palace 162-3
Scott, Sir Walter 11, 17, 22, 25, 72, 97, 182, 184, 186, 187, 227, 229, 230, **234-5**
Scottish Colourists 227, **235**
Selkirk 187
Shawbost 105
Shetland 143-7, **235**
Shieldaig 110
Skara Brae 10, **119**, 228
Skye 97-9, 217
Slattadale 111
Sligachan 98
Small Isles 97, **235-6**
Southend 86
South Queensferry 179
South Uist 102
Spean Bridge 59
Staffa 95, **236**
Stevenson, Robert Louis 22, 58, 152, 179, 198, 219, **236**
Stewart, Charles Edward; *see* Jacobites
Stewart, James Francis Edward; *see also* Bonnie Prince Charlie, Jacobites
Stirling 67, 78, **236-7**
Stonehaven 157
Stornaway 104
Stranraer 46
Strathpeffer 132
Strathyre 73
Stromness 119

Strontian 96
Sumburgh 143
Summer Isles 113

Tain 129-30
Tarbert (Harris) 103
Tarbert (Kintyre) 86
Tarbet (Highland) 114
Tarbet (Loch Lomond) 83
Telford, Thomas 112, 129, 153, 193, **238**
Thomson, Alexander 'Greek' 33, 35, 37, 193, **238**
Thornhill 79, **238**
Thurso 115, **125**
Tiree 95, **198**
Tobermory 95
Toft 145
Tomatin 61
Tomintoul 153
Tongue 115
Troon 51
Trossachs, The 72
Turnberry 47
Tyndrum **55**, 93
Tynet 138

Uig 101
Ullapool 112
Urquhart Castle 60

Wade, Gen. 60, 66, **220**
Wallace, William 11, 221, 230, 236, **238-9**
Wallace Monument 78, **237**
Wanlockhead 239
West Highland Way 71, 72, 222, **249**
Whithorn **45**, 234
Wick 126, **239**
Wigtown 44-5
Wolf of Badenoch 67, 207, **239**

Young Pretender; *see also* Bonnie Prince Charlie, Jacobites